D1627304

LEEDS BECKETT UNIVERSITY
LIBRARY
DISCARDED

71 0019302 9

TELEPEN

DISCARDED

**Victorian Spectacular Theatre
1850–1910**

Theatre Production Studies

Editor
John Russell Brown,
School of English and American Studies,
University of Sussex

Victorian
Spectacular Theatre
1850–1910

Michael R. Booth

Routledge & Kegan Paul
Boston, London and Henley

First published in 1981
by Routledge & Kegan Paul Ltd
39 Store Street,
London WC1E 7DD,
9 Park Street,
Boston, Mass. 02108, USA and
Broadway House,
Newtown Road,
Henley-on-Thames,
Oxon RG9 1EN

Set in 11/12 Plantin by
Computacomp (UK) Ltd
Fort William, Scotland
and printed in the United States of America by
Vail-Ballou Press, Inc.,
Binghampton, New York

© Michael R. Booth 1981
No part of this book may be reproduced in
any form without permission from the
publisher, except for the quotation of brief
passages in criticism

British Library Cataloguing in Publication Data
Booth, Michael Richard
Victorian spectacular theatre 1850–1910. –
(Theatre production studies).
1. Theater – Great Britain – History
I. Title   II. Series
792'.0941   PN2594   80–41729

ISBN 0–7100–0739–6

LEEDS POLYTECHNIC
291156
A V
38953
8.3 82
792 · (942)

710   019302-9

Contents

Illustrations

(between pages 118 and 119)

Melodrama

1 Military spectacle, *The Battle of the Alma*, Astley's, 1855. Courtesy Theatre Museum
2 Painted actors to swell a crowd. Stock Exchange setting, *The White Heather*, Drury Lane, 1897. Courtesy Theatre Museum
3 Elegance in costume. Violet Vanbrugh in *Hearts Are Trumps*, Drury Lane, 1899. Courtesy Theatre Museum
4 The sinking yacht, *The Price of Peace*, Drury Lane, 1899. From the *Graphic*. Courtesy Theatre Museum
5 Photograph of the set for the same scene, showing the electric bridges tilting and sinking. Courtesy Theatre Museum
6 Stables at the Horse Show, *The Whip*, Drury Lane, 1909. Courtesy Theatre Museum
7 The Great Hall, Falconhurst, *The Whip*. Courtesy Theatre Museum

Pantomime

8 The flies at Drury Lane, *Cinderella*, 1883. From the *Illustrated Sporting and Dramatic News*, 26 January 1884. Courtesy British Library
9 The Cave scene, *The Forty Thieves*, Drury Lane, 1886. From the *Illustrated London News*. Courtesy Theatre Museum
10 The Jubilee scene, *The Forty Thieves*. From the *Illustrated London News*. Courtesy Theatre Museum
11 The Court scene, *Puss in Boots*, Drury Lane, 1887. From the *Illustrated Sporting and Dramatic News*. Courtesy Theatre Museum
12 Dress rehearsal of *Cinderella*, Drury Lane, 1895. Arthur Collins standing behind the seated Augustus Harris. From the *Illustrated London News*. Courtesy Theatre Museum

Preface and acknowledgments

The purpose of this book is not to provide an examination of the principal characteristics of Victorian theatre production between 1850 and 1910, but to consider one aspect of it, the spectacular, which came to dominate certain kinds of production during that period. It was a remarkably consistent and unchanging style expressed in a variety of dramatic forms, and was carefully conceived in theory as well as practice. Spectacle was attended with much critical controversy which throws light on this theory and practice, and it grew, as I attempt to show, not from theatre alone but also from society, culture, and the pictorial arts. In order to focus the general account of spectacular theatre in the first three chapters and to give particular and extended examples of how the spectacle style worked in performance, I have tried in chapters 4 and 5 to reconstruct two important spectacular productions.

I am indebted to many people for assistance in the necessary research. I wish particularly to thank Jennifer Aylmer and the staff of the Theatre Museum, Victoria and Albert Museum, for the time and trouble they took to help me when the Museum was officially closed to the public; John and Barbara Cavanagh of Motley Books for making available to me the preparation book of *Faust* in the pleasant surroundings of Mottisfont Abbey; Ann Brooke-Barnett and Christopher Robinson of the University of Bristol Theatre Collection for guiding me through the labyrinth of Beerbohm Tree material; the late Margaret Morris Ferguson for granting me a personal interview about her choreography for Tree's *Henry VIII*; and Molly Thomas of the Ellen Terry Memorial Museum for virtually surrendering her office to me for my own research. I am also grateful to the Garrick Club for permission to examine the volumes of cuttings assembled by Percy Fitzgerald. Several people gave me useful advice on certain problems and showed me the way to material which I would not otherwise have come by, namely Alan Hughes, Terence Rees, Michael Reese, Christopher Calthrop, Denis Salter, and Linda Hardy.

1 · The taste for spectacle

The Victorian taste for spectacle in theatrical production has long been a subject of comment, often dismissive, but not, on the whole, a matter for explanation and understanding. The contrast with our own tastes in production is extreme. For both economic and artistic reasons, spectacle effects, at least in Britain, are now the province of ballet, grand opera, pantomime and musicals, and even here, for the same reasons, they are becoming rarer. When these effects intrude on a small scale into other kinds of theatre, audiences are surprised. Indeed, a positive austerity dominates contemporary Shakespearean production and the staging of much new drama. Actors move in an empty space defined and limited by light, against a selective and non-representational scenic background (if any), whose materials and textures are closely related to the world of the play. Lear and the Fool stand in light on a bare stage; the scenic illusion of a wild heath is not attempted. Half a dozen actors represent the coronation procession of Henry V; there are no cheering crowds, no scattering of flowers, no painted or built-up streets of London. The visual image can be strong, but there is no show, no mass, no profusion of colour, no picture-making, no rich splendour of lighting or decor, no sensual feast for the eye of the spectator – in short, nothing of what we mean by 'spectacle'. The current modes of taste in production are so antagonistic to Victorian styles that a real effort of historical understanding is necessary before the existence and importance of spectacle in the Victorian theatre can be properly appreciated. Yet such an effort should be made, since not only is a full comprehension of this theatre impossible without it, but also one finds in the development of the spectacle style a social and cultural microcosm of the age. Theatre is, after all, a social activity and never exists in isolation from the social and cultural pattern of its own age. This is as true of the Victorian theatre as any other, and the way in which society and culture nourished the spectacle style – as it did all the other styles of Victorian theatre – is of considerable interest in itself. Lastly, the knowledge of how the Victorians held entirely opposite views to ourselves about the production of Shakespeare and other drama and yet translated these views into effective, popular, and long-lasting practice should make us aware that there have been ways other than our own that worked, and that our methods may not be the only right ones. But that is another subject.

The dates chosen for the period of the study should not be taken to imply that spectacle did not exist on the English stage before 1850 or after 1910. The nature of spectacle had long been established in the shows, pageants and processions of Tudor and Stuart times, and the use of spectacle was essential to the court masque. In the eighteenth century, opera, pantomime and ballet were the proper theatrical habitats for display, and the coronations of George II and George III were occasions for elaborate productions of *Henry VIII* in the patent houses; other public ceremonials were also imitated in the theatre. The steady progression towards pictorialism and spectacle was also evident in the first half of the nineteenth century, a progression also determined by public taste and technological change. The sixty years from 1850 have been chosen because they represent the full flow of theatrical spectacle and the feeding into that mainstream of the tributary cultural influences which helped to shape its course.

It is significant that in the 1850s writers and critics became aware of what was happening to public taste in the theatre, and their views are remarkably consistent. William Bodham Donne, appointed Examiner of Plays in 1857, realised that what used to satisfy audiences satisfied them no longer, and that they wanted something different, something new. Writing in 1855, he declared:[1]

> we are become, in all that regards the theatre, a civil, similar, and im-
> passive generation. To touch our emotions, we need not the imaginatively
> true, but the physically real. The visions which our ancestors saw with the
> mind's eye, must be embodied for us in palpable forms ... all must be
> made palpable to sight, no less than to feeling; and this lack of imagination
> in the spectators affects equally both those who enact and those who con-
> struct the scene.

At almost the same time, commenting on Charles Kean's treatment of Shakespeare, his biographer noted that the taste of the age 'had become eminently pictorial and exacting beyond all former precedent. The days had long passed when audiences could believe themselves transplanted from Italy to Athens by the power of poetical enchantment without the aid of scenic devices.'[2] Observers felt that a drama could not succeed by the power of imagination or the power of words alone. E. T. Smith, then manager of Astley's and formerly of Drury Lane, told a parliamentary committee in 1866 that 'for a person to bring out a merely talking drama, without any action in it, or sensational effects, is useless; the people will not go to that theatre; they will go where there is scenic effect, and mechanical effects to please the eye.'[3] Over thiry years later Max Beerbohm was saying exactly the same thing: 'Our public cares not at all for the sound of words, and will not tolerate poetry on the stage unless it gets also gorgeous and solid scenery, gorgeous and innumerable supers. ... The poetry must be short and split; must be subordinated to the action of the piece, and to the expensive scenery and the expensive costumes.'[4]

The kind of theatrical taste described in these remarks cut across all social classes. A fondness for spectacle was not in origin exclusively East End or West End, working and lower middle class on the the the one hand, or upper middle class and fashionable on the other. It was a homogeneous, a ubiquitous taste that had nothing to do with income levels, employment, living conditions, or class position. In explaining the audience's enthusiastic reception of the Brocken scene in *Faust*, *Blackwood's* pointed out that 'Society, always more or less represented at the Lyceum, loves a spectacle as much as Whitechapel',[5] and there is a mass of evidence to suggest that both participated eagerly in the joys of theatrical spectacle and subscribed whole-heartedly to the predominant pictorial ethic.

Simply to note this change of theatrical taste and then go on to examine the spectacle style as it operated in the theatre is not quite enough. To attempt answers to the question of why such a change occurred is essential, since it illuminates the relationship between the audience in the theatre and the society and culture in which it lived, as well as placing the kind of theatrical production under discussion in a larger and more significant context than that of performance alone. Some theatre historians seem to have forgotten that people who went to the theatre had another, and to them probably more important, existence. It is unlikely that their standards of theatrical taste were formed only in the theatre. The desire for pictures and spectacle may well have come from elsewhere. Although the question is problematic and confident answers are difficult to give, it is necessary to look briefly at what may have created and sustained that desire outside the auditorium.

The elaboration of theatrical spectacle corresponded to the elaboration of urban architecture from the 1820s until after the end of the nineteenth century. The rapid growth of the metropolis and other cities, the concomitantly rising prosperity of the nation, and the spread of empire and mercantile imperialism meant the construction of docks, warehouses, bridges, factories, gasworks, railway stations, hotels, banks, department stores, office blocks, government buildings, insurance offices, and exhibition halls on a scale previously unimaginable: massive monuments to wealth, imperial glory, and commercial supremacy, self-important spectacle productions in real stone, brick, steel, iron, and glass. The fact that many of these same monuments appeared repeatedly on the canvas of scene painters is evidence that the new architectural environment was too significant and too much a source of pleasure to be left outside the theatre. Conditioned to mass, grandeur, and elaborate ornamentation in the buildings about them, it is not surprising that the public responded enthusiastically to the same sort of thing translated into the values of theatrical production. Indeed, demand, creation, and response must have been almost simultaneous: managers, scene painters, and stage carpenters were members of that same larger public and also moved in the world outside the theatre. The developing taste for luxury, ostentation, and outward show, which defined personal and public status in an age that could increasingly afford all three, was naturally reflected on the stage as well as on the street and inside the home. An examination of the late Victorian domestic middle-class interior will illustrate the same disposition to leave no space unoccupied, the same love of detail and mass as the Victorian stage.

There seems little doubt that nineteenth-century man saw the world – or, more specifically, used his eyes – in different ways from his ancestors. The demand in the theatre for the pictorial realisation of the word and the scenic recreation of the dramatist's setting was only a part of the extension and heightening of perception closely related to, if not caused by, a range of visual stimuli previously unknown or undeveloped. Urban architecture was one such stimulus; others were the product of new technology directed toward public and private entertainment. The great increase in urban populations and the intermittent but in the second half of the century steady rise in purchasing power created a whole new market for an entertainment industry of sizeable proportions, as well as leading toward a society of mass consumerism featuring the display and advertising of an immense variety of products.

The means for display and entertainment were soon available. Visual stimulus played an essential part. One can mention here only those developments which can clearly be related to the theatre. The new brilliance of the illumination of London streets by gaslight between 1814 and 1820 was the envy of foreign visitors and a source of delight and utilitarian satisfaction to the Londoner himself. In combination with plate glass, gaslight afforded greatly enhanced opportunities for the display of goods in shop windows. Plate glass was an expensive novelty at the beginning of the century, but by the 1830s it was common in superior shops and much better for display than the small leaded windows preceding it. Peering through a brilliantly lit rectangle of glass into a wonderland of attractive goods for sale was like looking into a peepshow or at a stage flooded with light behind a proscenium. The elements of a rectangular frame of vision, a bright light, a viewer, and the varied objects of his view were common to daily life and entertainment as well as the theatre. 'We go not so much to hear as to look,' wrote Percy Fitzgerald of the theatre in 1870. 'It is like a gigantic peep-show, and we pay the showman, and put our eyes to the glass and stare.'[6] The peepshow itself, refined and improved, was originally a sixteenth-century invention. The extensive employment of glass in public buildings – markets, shopping arcades, exhibition halls, conservatories, railway stations – did not occur before the end of the eighteenth century and the structural use of cast iron in buildings made possible by new engineering techniques. The lightness, purity, and sheer beauty of glass and its powers of reflecting and refracting bright light fascinated the nineteenth century; on the stage it was extremely popular, especially in pantomime.

Other inventions further stimulated and developed public taste for the visual image. Phillip de Loutherbourg's Eidophusikon, first presented to the public in 1781, was a sophisticated combination of lighting, sound, scene painting, transparencies, cutout scenery, and models in a miniature theatre 10 feet wide, 6 feet high, and 8 feet deep. The Eidophusikon presented pictorial images of landscapes and seascapes, shipwrecks and storms, sunrise and moonlight, even Milton's Satan and the raising of Pandemonium. De Loutherbourg had been Garrick's leading scene painter at Drury Lane and a master of the new romantic lighting effects and scenic methods. He was also, significantly, a painter of watercolours and oils, and became an Academician in the same year as he exhibited the Eidophusikon, one of the first of a long line of scene painters who attained reputations as artists. The magic lantern was greatly improved in the nineteenth century with the introduction into its mechanism of, first, a brighter and more efficient oil light, and then limelight. One variant, of American origin, was the Sciopticon, which appeared in British homes in the 1870s. A large domestic market in lanterns and slides followed, although the magic lantern, which dated from the seventeenth century, had long been used for public entertainment. It soon reached the theatre. Edward Fitzball employed it to project the image of the ghost ship in *The Flying Dutchman* (1829) at the Adelphi, and it had also been the source of kaleidoscopic flashes of light in Edmund Kean's *King Lear* at Drury Lane in 1821.[7] The kaleidoscope itself had been invented in 1817, but it never became a public amusement for paying audiences and remained a clever domestic toy for all classes of society. Another such device on the peepshow principle was the stereoscope, invented in 1832; much improved in 1849, it became suitable for home entertainment. Two photographs viewed side by side through two lenses gave an effect of three-dimensional perspective. The stereoscope became even more popular when the hand-viewer came into use, and thousands of sets of cards were sold containing views from all over the world. To travel widely in pictures the Victorian family did not need to leave its own parlour.

As Richard Altick has pointed out in his valuable work, *The Shows of London*, the stereoscope was no more than the immensely popular panorama domesticated. The panorama was a pictorial entertainment of sufficient public interest to occupy several important London public buildings from the 1790s until the 1880s. The first was what became Burford's Panorama in Leicester Square and opened under another name by Robert Barker in 1794 with a view of London seen from the roof of the Albion sugar mill in Southwark. Rival institutions followed Barker, and panoramas rapidly became a public craze. Landscape views – Rome, Florence, Dublin, the Alps, Naples, Cairo,

Niagara Falls; battles – Seringapatam, Agincourt, Salamanca, Waterloo; exploration, coronations, state visits, and other topics of immediate public and topographical interest formed the subject matter of the long-enduring panorama vogue. The most important feature of panoramas was their accurate depiction of this subject matter; 'fidelity to fact was a prime consideration. Here the literate public repaired to visualize what it read about in the newspapers, with the same expectations with which, in the twentieth century, it would watch first newsreels and then newsreels' successors, television news programs.'[8] The panorama itself was originally a huge picture painted in special perspective on a domed cylinder in such a way that it could be viewed from the centre of a circular building, sometimes from several levels in that building, as with Hornor's immense panorama of London from the cross of St Paul's exhibited at the Colosseum in 1829. The panorama soon diverged from the concept of circularity but always retained its great size. It was lit by daylight; when it became a flat picture with an illusion of depth and illuminated by special techniques it was called a diorama. The diorama had been invented by Daguerre and shown in Paris in 1822; the following year, specially housed on a site by Regent's Park next to the Colosseum-to-be, it opened with landscapes and interior views of famous cathedrals. A seated audience – in panoramas the audience strolled around the viewing area – looked through a rectangular frame and down a tunnel 30 or 40 feet long at a large picture painted on opaque and translucent materials and lit by daylight from back and front. Apart from the static nature of the experience, the resemblance between viewing a dioramic painting and a theatrical scene was very close, as it had been with the Eidophusikon. A cross between the diorama and the old peepshow was the Cosmorama, which opened in a building of that name in Regent Street in 1823 after a false start in St James's in 1820. Here the paintings were more numerous, much smaller, and seen through a convex lens with perspective effects created by mirrors. Again, the views shown were of Europe, Africa, and Asia, mixed in with public catastrophes such as the burning of the Houses of Parliament. It did not take long for toy diorama boxes for children to find their way into the home; the first one seems to have appeared in 1826. The fold-out or strip panorama was developed by publishers and the periodical press; it reached the heights (or lengths) of elaboration when the *Illustrated London News* printed a 22-foot fold-out of the Great Exhibition in 1851.

The theatrical advantages of the panorama or diorama – the terms soon became almost interchangeable and lost their initially precise meanings – were quickly realised. The basic principles of lighting and perspective were much the same in the theatre as in the exhibition room; the audience, it is true, was further away from the painting in the theatre, but lighting resources were more considerable, especially with gas and then limelight. It was the theatre that adapted the moving panorama, where pictorialism and technology united to satisfy the spectator's simultaneous desire for performance, scenic spectacle, and educational topography. *Harlequin and Friar Bacon* in Covent Garden in 1820 had a moving panorama, painted on a single canvas unrolling from one side of the stage to be rolled up again on the other, of a voyage from Holyhead to Dublin while a profile ship moved across the stage in the other direction. Thereafter pantomime harlequinades were frequently interrupted with not especially relevant views of the Welsh coast (Drury Lane, 1821), the scenery between London and Edinburgh (Covent Garden, 1822), a balloon ascent from Vauxhall Gardens (Covent Garden, 1823), and in the same year at Drury Lane a Clarkson Stanfield panorama of the new breakwater at Plymouth. The moving panorama entered Shakespearean production within a few years, and for the rest of the century was a feature of pantomime and spectacle melodrama. Mechanical and moving pictures were older than the nineteenth-century pantomime or the eighteenth-century Eidophusikon, but this was the first time they had been employed on such a large scale and with a purpose uniquely combining painting and performance.

The possibilities of the separate exhibition of moving panoramas, especially those depicting journeys, were obvious, and irregular shows of this kind culminated in the importation from America of an immense panorama, perhaps 3,600 feet long, of a journey down the Mississippi to New Orleans. It took two hours to unroll, and was exhibited at the Egyptian Hall in 1848. As it unrolled, portraying villages, sugar plantations, colonial mansions, Indian encampments, swamps, steam boats, and levees at different times of the day and night, a commentator spoke from a platform at the side, interspersing his narrative lecture with songs, poems, and jokes. Other monster panoramas, spectacles in their own right, followed: the Nile, the Ohio River, the Overland Route to India, and so on, the rage for these being equal to the demand a generation earlier for the fixed panoramas and dioramas of Burford, Hornor, and Daguerre. All such exhibitions were the visual equivalent of travel literature and a pictorial substitute for travel itself.

The illustrated book and magazine, together with the pictorial print, represented another source of visual stimulus to a public eager for self-improvement and amusement at the same time. The steel engraving, developed for commercial use in the 1820s but made cheaper and better by electrotyping about 1840, was well suited to the new mass market in travel and topographical books and prints; these, as well as reproductions of popular paintings and drawings, were sold in vast quantities in the 1840s and 1850s. The Victorian age was the great age of book illustration; it also saw the spread of the cheap illustrated periodical press, whose mass circulation fulfilled much the same function in print as the panorama on canvas. The illustrated paper also satisfied and expanded the taste for a pictorialisation of important events and foreign landscapes. The first proper illustrated magazine was the *Illustrated London News*, started in 1842, and in the next twenty years there were several more, including the *Pictorial Times* (1843), the *Illustrated Times* (1855), and the *Penny Illustrated Paper* (1861).

Looking at the world through the medium of pictures thus became a habit in the first half of the nineteenth century, and as the pictorial means of information and entertainment grew more sophisticated and better adapted to mass public consumption, the bombardment of visual and specifically pictorial stimuli became inescapable; the world was saturated with pictures. Only the big panoramas and dioramas could be described as pictorial spectacles, but the miniaturising of spectacle, as in the Eidophusikon, the cosmorama, and the toy panorama, was perfectly appropriate for people accustomed to see the wonders of the world unfold before them as they turned the pages of a book or magazine. The similarity of many of these means of pictorial amusement and education to theatrical productions does not need repeating, and the use of the same methods in the theatre and in the exhibition hall shows how close the two were. The essentially passive act of viewing a framed rectangular image of which the elements were colour, light, painting, the scene (moving and stationary), and the human figure was basic to both. Whether the chicken came before the egg or the egg before the chicken is the hardest question of all to answer; that is, whether the new pictorial technology created the taste for the recorded visual image of life or whether it was a response to some as yet unexplained demand for the pictorialisation of actual existence and romantic fantasy. Probably, as suggested above, both demand and response came near together and nourished one another. Certainly the whole movement was popular and universal, of which theatre was only an inseparable part.

In such a milieu it is not surprising that the art of painting played a much more significant role in the life of the people and the life of the theatre than it had before; the relationship between painting and the stage in our period was intimate and meaningful. The visual realisation of poetic beauty was fundamental to both. On the simplest level, as Hubert von Herkomer said, 'the proscenium should be to the stage picture what the frame is to the easel picture.'[9] Herkomer, himself a painter and experimenter in his own model theatre at Bushey with new scenic effects and lighting methods, clearly saw the resemblance between production on the stage and on the canvas, and thought one man could do both. In 1889 he produced at Bushey his own pictorial and musical play, *An Idyl*, in which largely pantomimic action took place to music he had written in front of village and landscape scenes he had painted. Speaking of his production, he believed that the painter 'could experiment in scenic art, in grouping figures, and in story-making, only changing the canvas for the stage in order to express with real objects and real people the thoughts he placed ordinarily upon canvas with brush and colour.'[10]

Herkomer was an exceptional case: an artist who dabbled in theatre to test out essentially painterly rather than theatrical theories. More common was the reverse, the scene painter who either left the theatre to establish or confirm a reputation as an artist, or exhibited professionally at the same time as he fulfilled his theatrical duties. De Loutherbourg has already been mentioned in this regard, but there were many others. Clarkson Stanfield, who became famous for his marine paintings, was a scene painter for the Coburg in the 1820s, and like his friend David Roberts then joined Drury Lane. He left the theatre in 1834 after exhibiting for several years at the Royal Academy, but sometimes painted scenery for friends, most notably the panoramas for Macready's *Henry V* at Covent Garden in 1839. Roberts was also a principal scenic artist who painted for Covent Garden as well as Drury Lane; he gave up the theatre in 1830 and was elected to the Royal Academy in 1838. He was noted for his illustrations of books on Spain and the Near East and his drawings of the same subjects. The great landscape painter David Cox was a principal scene painter on the Birmingham circuit in the first few years of the nineteenth century, and later at other provincial theatres and Astley's. A lesser artist but a most important scene painter was William Beverley, who pioneered the transformation scene in extravaganza and pantomime and was pantomime's leading scenic artist, particularly at Drury Lane, from the 1850s to the 1880s. He exhibited oil landscapes at the Royal Academy during this time, and his watercolours are of merit. These are only four of a considerable number which also includes George Chambers, Samuel Bough, John O'Connor, and William Leighton Leitch. Their training in the theatre was closely relevant to their work as easel painters, and they moved easily between the two.

Although painters like W. P. Frith and John Millais designed costumes for amateur theatricals, no painter of repute turned his attention to professional scene painting – not surprisingly, considering that a whole new set of technical problems would have to be solved in return for far less monetary reward. At the end of the century, however, it was not unusual for well-known artists to make scene designs which were translated into actuality by scene painters. Ford Madox Brown gave Irving some designs for the Lyceum *King Lear* (1892), and Edward Burne-Jones did the same for *King Arthur* (1895), as well as designing the costumes and armour. Lawrence Alma-Tadema was involved in designs for several productions: two for Irving, *Cymbeline* (1896) and *Coriolanus* (1901), and two for Tree, *Hypatia* (1893) at the Haymarket and *Julius Caesar* (1898) at Her Majesty's. An immediate and striking use of painting in the theatre was the widespread practice of 'realising' famous paintings by combinations of actors, scenery, and properties in imitation of the paintings themselves. This practice seems to have begun about 1830, although it may have been earlier, and lasted into the twentieth century. Charles Eastlake's three paintings of Italian brigands were realised in this way in J. R. Planché's Drury Lane melodrama *The Brigand* (1829); David

Wilkie's 'Distraining for Rent' and 'The Rent Day' in Douglas Jerrold's *The Rent Day* (1832), also at Drury Lane; Hogarth's 'Harlot's Progress' in J. T. Haines's *The Life of a Woman* (1840) at the Surrey; George Cruickshank's series of temperance engravings, 'The Bottle', in a play of the same name by T. P. Taylor at the City of London in 1847; and a painting by Abraham Solomon, 'Waiting for the Verdict', in a play of this title by Colin Hazlewood at the Britannia in 1859. Alma-Tadema declined a request from Irving to imitate Gérôme's 'The Death of Caesar' for a scene in a prospective Lyceum *Julius Caesar*, and Tree toyed with the idea of realising Edwin Abbey's 'Trial of Queen Katharine' in his 1910 *Henry VIII*. In 1895 Tree's production of *Trilby* at the Haymarket opened simultaneously with an exhibition of George du Maurier's drawings from his novel at the Fine Art Society, which *The Times* (31 October 1895) said influenced Tree's production. According to the reviewer, Dorothea Baird was instantly recognisable as Trilby from the drawings. Art, the theatre, and the novel came together in this moment, and it should be remarked in passing how pictorial and how theatrical in character is the work of novelists like Scott, Dickens, and Thackeray. The stage presentation of a famous painting took the form of a tableau at the end of a scene or act. The tableau method was used to depict a climax of action in melodrama and was entirely pictorial in groupings, attitudes, and the sense that all motion was absent; it could also be used – as in Tree's *Henry VIII* – as a form of curtain-call. The term for it in stage directions was often '*picture*'.

An interesting aspect of public taste and the public knowledge of art is the fact that the audience immediately recognised the painting and applauded the resemblance rather than the stage performance. To some extent, at least, it was therefore the same public that bought prints of paintings and visited art galleries, which it could do more easily as the century wore on. Single paintings that attracted great interest, such as Theodore Géricault's 'The Raft of the Medusa' (1819), John Martin's 'Belshazzar's Feast' (1820), and Holman Hunt's 'The Finding of the Saviour in the Temple' (1854–60) were given special exhibitions of their own and, like plays, were then taken on provincial tours. Engravings of each painting were printed and sold in their thousands. After the opening of the National Gallery in 1824 and the growing popularity of the Royal Academy's annual exhibition, the number of art galleries where people could see collections of modern paintings slowly increased. These exhibitions received lengthy reviews in the daily and weekly press as well as the specialist art periodicals, and were as much a matter for critical comment as theatrical performances. In fact the *Era*, a specialist theatrical journal, devoted considerable space in the 1880s to reviews of art exhibitions.

To look at the stage as if it were a picture was by 1850 an automatic response in audiences, and to make performance resemble painting was a habit of managers and technical staff. The examination of Irving's *Faust* will

give a specific example of both processes, but several related developments
should be mentioned that rendered these processes inevitable and, by 1880,
completed them. The pictorial actualisation of poetic beauty and historical
setting has already been mentioned and will be discussed more fully in later
chapters; suffice to say here that the doctrine of illustration espoused by the
Victorian and to some extent the pre-Victorian theatre made pictorialisation
of the drama inevitable. This was especially so in the case of Shakespeare.
Acting was also traditionally pictorial, and the use of stylised and sometimes
stereotypical gesture, attitude, and facial expression – at least in tragic and
poetic drama, and certainly in melodrama – pictorialised character and
emotional response. Scenically, improved methods of lighting meant that
illumination behind the proscenium was now strong enough for the actor to
retreat behind it and no longer feel the need to play right down stage to catch
the light from the footlights and the auditorium. When this happened he was
no longer performing well in front of a pictorial background of wings and
backshutters but integrated with a scenic unit, a part of a pictorial composition
in three dimensions as well as of a dramatic event. The union of stage and
painting was publicly and officially consummated when Squire Bancroft had a
2-foot wide picture-frame moulded and gilded right round the proscenium of
the Haymarket in 1880, the bottom of this frame corresponding exactly with
the front of the stage. Other theatres followed suit.

It was, then, common to consider a stage production from the point of view
of artistic composition, light and shade, and colouring. Two quotations,
separated by nearly a hundred years, demonstrate this attitude and show how
it was developing well before 1850 – indeed, it probably started with similar
responses to de Loutherbourg's settings and lighting at Drury Lane in the
1770s – and how long it lasted. The first, by Leigh Hunt, concerns a setting
in Planché's *The Vampire* at the English Opera House in 1820, a production
entirely characteristic of the popular pictorial romanticism of the
contemporary theatre.[11]

> To the splendour of a transparency were here added all the harmony and
> mellowness of the finest painting. ... The hue of the sea-green waves,
> floating in the pale [moon] beam under an archway of grey weather-beaten
> rocks, and with the light of a torch glaring over the milder radiance, was in
> as fine keeping and strict truth as Claude or Rembrandt, and would satisfy,
> we think, the most fastidious artist's eye.

The second relates to the production of Louis N. Parker's *Joseph and his
Brethren* in New York in 1912 and then at His Majesty's in 1913; the spirit
is of archaelogical recreation, but the pictorial romanticism is still there:[12]

> Every scene was like a composition by an old master: Down in the Valley
> of Schechem, the wells of Dothan, Potiphar's garden, Zuleika's room,
> with the huge sinister statue of Ashtaroth. Pharoah's palace, in which we
> used the whole depth of the enormous stage, and reproduced the Temple

of Karnak in its glory, was grand and awful; but the most terribly beautiful and impressive scene was the foot of the great pyramid at night, with an Egyptian star-lit sky, and, at the close, a huge full moon leaping up and flooding the auditorium with light.

Although it is relatively easy to identify and describe the pictorialism of the Victorian theatre and to illustrate the closeness of production to painting, it is also necessary to view the question from the other side and briefly consider the theatrical nature of Victorian art and the parallels to the stage one can find in the paintings themselves. The nineteenth century developed spectacle painting akin to spectacle theatre in the manipulation of setting and mass. William West's 'The Israelites Passing Through the Wilderness' (1845) presents the viewer with a vast desert set: huge cliffs, narrow defiles, an immense host winding from the left background to the right foreground, moon, stars, and a concentrated and brilliant shaft of heavenly limelight pouring straight down onto the Ark of the Covenant. The most striking painter in the spectacle style, and one of the most relevant to the theatre, is John Martin, whose apocalyptic subject matter includes the fall of Babylon, the destruction of Nineveh, and the Last Judgment itself. In painting like this the world is afflicted with dissolution: the earth opens and crumbles, buildings rear up and disintegrate, pillared colonnades topple, floods rise, lightning flashes and destroys, fire consumes. Martin was hugely popular in his time and after it, and mezzotints of his paintings were sold in their hundreds of thousands in the 1820s and 1830s. Although he was not the first British painter of catastrophes, divine and natural, his are on a titanic scale. He was soon imitated in the apocalyptic mode by Francis Danby, with 'The Delivery of Israel' (1825), 'The Opening of the Seventh Seal' (1828), and 'The Deluge' (c. 1840). David Roberts's 'The Flight of the Israelites' (1829) is also a direct imitation. The point of mentioning these paintings, apart from the vastness of their stage sets and their dramatic arrangement of huge mobs of fleeing supers and frantically gesticulating leading actors, is that catastrophes like shipwrecks, explosions, fires, avalanches, and earthquakes were the stock-in-trade of sensation melodrama. In the last thirty years of the century, with the steady improvement of machinery and the technology of disaster, such catastrophes could be impressively and credibly produced in well-equipped theatres with large stages like Drury Lane and the Standard in the East End. Indeed, nineteenth-century melodrama, with its own apocalyptic character and its own titanic conflict between good and evil – which manifested itself in physical as well as moral symbols – was obsessed with catastrophe.

A different kind of spectacle painting, social and contemporary rather than supernatural and biblical, can be seen in the many pictures of public gatherings and sporting and social events. Here too mass and scale of setting are important, but in a topical and socially realistic way. Such art is best

represented by W. P. Frith – the leading one in this style – and G. E. Hicks.
Pictures like Frith's 'Ramsgate Sands' (1854), 'Derby Day' (1858), and
'The Railway Station' (1871) are social landscapes conceived in terms of a
mixture of classes, great numbers of people grouped according to motives of
purposeful activity or passive indolence, a well-known public setting, and
careful realism of place and person alike. Both 'Derby Day' and 'The
Railway Station' were realised on stage, and places of public resort where
large crowds gathered were a regular feature of spectacle melodrama. More
fashionable settings also found their way into the theatre, and were annually
reproduced in Augustus Harris's autumn dramas at Drury Lane in the
eighties and nineties. An exactly parallel social upgrading of the Frith–Hicks
school can be found in art. Frith himself contributed 'The Salon d'Or
Homburg' (1871) and 'The Private View at the Royal Academy' (1881);
typical of this genre were 'The Four-in-Hand Club in Hyde Park' (1886)
and 'The Lawn at Goodwood' (1887) by Frank Walton and T. W. Wilson
collaboratively. The general parallels between spectacle painting and the
spectacle theatre were close, and particular styles of painting – given the
difference between the media, of course – closely resembled particular styles
of production.

The realistic approach of painters like Frith and Hicks to the social scene
was part of a general movement including art, the theatre, and the novel
toward greater realism of technique and content. In the case of painting and
the theatre this could be a matter of style rather than substance, especially
when it came to the treatment of contemporary social and economic
questions. Nevertheless, the recreation of reality was a vitally important
doctrine in the pictorial and spectacle theatre, and some introductory attention
must be paid to the idea and its execution. The best parallel in painting, and a
good example of the way in which theory and practice are close to each other
in different art forms, is the work of the Pre-Raphaelites. There is in Pre-
Raphaelite painting a minutiae of external detail and a feeling that the setting
is as important as the figures. Holman Hunt, for instance, first painted the
background and foreground of 'The Hireling Shepherd' (1851) out of doors,
and then added the figures from studio models. The Brotherhood's
commitment to the recreation of history, in their case notably medieval
settings and legends and what they believed to be the everyday environment of
biblical stories, could simultaneously be found in the theatre. Their
painstaking research techniques for the duplication of historical reality were
identical with those of that enthusiastic contemporary and Fellow of the
Society of Antiquaries, Charles Kean. What excited some and offended many
was the vivid and often lurid colouring of Pre-Raphaelite paintings. Here
Blackwood's drew the likeness between 'the Pre-Raphaelites of the stage and
of the picture galleries':[13]

The more narrowly we examine the sister arts, the more nearly do we find that they assimilate. In the pictorial art we find the same symptoms of dis-integration and decay as in the dramatic; in both we find the same elements of promise. ... In how many of these pictures do we find the artists compensating for bad drawing with gaudy colour, hiding vacancy of expression in a blaze of light, feebleness and passion in a tornado of shadows and blundering perspective, aerial and linear, in a mist. ... The very faults we find in the theatre!

Blackwood's, thinking of the 'historic fidelity' of Kean's Shakespeare revivals at the Princess's, nevertheless defended the right of the theatre to adopt realistic methods.

Indeed, if there is any age in which visual taste has been less abstract, it is the Victorian. The general public and the theatre audience included in that public craved concrete images of historical and contemporary reality in the book and magazine illustrations, prints, magic lantern slides, panoramas and paintings they saw. Legend and history had to be actualised and made visually familiar and accessible. The domestic feeling that permeated Victorian taste and Victorian art meant that the reality of the everyday or historical environment – the streets, public buildings, taverns, restaurants, and parks of London, or the Rialto, the villa of an Ephesian courtesan, Juliet's bedroom, and Faust's study – were re-created in art forms for public consumption. A tremendous stimulus to this process was the invention of the camera, which became a practicable instrument for professional use in the 1840s and increased rapidly in popularity. After the Kodak roll-film camera appeared in 1888, followed by celluloid film and the light-proof spool, photography became the pastime of the people. In 1851 the census figures show fifty-one professional photographers, in 1901, 17,628. In 1880 there were fourteen photography clubs in Britain, in 1900, 256. In 1905 it was estimated that there were 4,000,000 amateur photographers in the country, about 10 per cent of the population.[14] Exhibitions of photographs had been open to the public since 1839, and by the 1850s the camera was making the panorama obsolete; photographic views replaced painted slides in the magic lantern and were widely sold with the new stereoscope. Painters like Frith worked from photographs in creating canvases of the 'Derby Day' variety. Beerbohm Tree could say of theatrical taste at the end of the century, with perfect truth, that 'the public demand absolute exactitude, they delight in photographic accuracy, and are satisfied if the thing produced exactly resembles the original without stopping to think whether the original was worth reproduction.'[15] The arrival of the cinema, whose first London showing was in 1896, and the consequent improvement in the realistic fidelity of the visual image, was not at all the culmination of a teleological process in which the theatre struggled clumsily toward the divine glory of cinematic realism, but simply one of the many responses of an increasingly sophisticated entertainment technology to the demand for pictorial realism.

What the realistic movement meant to the theatre was that the spectator required and was supplied with a great deal of factual, visual information. The environment of the actor solidified around him; it had to be, as Donne observed, 'embodied in palpable forms', not imaginatively true but physically real. The reproduction, as well as the theatre could achieve it, of all the paraphernalia of corporeal existence was one aspect of this realism, which satisfied the taste for the recycling of contemporary visual experience from the spectator's own contact with the diurnal world through stage production back to his storehouse of material images. Percy Fitzgerald noted the perfection of this kind of theatrical scenery in 1870:[16]

> The most complicated and familiar objects about us are fearlessly laid hold of by the property man, and dragged upon the stage. Thus, when we take our dramatic pleasure, we have the satisfaction of not being separated from the objects of our daily life, and within the walls of the theatre we meet again the engine and train that set us down almost at the door; the interior of hotels, counting-houses, shops, factories, the steam-boats, waterfalls, bridges, and even fire-engines.

The Bancrofts, who were at the Prince of Wales's in the 1860s and 1870s, claimed that they were the first to put every piece on the stage in a realistic way, but like many claims for innovation in the nineteenth-century theatre the truth is somewhat different. Although the claim might be correct in a literal sense, the Bancrofts represent an intermediate point in the movement of the stage toward realism, not a beginning. A few illustrations will show what was happening. For Boucicault's *Janet Pride* at the Adelphi in 1855 the entire Central Criminal Court at the Old Bailey was reproduced for the last act; so praised was this scene that Boucicault repeated it at the Westminster in 1863 with *The Trial of Effie Deans*. The first two acts of a revival in 1882 at the Haymarket of Tom Taylor's *The Overland Route* were set on board a P. & O. steamer. After months of labour, the head carpenter successfully replicated, as far as possible for stage purposes, the saloon and part of the upper deck of the *Poonah*, an older vessel of the P. & O. fleet. Since Bancroft had sailed to Malta the year before on the *Deccan* of the P. & O., he felt well qualified to use details of shipboard life in the production, adding with pride that 'we were also fortunate in securing some real niggers, lascars, and ayahs, who lent great reality to the picture.'[17] In 1892, to lend the same kind of reality to the last act of his adaptation of Sardou's *Divorçons*, *To-day*, set in the dining-room of the Savoy, Charles Brookfield borrowed from the hotel management napery, cutlery, glass, and a group of waiters, who served on the stage of the Comedy every night during the run of the play. A writer for the *Stage* noted the use of a hand-woven Aubusson carpet in Offenbach's *Madame Favart* in 1879 at the Strand and a sixteenth-century carved oak cabinet in another Offenbach opera, *La Belle Lurette*, at the Avenue in 1883.[18] The replacement of the property man by the antique dealer, the modish shop, and the professional decorator was a striking instance of the stage's devotion to fashionable verisimilitude and the lengths to which it was pursued.

The doctrine of realism and its practice, which could be intimate, as at the Bancrofts' Prince of Wales's, or spectacular, as on the stage of Drury Lane or Tree's Her Majesty's, were matters of controversy throughout our period. Essentially the problem was as Sir Frederick Pollock put it at a meeting of the Society of Arts in 1887. Audiences, he said, 'need not bring any mind at all to the theatre; they were not expected to do so; it was all done for them by carpenters and scene-shifters ... what were the real limits of dramatic illusion?'[19] Fitzgerald had no doubt that the trend toward greater and greater realism was bad for the theatre and destructive of true illusion. Arguing carefully and thoughtfully for the suggestiveness of earlier scenic styles and the superiority as illusion of scene painting over built-up scenery, he said that the closer reality was imitated the more nearly effect was produced rather than the illusion of reality itself. The more the reproductions of reality, such as curtains and furniture, clashed with flat surface painting and the absence of shadows, except the coarse ones cast by artificial limelight, the more unnatural was the result. Real furniture in place of property furniture looked shabby and unreal when viewed from a distance never appropriate to ordinary domestic life. The danger and the paradox in the over-elaboration of stage effect was that 'the more realism is aimed at, the more surely will the eye discover where it falls short.' Archaeological exactitude is not feasible because 'we become pledged to a minuteness of detail which the play does not require, and which is an insufferable burden to those who get up the play.'[20] That was one point of view. Another was the view of a critic who, in praising E. W. Godwin's production of *As You Like It* in the woods of Coombe House in 1884 and 1885, said that 'when the opportunity is afforded of replacing artificial scenery by a natural stage ... there can be no doubt as to the advantage of change, especially as the object of all histrionic art is to represent as faithfully as possible, even to the smallest detail, whatever subject may be introduced.'[21] The dogma of exact imitation explicit in the latter half of the quotation, though entirely opposed to Fitzgerald's views, was the very gospel of archaeologically-minded theatre practitioners. Paradoxically, then, the nineteenth-century theatre moved steadily toward a simultaneous affirmation of realism and art; that is, while it was framing its stage as a painting would be framed, and bringing much stage art close to the art of painting, it was also insisting that the content of the frame should be as life-like as possible. This is an old artistic paradox, but perhaps it is at its most extreme in Victorian theatre.

Basically, the complaint about realism in production was that it rendered audiences mentally passive and anaesthetised the imagination. Making pictures on stage was one means of this realism, and it was disapproved of for the same reason. Thus one critic could object to the generally much praised scenery at Irving's Lyceum because it was too distinctly painted and too realistic, ceasing to be the background it should be to the pictures made by the actors.[22] *Faust* was also thought to leave too little to the imagination because it was so splendidly produced.[23] This kind of criticism occurs repeatedly in attacks upon spectacular Shakespeare. Another critic of *Faust* believed that the attempt to combine poetry with elaborate realism was bound to be unsuccessful, that to appeal to the imagination at the same time as gratifying the senses with mechanical effects was impossible, and that the very excitement and curiosity aroused by the wonders of spectacle and technology destroyed the reflective and creative faculties.[24] If anyone solved the inherent problems of theatrical spectacle Irving did in *Faust*, but even Irving could not silence the voices of intellectual dissent from the prevailing and enduring fashions of realism and spectacle. These voices were, however, those of a minority, a thinking minority certainly, but not at all representative of the great mass of public and journalistic opinion. This mass hailed every new refinement of realism and every further elaboration of spectacle with almost unqualified delight. It was in tune with the visual temper of the age and opposing critics were not. In the nineteenth century only audiences kept theatres in business, and audiences thought as Charles Kean, Irving, and Tree thought. This unity of taste between actor-manager and spectator is one of the most interesting and impressive phenomena of the Victorian theatre; it kept the pictorial and spectacle style going for a very long time, well after critical hostility had been translated into reformist practice.

The realistic movement on stage was not just concerned, as a reading of Fitzgerald might suggest, with the replication of contemporary and daily life. The movement was also purposefully historical, an interest in the past and the recreation of history in painting, poetry, the novel, the theatre, and scholarship being one of the most important features of late-eighteenth- and nineteenth-century thought and creative art. Originally medievalist and romantic in character, this movement became catholic in scope and by 1850 was fully fledged in both theory and practice. Macaulay, Carlyle, Lingard, Scott, Bulwer-Lytton, and Harrison Ainsworth were immensely popular authors in the early Victorian period. The cheap popular illustrated history was made possible through the development of lithography. Public interest focused upon the particular way people lived and behaved in past times as well as upon the general sweep of history. Social history and antiquarian scholarship proliferated. Joseph Strutt published *A Compleat View of the Manners, Customs, Arms, Habits, etc. of the Inhabitants of England* (1775-6) and *A Complete View of the Dress and Habits of the People of England* (1796-9). Planché's *History of British Costume* and F. W. Fairholt's *Costume in England* each ran through several editions between 1834 and 1885. C. A. Stothard's *The Monumental Effigies of Great Britain*

(1817–32) and Samuel Meyrick's *A Critical Inquiry into Antient Armour* (1824) were specialist studies into subjects of considerable antiquarian interest. Henry Shaw's *Specimens of Ancient Furniture* (1836) and *Dresses and Decorations of the Middle Ages* (1834) were standard works. These books were also extremely influential in the theatre. The vogue for historical and archaeological truth in production could not have taken the direction it did without the existence of such necessary aids to the actor-manager, costumier, property man, and scene painter.

The artist was as much beholden to the scholar as the theatre practitioner was, for the Victorian period was the great age of British historical painting. Much of this was mixed up with the narrative genre and sometimes sentimentalised, but both idealism and sentiment were essential aspects of stage art as well as easel painting. Yet a great deal of Victorian historical painting was a serious and detailed attempt to recreate the national past. The competition for the decoration of the new Houses of Parliament in 1842 was evidence of this, and the exhibition of the 140 cartoon entries the following year drew thousands of spectators every day; the subjects had to come from Shakespeare, Spenser, Milton, and British history. Learning through history was important for Victorians, as apparent in their response to the Shakespearean productions of Charles Kean as in their appreciation of historical painting. One of Kean's most significant ventures into historical re-creation through period detail was *Henry VIII*, as it was also for Irving and Tree. In all three productions (not to mention those by John Philip Kemble) one of the big scenes was the Trial of Queen Katharine. It is worth noting that between 1790 and 1900 there were exhibited at the Royal Academy six paintings of the Trial, including the one by Abbey which Tree wished to realise, three more of Katharine's Dream – a spectacle feature of all three productions – and a total of forty relating to Shakespeare's play or to aspects of Henry VIII's reign.[25] Interestingly, the act of stepping out of the frame of a picture onto the stage occurs in several nineteenth-century plays; one of them was Planché's *The Court Beauties* (1835) at the Olympic, and 'the scene in which King Charles II's Beauties were represented in their frames, from the well-known pictures at Hampton Court, by ladies of the company, was a *tableaux vivants* [sic] as novel as it was effective.'[26]

A footnote to the examination of history painting and its contextual relationship to the stage is the existence of the *tableau vivant* itself, an elegant social entertainment that combined history painting and theatrical performance. Historical painters themselves went to a lot of trouble to get their details right, and often clothed their models in genuine historical costumes. The *tableau vivant*, usually a presentation of subject matter from art, classical myth, or history, had to be authentically dressed, and the marriage between costume archaeology and pictorial attitude was characteristically theatrical. A great deal of money could be and frequently was spent on costumes and properties for the *tableau vivant*, which thus satisfied a taste for private spectacle in one's own richly appointed drawing-room. These *tableaux vivants* were in their frozen pictorialism closely related to the climactic 'pictures' of melodrama and the realising of paintings on stage. Andrew Ducrow's 'living statues' in the 1820s at Astley's and on tour, in which he posed in a picture frame behind a curtain in the precise attitudes of classical statuary, was another transposition of the *tableau vivant* to theatrical performance. By the 1830s *tableaux vivants* had become public entertainment, known sometimes as *poses plastiques*, and eventually found their way into the music hall.[27]

Archaeological research embraced not only dress and artefacts, but also architecture, social life, warfare, the trades, and a hundred other aspects of a past which fascinated the nineteenth century. Antiquarian and archaeological investigation was part of the realistic movement and the general absorption in history; the impulse to recreate the past as accurately as possible was only the other side of the coin from the desire to make pictorial images of contemporary life. The Victorian public responded enthusiastically to a whole series of splendid discoveries, although of course archaeological excavation and the stimulus of ancient cultures did not start with the reign of Queen Victoria. The Elgin Marbles were placed in the British Museum in 1816, and the next really significant impact of ancient architecture upon the public was the discoveries by Layard and Rawlinson at Nimrud and Nineveh in Assyria between 1845 and 1855. The *Illustrated London News* printed many drawings of their excavations, and from its beginnings disseminated pictorial views of archaeological discoveries to an eager readership. People could read the scholarly literature as well as see the Assyrian sculptures in the British Museum. Layard published four books on Nineveh between 1849 and 1853, and finds from the various sites were shown at the Great Exhibition in 1851 and at the Crystal Palace in 1854. Like other discoveries, those at Nineveh soon appeared in the panorama and diorama, and photographs of archaeological sites and antiquities in museums became available to the public, as well as to artists and the theatre. After Nineveh came Pompeii in the 1860s, Ephesus in the sixties and seventies, Schliemann's Troy and Mycenae in the 1870s – each one a further stimulus to exhibitions, entertainments, learned treatises, and the arts, and each one creating a further demand for pictorial realisation.

Painters were soon inspired by archaeological subject matter and the necessity for careful archaeological research. The paintings of John Martin, though not in the least motivated by the historical spirit, were the spectacular equivalents of historical and archaeological research, the pictorialisation on a huge scale of a visionary concept of the ancient and mythical past. The endless and gigantic colonnades of Martin's theatrical sets, as in 'Belshazzar's Feast' (1820) and 'The Fall of Nineveh' (1828) are not unlike the designs for

Kean's *Sardanapalus* at the Princess's in 1853. In its turn *Sardanapalus* influenced a painting like J. P. Pettit's 'Golden Image in the Plain of Babylon' (1854), and both Kean and Pettit owed an artistic debt to the discoveries of Layard, whom Kean acknowledged in his programme notes. Kean's purpose was not only to perform Byron's tragedy, but also (and perhaps more importantly) 'to render visible to the eye ... the costume, architecture, and the customs of the ancient Assyrian people, verified by the bas-reliefs'. A performance of *Sardanapalus* 'with proper dramatic effect' had not been possible until the present time, said Kean, because 'until now we have known nothing of Assyrian architecture and costume', an interesting condition for the performance of a historical drama. Kean also 'rigidly followed' the British Museum sculptures. Thus he endeavoured 'to convey to the Stage an accurate portraiture and a living picture of an age long since past away',[28] and thus the production contained a Palace scene with '*huge winged lions [sic] with human heads supporting the columns upon which the roof rests*', the Hall of Nimrud with appropriate furniture – and much spectacle. A huge procession opened the play of spearmen, musicians, dancing-girls, archers, nobles, officers, eunuchs, standard-bearers, and Sardanapalus himself in an authentic chariot drawn by two cream horses. The play ended with a *Götterdämmerung*-like funeral pyre and dissolution reminiscent of Martin: '*MYRRHA springs forward and throws herself into the flames; the smoke and flames surround and seem to devour them – the Palace bursts into a general and tremendous conflagration – the pillars, walls, and ceiling crumble and fall – the pyre sinks – and in the distance appears a vast panoramic view of the Burning and Destruction of Nineveh.*'

Both Pettit and Kean were undoubtedly influenced by Martin and, as already mentioned, the Victorian stage was devoted to catastrophe. Other painters were historically more scrupulous than Martin; their methods were just the same as Kean's and those scene painters and stage carpenters who strove to represent the contemporary world. Millais put Elizabeth Siddal in a bath in order to paint 'Ophelia' (1851–2) and filled his studio with smoke in order to reproduce the effect in 'The Rescue' (1855). For 'The Doctor' (1891) Luke Fildes sketched cottages in England and Scotland and then constructed a life-size fisherman's cottage in his studio. A weekly shipment of fresh roses from the French Riviera arrived for Alma-Tadema throughout four winter months so that he could with perfect accuracy paint every one of the thousands of petals in 'The Roses of Heliogabalus' (1896). His 'Caracalla and Geta' (1907), a view of the Colosseum, was a spectacle scene with 2,500 spectators in the picture, each of them separately painted – an effect strikingly similar to the common theatrical practice of painting figures on a backcloth to swell a crowd scene in the foreground. Alma-Tadema, whom Tree and Irving involved in designing Shakespeare, had visited Pompeii and the ruins of Rome when young, and made determined and

successful efforts to duplicate on canvas the architecture, costumes, and properties, if not the spirit and substance, of the classical world. His research methods, as will be seen from his work on *Coriolanus*, were extraordinarily thorough; even more dogged and persistent was Holman Hunt, who brought a goat and some Dead Sea mud back with him from the Holy Land for 'The Scapegoat' (1854). His notes for the exhibition of 'The Shadow of Death' (1873) read just like Kean's scholarly gloss on Shakespeare bills, describing the archaeological provenance of a variety of ancient carpenters' tools. By the second half of the century, the artist as well as the theatre could call upon all the considerable resources of antiquarian scholars and archaeological research. These resources were fully employed by Kean and Irving, as well as by Alma-Tadema and Edward John Poynter, beside Tadema the leading painter of the classical world. Poynter's 'Israel in Egypt' (1867) is an outdoor spectacle whose every object was recreated from archaeological study; its size and scale foreshadow Tree and the production of plays like *False Gods* (1909) and *Joseph and his Brethren*. The massive columned palace, huge cast, and brilliant colour of 'The Visit of the Queen of Sheba to King Solomon' (1890) simultaneously look backward to *Sardanapalus* and forward to Tree's *Antony and Cleopatra* (1906), for whose sets Poynter would have been a most suitable designer.

Art and archaeology came together on the stage as well as in painting, but it was easier to advocate archaeological principles than to ensure that they were satisfactorily implemented. For those who believed that anachronisms and historically inaccurate costuming weakened in the educated mind the illusion produced by good acting, it was essential, despite the enormous labour involved, to pay attention in costuming, for instance, to the smallest matters of archaeological detail. However, there were problems in obtaining approval from a theatre-going public containing few trained archaeologists. One person who refused to be daunted by any such problems was E. W. Godwin, the most extreme and the most dedicated of archaeological theorists and practitioners, and one who, with the possible exception of Wingfield, involved himself most completely in theatre. Godwin's *credo* is an excellent summation, not only of archaeological principle, but also of the high-minded educational motives of the whole historical-realist movement in the Victorian theatre. We do not go to the playhouse, Godwin said, merely to observe the passion of the actor or listen to funny speeches, 'but to witness such a performance as will place us as nearly as possible as spectators of the original scene or of the thing represented, and this result is only obtainable where accuracy in every particular is secured.'[29] In 1874 and 1875 Godwin published in the *Architect* an exhaustive series of thirty-two articles on 'The Architecture and Costume of Shakespeare's Plays', later reprinted in the *Mask* by Gordon Craig, and in 1885 contributed several articles on 'Archaeology on the Stage' to the *Dramatic Review*. In the latter series he argued that the archaeologist must be an artist, and that comedies of manners and customs require exact archaeological treatment, not to mention the artistic treatment of costume, scenery, and properties demanded by the higher poetical drama represented by Shakespeare. Godwin even suggested that the critic ignore acting and 'give undivided attention to the externals of architecture and costume'.[30] Elaborating this idea, he outlined a plan whereby one critic should review the acting, another the literary content of the play, and a third the setting – this last critic obviously being the most important.

Godwin was active in the theatre in the 1870s and 1880s, being especially involved with Wilson Barrett at the Princess's in productions of W. G. Wills's *Juana* (1881), a play with a fifteenth-century Spanish setting, the same author's *Claudian* (1882), set in fourth- and fifth-century East Asia, and *Hamlet* (1884). It was Godwin who designed and produced the outdoor *As You Like It* in 1884 and *The Faithful Shepherdesse* in the same setting next year. His productions attracted much interest but were not always successful, and Godwin himself was irritated by the compromises he had to make with archaeological principle in order to satisfy actors and managers. It was partly a failure to compromise that damned his revival of Tom Taylor's *The Fool's Revenge*, which opened his ill-fated management at the Opera Comique in 1886. Godwin stage-managed the production, designed the scenery, and superintended the costumes. No amount of archaeological accuracy compensated for the deficiencies of the performance as a whole. The *Dramatic Review* (7 August 1886) objected that 'while its archaeological completeness is carried to an extent far beyond the comprehension of anyone save an expert, much more important matters are left to chance. ... Archaeology, which is, after all, an essential but subordinate part, has had to do duty for the whole of Art, and has proved unequal to the task.' Too much archaeology was beyond audience understanding and the patience of actors, as well as producing inartistic and unaesthetic effects on stage. Too little aroused the wrath of those archaeologically zealous critics and members of the public who delighted in reviews and letters to the papers in exposing anachronisms and other inexactitudes. The general desire of audiences was for as much archaeology as possible, but only if expressed with poetic and pictorial beauty. The archaeologising of spectacle, at least in serious drama with historical settings, became *de rigueur*, but archaeology on the Victorian stage was in any case, from the time of Charles Kean, closely akin to display, a visual flourish of scholarship and resources combined. It was the outward show of things that tended to be most archaeological: the elaborate procession, the crowded market-place, the banquet in the palace. The authentic hut, little shop, or mean street did not win such favour. Thus a taste for archaeology was entirely compatible with a taste for spectacle. No manager solved the problems posed by archaeology, although Irving, himself not a fanatic devotee of the faith, came nearest. He did it, however, through artistry rather than archaeology.

Despite the difficulties, the impulse to archaeological correctness pervaded the Victorian theatre and extended to lighter forms of drama. George Augustus Sala wrote a burlesque, *Wat Tyler, M.P.*, for the Gaiety in 1869, and *The Times* (22 December 1869), describing it as 'one of the most costly and elaborate spectacles ever seen at any theatre', also observed that it set out to illustrate a particular period of costume and architecture and did it to perfection. John Hollingshead, the manager, declared that he had placed *Wat Tyler* on stage as carefully as Charles Kean did his Shakespeare.[31] Godwin's view that comedies of manners necessitated full archaeological treatment had already been put into practice by the Bancrofts, whom he advised on *The Merchant of Venice* in 1875. At the Prince of Wales's in 1874 the Bancrofts revived *The School for Scandal*, in 1884 *The Rivals* at the Haymarket. They conceived of the former as an exact picture of its period; this was the spirit in which it was produced and the spirit in which the public took it. In preparation Bancroft and his principal scenic artist, George Gordon, followed approved paths. Research visits were made to the Print Room and Reading Room in the British Museum, and to Knole in order to choose the type of room, pictures, and furniture wanted on stage. Months of work followed, and the results were lavishly praised. Clement Scott in the *Daily Telegraph* (6 April 1874) gave full marks to the reality of everything and to the 'beautiful pictures' placed before the audience, taking it for granted that the primary intention in reviving *The School for Scandal* was to reproduce the society of 1777. Much of his review is a description of costumes, carpets, curtains, and other properties. Dutton Cook compared this 'highly embellished edition' of the play with the work of Kean, praised the rich appointments and painstaking reproduction of scenes of eighteenth-century life, dismissed the reservations of those worried by 'the first invasion of comedy by the spirit of spectacle', and admired the dress and attitude of the actors, 'who wear the look, indeed, of animated portraits of Gainsborough and Sir Joshua'.[32] The idea of doing a play as if one were illustrating a book runs right through the period; it is apparent in Dutton Cook's remarks and stated explicitly by the actor and manager William Creswick in a letter to the Bancrofts praising the revival: 'I have ever thought that the revival of a great dramatic work should resemble the production of a grand book. The illustrations should be original, new, and more brilliant and appropriate than any upon the same subject that may have preceded it.'[33]

The Rivals was produced on the same principles as *The School for Scandal*: picturesqueness and historicity, and scenes were rearranged to prevent too frequent changes and 'to allow of the intended elaborate picture of old Bath'. (In pictorial and spectacle theatre the text of a classic play was frequently cut for this reason, to avoid too many scene changes and too much scenery, to make room for the often time-consuming changes that were necessary, and to accommodate the lengthy entry and exits of large numbers of actors, notably in processions, marches, festivities, and the like.) William Telbin, the principal scene painter on this occasion, went off to Bath to consult authorities and make sketches, and the British Museum was once again a place of scholarly resort. *The Rivals* was not nearly as successful as *The School for Scandal*. The Bancrofts blamed this partly on its unsuitability for 'elaborate illustration' and detailed treatment; some critics said that their company, used to playing the comedies of Tom Robertson, simply did not have the style for the older comedy. However, few voices were raised against the pictorial and archaeological approach, and these methods continued to be applied to modern comedy, as they already had been to Shakespearean comedy. David Belasco, for instance, produced his period comedies in New York in the same way as the Bancrofts, but more lavishly and expensively. His own play, *Sweet Kitty Bellairs* (1903) was also set in eighteenth-century Bath and had the same pictorial and archaeological motivation. He had even purchased the principal properties in Bath itself, as Irving had shopped for *Faust* in Nuremberg some years earlier.

The general sumptuousness of stage setting could easily overwhelm archaeological detail, and audiences cared more for the former than the latter in any case. Splendour of mounting could be grossly inappropriate to the content and actual setting of a play. Drawing-rooms looked like state reception-rooms in palaces; a garden scene opened into visions of park-like beauty. The varied brilliance of colour on stage in a spectacle scene could have an overpowering effect; a writer in 1896 thought that the current fashion for dressing each actor of a group in a different colour – musical comedy and pantomime seem to be the references here – was not effective, 'giving the stage the appearance of a grand fancy dress ball; whereas the fewer colours, and those in large masses, must be like somebody's cocoa, both grateful and comforting – but in this case to the eye.'[34] All pantomime producers did not make this alleged mistake, however, and there is evidence that both Augustus Harris and his successor Arthur Collins at Drury Lane thought in terms of toning blocks of colour rather than a large group containing different individual colours.

The spectacular display of mass and colour would have been impossible without advances in lighting technology. The various forms of lighting introduced through these advances had more or less the same objective: to throw more and brighter light upon the actor and the scene, to control the intensity and the area of lighting, and to extend its colour range. The arts of scene painting and costuming in the context of gas, limelight, and electric light could not be the same as in the days of candlelight and oil lamps; better lighting also led to the development of new scenic and dress materials. Gaslight was used on stage in 1817, limelight in 1837, the electric carbon-arc in 1848, and the incandescent carbon-filament light in 1881. All these took some time to improve and perfect. Innovations in lighting on the English stage go back a long way before 1817, of course. De Loutherbourg's experiments with coloured silk screens and transparencies at Drury Lane in the 1770s had important and far-reaching effects in the romantic theatre, and rudimentary methods of brightening and darkening the scene had been developed for candles on wing-ladders and footlights. Yet it was not until the use of limelight that really spectacular display became feasible, and the introduction of the focused lime (in Kean's *Henry VIII* in 1855) made it possible for beams of concentrated and resplendent light to create wonderful effects in combination with new colours and new materials, as well as to bathe the face, costume, and body of the individual actor in a powerful light. The strength and brilliancy of limelight made lighting through or behind transparencies – scenes painted on gauze-like material – technically superior and more impressive. The use in sets and costumes of any substance that would reflect or refract light became common; gilt foil, glass, crystal, and spangles were sown into dresses and glittered from the scene. Bright satins, plush, silks, brocades, and rich velvets showed up well in light of this quality, which also shone dazzlingly from a great array of silvery armour, shields, and helmets.

The same revolution, then, occurred in costuming as in lighting. Although coarseness and clumsiness in costuming still existed at many theatres, by the 1870s and 1880s there had been significant improvements. Costumiers worked with new models, new materials, and new ornamentation. Breastplates and shields were no longer tinselled, gauntlets and boots no longer smeared with yellow ochre, glazed calico no longer substituted for real satin in court dresses worn at the back of the stage. The proliferation of light-reflecting substances and highly coloured costume material on the person of the actor, together with a new brilliancy of illumination that could penetrate all corners of the stage, enabled managers to employ large groups of attractive young women attired in this way as extensions of the scenery, ranged around the back and sides of the stage.

Limelight, in particular, could penetrate and illumine where less powerful light was ineffective, and it was especially brilliant when its coloured rays reflected from jewelled armour. It was also romantically appropriate to sunrise, sunset, and moonlight, and the number of scenes written to incorporate such effects multiplied enormously. Dawn, twilight, and very subtle gradations of colour change were harder to manage, and only mastered by the best gasmen and most artistically inclined managers. Lighting was closely related to scene painting – sunlight and moonlight were often painted on the scene – and it was found that gaslight coarsened or killed some colours and altered others. For the same reason greys and very quiet colours were not particularly effective. Red limelight thrown on the white smoke created by lycopodium flares could convincingly simulate fire, and bright coloured flares from mixtures of chemical powders which were combinations of sulphur, arsenic, charcoal, strontium, etc., burnt in metal boxes in the wings and

known as 'blue fire', 'red fire', 'green fire', and 'white fire' – depending on
the mixture – cast a lurid glare on many a melodramatic *'picture'* and
pantomime transformation.[35]

Obviously, the brighter and more colourful the light on the one hand and
the scenic and costume material on the other, and the more dazzling and
peacock-like the relationship between the two, the more impressive and
spectacular the display. The very existence of a rapidly improving technology
which could facilitate such a relationship inevitably impelled the stage,
through an unstoppable force of its own, to greater and greater heights of
spectacular effect, given the accompanying presence of favourable public taste
and appropriate financial resources. The possibility of increasing light
intensity meant that it *was* increased, and critics soon began to complain of
the result and its effect upon the scene, the actor, and the audience. The
fierceness of light seemed to eliminate distance and throw everything into the
same plane. This light was also, in unskilled hands, an entirely unnatural light
– a cause of worry in an age of stage realism, and effects of sunlight and
shadows, except for the coarse shadows cast by limelight, could not be
managed in the equable glare of gaslight coming from the front, the sides, and
above; thus it was often necessary to paint shadows with colour. Before
Irving's tenure of the Lyceum it would seem that area lighting hardly existed
and that the general idea, except for specifically romantic effects, was to throw
as much indifferentiated light as possible upon the actors and the scene. Even
in the 1880s and 1890s objections to too much light were frequently heard,
perhaps more applicable now to pantomime and ballet than other kinds of
theatre. The complaint of a well-known costume designer in 1895 is worth
recording:[36]

> I want to see a stage illuminated with a suggestion of real sunlight, with
> shadows from the figures in one direction only. In processions and big
> spectacles, the habit of reinforcing the fiery furnace of the footlights with
> enormous lime-boxes; and of supplementing these by others at the various
> entrances, is utterly destructive of light and shade; and drapery subjected
> to this searching glare loses all its beauty and meaning. Again, a partiality
> for coloured rays of light threatens to extinguish all colour in the dress, and
> is greatly to be deplored.

The consequences of such a glare of light upon the actor were noted with
disfavour. Actors were perceived to move in a ring of fire, and the word
'furnace' was sometimes applied to the way in which the stage was lit.
Spectators were distracted by glitter and found it hard to concentrate their
attention on the individual actor. The conditions arousing protests of this kind
persisted well after the arrival of electric stage lighting. In fact they continued
to exist for some years, as witness critical reaction to some aspects of lighting
in Tree's Shakespeare productions. The importance of the actor was
diminished by this super-abundant light, unless he were part of a brightly

coloured mass, in which case his identity was absorbed into that of the group. Right to the end of our period the proper relationship of light to colour, the actor, and the scene, as well as the necessity of chiaroscuro and the reproduction of the natural effects of light, were difficulties, most obviously in spectacle theatre.

The problems which the actor encountered in spectacle theatre were manifold. Not only could his individuality be nullified by the effects of light, mass, or colour, but also there was no easy way of distinguishing him from a scenic environment into which he was now fully integrated. In some theatres disharmonies resulted from the absence of artistic control by a single mind, and it is certainly true that a strong-willed manager with taste could obtain better artistic results in his theatre than in a theatre where scene painter, costume designer, and property master each went more or less his own way. Harmoniously produced or not, ostentatious show was a substantial box-office attraction in its own right, a proposition annually demonstrated by the success of Augustus Harris at Drury Lane in pantomime and melodrama, in which acting performances were never of much consequence to audiences. Since the end of the eighteenth century actors had been struggling to project style from large stages into vast auditoria, and the big theatres – Drury Lane, Covent Garden, the Standard, Astley's, the Pavilion, the Britannia – were still dominated by spectacle in the second half of the nineteenth century, despite the existence of many smaller theatres suited to a more intimate and natural acting style. Irving's and Tree's approach to the problem of the identity of the actor in pictorial spectacle will be outlined in the chapters on *Faust* and *Henry VIII*, but the problem was never fully solved. Indeed, it was inherent in the spectacle style. The solution advocated and eventually implemented by the reformers was to abolish the spectacle style and concentrate on the actor's relationship to light and space rather than the pictorial replication of the modern or ancient world and the filling of space with as many people and as much light and colour as possible.

Controversy over stage spectacle had long been established in English criticism, going back to the Dryden–Davenant *Tempest*, the Italian opera of the early eighteenth century, and virtually the whole career of pantomime. In the nineteenth century, however, after the perennial subject of the decline of the drama had been exhausted in the years before 1850, the problem of spectacle became more pressing, as we have seen in the comments on the use of light. The conventional view of the function of pictorial scenery and effects did not change and was repeatedly expressed. In 1853 Donne believed that the conditions of scenic effect were not difficult to define; 'they are the framework of the picture, not the picture itself. ... The object of pictorial illustrations on the stage, is not so much the historical as the practical element of the drama. ... So much of the costume or the scenery as calls off attention from the actor, is excess.' Donne did not think that exact copies of swords, helmets, mantles, or reproductions of actual streets were necessary; the main thing was that 'an artistic sense of the beautiful should preside and predominate over scenical representations'.[37] One should go to a panorama if one wanted a splendid view of Venice, and the actual exhibition of pomp and ceremony, of battles and processions, merely detracted from the actor and the proper business of the scene. Donne was writing in the same year as Kean's production of *Sardanapalus*, and the battle he was fighting was already lost. Nevertheless, over forty years later William Archer was almost of the same opinion, but with significant concessions to the principle of realistic illustration: 'The fundamental axiom, I take it, is that scenery should as nearly as possible express to the eye the locality which was present to the author's imagination, without distracting the attention of the audience from the action of the play, either by too great ingenuity and luxury or by ludicrous inadequacy.'[38] This was the received point of view at the end of the century and one that managers such as Irving tried to adhere to in practice.

A practitioner like Godwin argued strongly that acting was a subordinate art and must, if necessary, be sacrificed to pictorial and realistic effect. This was an extreme, though not unheard-of position, and the public's acceptance of spectacle was matched by the readiness of a handsome majority of critics to defend it. The more educated critics cited Wagner as eminent precedent for advocating the legitimacy of a union on the English stage of pictorial spectacle and the art of acting. Henry James pointed out that such a union never worked in practice, since 'there is evidently a corrosive principle in the large command of machinery and decorations — a germ of perversion and corruption. It gets the upper hand — it becomes the master. It is so much less easy to get good actors than good scenery and to represent a situation by the delicacy of personal art than by 'building it in' and having everything real.'[39] A few years later, however, Max Beerbohm professed that he could not understand Sidney Lee's strictures upon elaborately scenic productions. As long as scenery was kept in the same relation to the actors as the surroundings of people in real life bore to them, there should surely be no distraction. A paucity of scenery would only draw attention to itself. When a play is acted, 'the characters are there, as large as life, before your very eyes. Surely, their surroundings ought to be there too. You imagine either everything or nothing. The only justification for no scenery would be invisible mimes.'[40]

Clearly, the nature and operation of the imagination in the theatre was almost as much a matter of dispute as the actual merit or demerit of spectacle itself. Those in favour of spectacle argued that the pictorial recreation of contemporary and historical reality, together with the beautiful and ornamental additions of fine paintings, rich costumes, and lavishly executed properties, supplied inevitable deficiencies in the imagination of a modern audience no longer content with simplicity of staging, the voice of the actor, and the spoken word. Those against argued the reverse: that spectacle suffocated the imagination rather than nourished it, that it distracted attention from the actor and the spoken word, and that a gorgeous picture was an inadequate substitute for the skills of the actor and dramatist. Both were generally agreed, in theory, that harmony between background and foreground, between picture and actor, was desirable, and that the latter should not be subordinated to the former. Pictorial illustration itself was rarely attacked, because it was considered beautiful and appropriate by all parties, pleased audiences, and was a dominant cultural mode. However, practice was another matter, and the opponents of spectacle were rarely satisfied with that. The compelling actor might through his own abilities make the spectator forget all about stage accessories, but it was difficult to mark the exact point when pictorial illustration became spectacular excess. Perhaps the decision could be left to the individual playgoer or the intelligent audience. But what was the intelligent audience, and where could one find it? A fair amount of criticism in the second half of the nineteenth century tried to prove that no such audience existed, and that too many playgoers were really rather stupid and without taste. These playgoers, because of their limitations, were supposed to thrive on spectacle. A Lyceum audience for an Irving production might be considered the best intelligent audience available, but it enjoyed the Irving brand of spectacle as much as the allegedly unthinking audience at lesser theatres revelled in lower forms of display.

Spectacle theatre carried with it the taint of vulgarity and tastelessness, and could never entirely avoid the critical sniff, the upturned nose. Certainly much of the audience liked glare and glitter, and the more gorgeous the stage appeared the more they admired it. The degeneration of popular taste, the pictorial aims of managers, the domination of scene painters and carpenters and gasmen, the lack of strong actors, the enthusiasm of archaeological advisers — these were all reasons advanced for the supremacy and long continuance of stage spectacle. Near the end of the century spectacle was defined as 'an abundance of tinsel, silks, and satins, gorgeous trappings, and an exuberance and a brilliancy in effects of colour and light';[41] these are indeed both its outward manifestations and much of its substance. However, the reasons for its existence are complex and are to be found in society and culture at large as much as in the theatre itself. The relationship between spectacle, realism, historicity, archaeology, and pictorialism is most richly illustrated in the staging of Shakespeare. So many of the ideas and so much of the style of spectacle theatre come together in the Victorian production of Shakespeare that it is fruitful ground for further investigation.

2 · Shakespeare

Shakespearean performance in the Victorian period became a battleground between supporters and opponents of the spectacle style, a territory contested with particular bitterness toward the end of the century and during the reign of Edward VII. Spectacle's conquest of melodrama and pantomime merely signified the loss of outposts remote from the heartland of the legitimate drama, but to strike at Shakespeare himself endangered the very capital of the country. Despite protests against the spectacle production of Shakespeare, however, it remained the dominant mode even at the height of contrary argument in the years from 1890 to 1910. Those favouring it, or at least those favouring the general application of pictorialism, historical realism, and archaeological principles to Shakespeare, could and did argue from the educational point of view as well as the theatrical; there was, indeed, more than a touch of missionary zeal about the frequent justification of such theories by educational imperatives. The teaching of history through the production of a pictorialised and archaeologised Shakespeare was a worthy goal in itself. Such an attitude is especially noticeable in Charles Kean, but others held it also, and this often ostentatiously stated nobility of purpose distinguishes pictorial and spectacle Shakespeare from other kinds of theatre. The already long-existing tradition of Shakespearean illustration and paintings of Shakespearean scenes gives additional respectability as well as important antecedents to a particular style of Shakespearean production, and frequently painstaking scholarly research was necessitated by and also dignified archaeological presentation.

The articulation of a theory of spectacle appropriate to the performance of Shakespeare goes back at least to the ideas of Macready in the 1830s. It was he who resolved to stage *The Tempest* at Covent Garden in 1838 as a physical and pictorial realisation of the text. Taking the hint from his stage manager, Serle, that the choruses in *Henry V* would 'admit of illustration', he commissioned Stanfield's panoramas in 1839. It was not generally until much later, however, that managers and critics began assuming that Shakespeare himself, fondly desirous of the glories of theatrical spectacle, was a confessed apologist for the alleged poverty of effects in his own theatre. The choruses in *Henry V* were a case in point. In the first chorus Shakespeare obviously regretted the deficiencies of his own stage and implored the spectator to correct them by means of his own imagination. Henry Arthur Jones assumed that Shakespeare, if he were alive, 'would rejoice in the beautiful illustration of his plays that is now always accorded to them by the better West-End theatres.'[1] The notion of a grateful Shakespeare seated comfortably in the stalls, delighted at the full expression of the pictorial and spectacular possibilities of his plays finally attained by the late Victorian theatre, is essentially a teleological one, and was not uncommon. Tree expounded it again when he considered the stage directions in *The Tempest* and *Pericles* and the whole scenic tenor of *Henry VIII*. Summoning Shakespeare as a witness to the current controversy, he declared that he foresaw as well as desired spectacle production. The Vision scene in *Henry VIII* proved the point. 'Surely no one reading the vision of Katharine of Aragon can come to any conclusion than that Shakespeare intended to leave as little to the imagination as possible, and to put upon the stage as gorgeous and complete a picture as the resources of the theatre could supply.'[2] The creation of a Shakespeare in the image of the late Victorian producer was the theatrical equivalent of an etymological backformation. To compare the rich and opulent mode of contemporary practice with a supposedly austere and barren Elizabethan style was one aspect of it, but to go on from there to posit an Elizabethan audience as unimaginative as a Victorian audience was deemed to be, and an Elizabethan Shakespeare hemmed in and frustrated by the absence of Victorian spectacle on his own stage, was an assertion of theatrical progress and perfectibility breathtaking in its sheer confidence, audacity, and – we might add with the unfair advantage of hindsight – smugness.

There was something of a defensive posture in all this, since toward the end of our period the spectacle style in Shakespeare was under heavy attack. Much earlier in the nineteenth century, however, it was realised that new ways of doing Shakespeare had to be found to suit the taste of the age, and that it was no use going on in the old ways. Talking to Lady Pollock about Charles Kean's *Winter's Tale*, Macready admitted partial responsibility for a style in which accessories swallowed up both poetry and action, since he had himself endeavoured to enrich Shakespeare's poetry with appropriate scenery, to give the tragedies due magnificence and the comedies due brilliance. Yet the example he gave, he now recognised, was 'accompanied with great peril, for the public is willing to have the magnificence without the tragedy. ... Did *I* hold the torch? Did *I* point out the path?'[3] Whether he did or not is not really relevant to the fact that Macready believed it necessary to approach Shakespeare afresh and evolved elements of a spectacle style which Kean later enlarged and intensified. George Henry Lewes, no friend of Kean's, nevertheless said in reviewing the latter's *King John* in 1852[4] that clearly

we must have some accessory attraction to replace that literary and historical interest which originally made Shakespeare's historical plays accept-
able; and that therefore Macready was wholly right in the principle of his
revivals. Scenery, dresses, groupings, archaeological research, and pictorial
splendour, can replace for moderns the poetic and historic interest which
our forefathers felt in these plays.

Although Shakespeare's descriptions were part of his imaginative method,
they were considered undramatic, despite their beauty. Scenery, for instance,
explained itself and immediately informed the audience of the surroundings
and the period.

Even if Shakespeare had been unable to fill the agreeable role of witness for
the prosecution, the production of his plays would have taken precisely the
same course. The requirements of historical realism, archaeological accuracy,
and pictorial realisation necessitated full and elaborate scenic treatment. Tree
claimed that in order to represent Shakespeare worthily 'the scenic
embellishment should be as beautiful and costly as the subject of the drama
being performed seems to demand' – the possibilities of 'seems to demand'
obviously developed and defined by the manager rather than the text.
Furthermore, such embellishment should not necessarily be subordinate to
the dramatic interest of the play, but in harmony with it.[5] The parallel
between Shakespearean production and the methods of Bayreuth was clearly a
desirable one for Tree, and even a less sybaritically inclined theorist like
William Archer professed himself unbothered by the current overindulgence
in expense and show, and denied the charge that Shakespeare was distorted
and obscured by rich decoration. Archer said that the techniques of spectacle
came to Shakespeare from melodrama and pantomime, and that a happy
medium of illustrative decoration would be reached after the enthusiasm for
splendour and archaeological pedantry died away. In the meantime, if the
public enjoyed ostentatious presentation of the text, why should they not have
that pleasure?[6]

The opposition to spectacular Shakespeare came in statements of theory
and assertion of critical dogma as well as in practical experiments like those
carried out by William Poel, whose work is too well known to need comment
here. This critical opposition had little influence in the commercial theatre,
where the pictorial and spectacular style dominated throughout our period
despite the restraint of an occasional production like Tree's *Hamlet*, revived
for his Shakespeare Festivals at His Majesty's between 1905 and 1910, and
played simply in front of curtains or tapestries. In 1844 Benjamin Webster
had staged *The Taming of the Shrew* at the Haymarket in Elizabethan
costumes, a tapestry curtain upstage, a pair of screens, placards pinned to the
curtain to indicate the place of action, and a stage audience (but no stage
apron).[7] This was, however, an isolated experiment for its time. The point of
view taken by Lewes and others was that something had to replace the

audience's former but now lapsed poetical and historical interest in the text.

The principal objection to the spectacle style was, obviously, that it overpowered Shakespeare's plays with effects. Examples of these effects will be given below, but it is worth-while referring briefly to one or two general critical positions representative of a considerable agglomeration of similar views. Complaints about the subordination of acting to spectacle were more commonly heard with regard to Shakespeare than to any other dramatist in the nineteenth century. In writing of Mary Anderson's *Romeo and Juliet* at the Lyceum in 1884, Clement Scott declared that it was no longer a question of how a Shakespearean character should be played, but of how much money should be spent on the scenery. Scott was on the whole a great admirer of the scenic style of the Lyceum under Irving, but he came down hard upon Mary Anderson. 'Silks and satins, stuffs and tapestry, the shape of a shoe, the cut of a gown, the form of a lamp, the topography of a street are preferred to the interpretation of any one given part.'[8] Scott had always been able in a review to recreate, with life, colour, and detail, an actor's performance, and it is not surprising that his main concern with modern productions of Shakespeare was the effect of spectacle upon the actor. Other critics worried about the use of mass, space, and light, as well as costume and scenery. Sidney Lee, a critical conservative in direct line of descent from William Bodham Donne, strongly attacked the modern spectacular method of staging Shakespeare. Lee objected to doing anything more than merely suggesting the scenic environment, and condemned the presence of more actors than were actually necessary to conduct the proper business of the scene, arguing against superfluous processions of psalm-singing priests, monks, and hosts of Venetians hanging about the Rialto. 'No valid reason can be adduced why persons should appear on the stage who are not precisely indicated by the text of the play or by the authentic stage directions'[9] – is an injunction to make Victorian managers recoil in horror; it was, of course, together with fiats of a like nature, aimed at Tree and producers of his school. Tree himself was betrayed from within the commercial theatre by a fellow-manager, Herbert Trench of the Haymarket, who savaged spectacular Shakespeare in print a short time before the opening of Tree's *King Henry VIII* at His Majesty's. Trench condemned the alleged vices of such as Tree:

> The eye must not be sodden and satiated in vulgar profusions of loud glar-
> ing colours, trumpet-notes of satins, rich textures and spangled stuffs,
> ballet dances or farcical ceremonies – in which courtiers are ever prancing
> about in their best. The stage must not be, as it always is now-
> adays, a fierce blaze of evenly shed, unflickering and merciless electric
> light. Packed and innumerable crowds ... are totally unnecessary for
> Shakespearian performances ... no effort [should be made] at squalid real-
> ism of costly stuffs or expensive timbering.

In place of all this scenic lumber there should be a platform stage, stress on poetry, area lighting, suggestive scenery, simplicity in pictorial effects where these are necessary, and rapid changes of scene through the swift interchange of painted cloths.[10]

Both Trench's article and Tree's *Henry VIII* appeared in 1910. By this time the tradition of pictorialised, historically recreative, and increasingly spectacular productions of Shakespeare had lasted for nearly a century. Older still than this tradition was another way of approaching Shakespeare, through painting and book illustration. This kind of approach, defining Shakespeare in a series of historical and romantic pictorial images, gave him a strongly visual character which was appropriated and strengthened by the stage. A substantial public, well acquainted with paintings of Shakespearean characters and scenes, and well educated in printed Shakespearean iconography by a steady stream of illustrated editions of the plays, took new visual expectations to Shakespearean performances early in the nineteenth century. In combination with the social and cultural trends discussed in the previous chapter which were creating and enhancing an intensely visual and pictorial context for daily life, these expectations must have profoundly affected Shakespearean production.

The man responsible for the first extensive iconography of Shakespeare was John Boydell, alderman and later Lord Mayor of London. In the 1780s Boydell was a print dealer with a large and profitable business. He was struck with the idea of founding a school of British historical art by commissioning paintings of Shakespearean scenes from a wide variety of artists, some of great eminence. Sir Joshua Reynolds contributed 'Puck', 'The Death of Cardinal Beaufort', and 'Macbeth and the Witches'; Benjamin West a fine 'Lear in the Storm' and 'Ophelia before the King and Queen'. Romney painted the shipwreck in *The Tempest*, Joseph Wright of Derby 'Prospero's Cell' and 'Antigonus Pursued by a Bear'. William Hamilton did twenty-three pictures, Francis Wheatley thirteen; other well-known artists commissioned by Boydell included Robert Smirke, Richard Westall, and James Northcote. Henry Fuseli painted several pictures for Boydell, including one of *The Tempest* and two of *A Midsummer Night's Dream*, 'Titania and Bottom' and 'Titania's Awakening'. In 1789, in order to exhibit the paintings, Boydell opened the Shakespeare Gallery in Pall Mall. The first thirty-four canvases went on exhibition that year, to be joined the following year by thirty-three more. The final total was 167 paintings and three pieces of sculpture, altogether involving thirty-five artists. To pay for all this, and indeed to make a profit, it was decided to collect engravings of the paintings in a splendid folio edition, and also to bring out in parts an edition of the plays accompanied by smaller reproductions. The folio edition did not appear until 1805, the year which also finally saw the completion of the parts, a project started in 1791. In the 1790s Boydell ran into serious financial difficulties, and had to raffle the paintings in the Gallery in 1804 in order to recover his losses. Abortive though the grand plan proved to be, it nevertheless had a considerable influence in stimulating the publication of illustrated editions of Shakespeare and in firmly associating Shakespeare with British history and the easel artist. Enthusiasm for the historical settings and pictorial images of nineteenth-century stage Shakespeare is easier to understand after a study of Boydell's venture.

Other paintings besides those commissioned by Boydell and many more illustrated editions of the plays further extended the pictorialising of Shakespeare. Of the artists, Fuseli and William Blake were the most notable, and their conceptions of Shakespeare were strongly romantic. *Macbeth* and *A Midsummer Night's Dream* were the plays that keenly interested Fuseli, but most of Blake's drawings were unknown to the public. John Martin did a characteristic painting in 1820 of Macbeth and Banquo confronting the witches, in which a vast landscape of rocks and towering clouds forces the main figures into gesticulating insignificance. Engravings after Fuseli's Shakespeare drawings were published by Rivington in a ten-volume edition in 1805; from the time of Boydell and for over a century afterward illustrated editions of Shakespeare came out with unfailing regularity. The Wheeler edition appeared in 1827 with 230 wood engravings; the Boydell engravings were reissued by Valpy in fifteen volumes in 1832–4. C. R. Leslie was one of the illustrators of Heath's *The Shakespeare Gallery* (1836), which concentrated on the female characters, and Heath also published an illustrated folio of *The Heroines of Shakespeare* in 1848. Knight's *Pictorial Edition of the Works of Shakespeare* in eight volumes (1839–42) was long a standard iconography. Baudry's edition of 1843 contained thirty-eight wood and forty-two steel engravings, and in the same year the *Works* were published in three volumes with over 1,000 wood engravings by Kenny Meadows. In the 1850s came the Halliwell Shakespeare and Samuel Phelps Shakespeare, in the next decade the *Cassell's Illustrated Shakespeare*. The *Henry Irving Shakespeare* (1887–90) was illustrated by Gordon Browne, the *Comedies of Shakespeare* (1896) by Edwin Abbey. These are only a selection of the numerous illustrated anthologies of the nineteenth century; individual plays were also illustrated by known and popular artists. To take only two, *The Tempest* was illustrated by Birkett Foster, Gustave Doré, and others in 1860, by R. A. Bell in 1901, by Walter Crane in 1902, and Edmund Dulac in 1908; *A Midsummer Night's Dream* was illustrated by J. Moyr Smith in 1892, R. A. Bell in 1895, and Arthur Rackham in 1908.

The Tempest and *A Midsummer Night's Dream* had the same popularity with painters as with illustrators. Reynolds's 'Puck' and Fuseli's two paintings for Boydell were early examples of an artistic obsession with what were considered to be Shakespeare's fairy plays, and foreshadowed that minor but distinct genre of Victorian art, fairy painting. Throughout the period, the number of paintings of both plays is extraordinary, and the subjects are almost

invariably the fairies and sprites (or monster, in the case of Caliban) among
the *dramatis personae*. Oberon, Titania, Puck, and the fairies are the major
figures in paintings of *A Midsummer Night's Dream* such as David Scott's
'Puck Fleeing before the Dawn' (1837); Richard Dadd's 'Puck' (1841) and
'Contradiction: Oberon and Titania' (1854–8); Robert Huskisson's 'The
Midsummer Night's Fairies' (*c.* 1847), of Titania sleeping; Joseph Noel
Paton's twin canvases 'The Quarrel of Oberon and Titania' (1849) and 'The
Reconciliation of Oberon and Titania' (1847); Edwin Landseer's 'Titania
and Bottom' (*c.* 1851); and two watercolours and one oil by John Simmons
of Titania – standing, flying, sleeping (1866–72). *Tempest* paintings naturally
concentrated on Ariel and Caliban, especially the former, although Richard
Dadd's 'Come unto these Yellow Sands' (1842) is a view of fairies dancing
upon the sand and in the air over Prospero's island. Millais and John Anster
Fitzgerald both painted Ariel (1849 and 1858–68), and David Scott's 'Ariel
and Caliban' (1837) is a sharp juxtaposition of beautiful sprite with dark
monster. Many of the *Midsummer Night's Dream* paintings, especially those
depicting Oberon and Titania, show attendant hosts of fairies grouped in
poses of dramatic action and – particularly in Paton's twin paintings – filling
the canvas as full as Augustus Harris ever filled the Drury Lane stage with
pantomime fairies.[11] They are truly spectacle paintings in the theatrical sense.

The genre of fairy painting extended further than paintings of Shakespeare.
Stories from folklore and legend were also popular, as were literary tales.
Indeed, the acceptance and rapid growth of fairyland as fit subject matter for
literature, painting, and the stage from the 1820s to the 1840s and its survival
at least until the First World War is one of the most remarkable phenomena
of nineteenth-century culture. It was a phenomenon by no means confined to
Britain. This was also the great period of the romantic ballet, whose early
development was closely related to fairy themes. Those two great fairy ballets,
La Sylphide and *Giselle*, appeared in 1832 and 1841 respectively: in opera
Wagner wrote *Die Feen* in 1834 and Lortzing's *Undine* was performed in
1845. For some years before that the British had been able to read Thomas
Keightley's *Fairy Mythology* (1828) and T. Crofton Croker's influential
Fairy Legends and Traditions of the South of Ireland, published in three
parts between 1825 and 1828 and illustrated by several hands, including the
as yet unknown Daniel Maclise, who went on to become a history painter; in
1832 he turned to Shakespeare with a 'Puck Disenchanting Bottom'. In the
third part of his study Croker included a seventy-five-page survey, 'On the
Nature of Elves', comprising sections on, among others, Form, Dress,
Habitation, Food, Mode of Life, and Connexion with Mankind. There is
every reason to believe that this sort of information, combined with the
content and style of so many fairy paintings, influenced the visualisation of
fairies on stage, especially in *A Midsummer Night's Dream*.

Meanwhile, the fairy boom continued. A stream of fairy stories appeared in

Europe as well as in Britain. The fairy folktales of Jacob and Wilhelm Grimm, first translated in the 1820s in an edition illustrated by George Cruikshank, were published regularly in English from the 1840s, the peak decade for fairy stories and fairy extravaganzas on stage. *The Fairy Tales and Stories* of Hans Christian Andersen began to appear in English from 1846, in dozens of editions between then and the end of the century. Cruikshank's *Fairy Library* (1853–4) contained four well-known fairy tales; Ruskin and Thackeray published *The King of the Golden River* (1851) and *The Rose and the Ring* (1855) respectively. Later came Christina Rosetti's 'Goblin Market' (1862), Kingsley's *The Water Babies* (1863), *Alice's Adventures in Wonderland* (1865) and a long series of 'Fairy Books' by Andrew Lang: Blue, Green, Red, Yellow, Orange, Crimson – thirteen of them altogether between 1889 and 1910. The whole movement culminated in late Victorian pantomime, the illustrations of Rackham and Dulac, and Barrie's *Peter Pan* (1904), but it was to last years longer, as evidenced even in the middle of the War by the controversy over the Cottingley fairy photographs and Conan Doyle's spirited defence of the truth of the Cottingley fairies in *The Coming of the Fairies* (1922). The reasons for the immense popularity of fairy art, fairy literature, and fairy theatre are complex; they are also related to the fashion for spiritualism, spirit photography, levitation, and automatic writing. Critics have suggested a reaction against the rationalism and scientific materialism of the age, the realism of photography, and urban growth; and a hearkening back to an older, simpler, rural Britain in which contact with another world of shadows and spirits was a meaningful aspect of daily life.

Whatever the reasons for the existence of this movement, it was one in which theatre played a considerable part, especially Shakespeare and pantomime. Not only did the fairy cult influence *The Tempest* and *A Midsummer Night's Dream* on stage and perhaps even stimulate their production, but new pictorial conventions of depicting fairies in paintings and book illustrations also reached the stage in the same productions, which were commonly spectacular in all the theatrical senses of the word. The Victorian stage history of *A Midsummer Night's Dream*, for instance, properly begins with Madame Vestris's revival at Covent Garden in 1840, the beginning of the great fairy decade. The production was not as spectacular as Kean's in 1856, and, unlike Kean, Vestris retained 1,700 of the 2,100 lines of the play. It was, however, highly pictorial; the sylvan scenery was most beautiful, and a panorama was used to indicate changes of scene within the woodland, as in the change from II.i to II.ii. The last scene of Act V heavily stressed both the fairy and spectacle elements: the apartment in the palace of Theseus was lined with galleries and built up with flights of stairs, and a large number of fairies, upon Oberon's 'Through the house give glimmering light', moved about the galleries, up and down the stairs, and over the floor of the stage with twinkling coloured lights. This scene remained a fairy spectacle throughout the century, and was treated much like a pantomime transformation.

Samuel Phelps's *Midsummer Night's Dream* at Sadler's Wells in 1853, quite possibly the century's best, was just as pictorial as Vestris's and also used a panorama to indicate changes of place. The dream aspect was much more strongly emphasised and the play set more firmly in fairyland by the use of a green or blue gauze between the stage and audience for the second, third, and fourth acts, and by the use of subtle lighting effects behind the gauze. Henry Morley in the *Examiner* (15 October 1853) noted that 'as in dreams, one scene is made to glide insensibly into another'; the gauze subdues 'the flesh and blood of the actors into something more nearly resembling dream-figures, and incorporates more completely the actors with the scenes, throwing the same green fairy tinge, and the same mist over all. A like idea has also dictated certain contrivances of dress, especially in the case of the fairies.' Douglas Jerrold enlarged upon this feature of the production in *Lloyd's Weekly* (23 October):[12]

> It is dreamland with its curious population of fairies and elvish sprites, whose fantastic outlines the eye can scarcely make out, presented most dreamily before the spectator. There is a misty transparency about the figures that gives them the appearance of flitting shadows more than of human beings. You fancy you can see the moon shining through them. There they dance and whirl, and are puffed about first from one side and then to another, like a cloud of silver dust; and as the endless atoms of which the cloud is composed keep springing into the air, in one heap of joyous confusion, you may almost imagine, in the dreamy state which the play engenders, that the little fairies are being tossed in a big sheet of the moon, and that Puck is looking on and enjoying the fun. It is a play, in truth, to dream over.

For the last scene of all, Phelps put gas jets inside the columns of Theseus' palace and covered the columns with gauze. The jets were turned up on a darkened stage as soon as the limelight moon (moonlight dominated the production) streamed into the grand hall, thus making the columns shine with a strange and mysterious light, partly moonlight, partly fairy light. (Tree did almost the same thing in 1900, except with electric light.) The dreamlike nature of fairyland, carefully established by pictorial and technical means in the 1853 production, was a little darkened in the 1855 revival. Puck wore a grotesque outsize pantomime head, and some fairies were given a bizarre appearance, like those with large hands, who were even more noticeable as they mingled with the ideal-looking fairies. This reminded *The Times* reviewer (27 November 1855) 'forcibly' of the illustrations to Croker's *Fairy Legends*. Such misshapenness can also be found in paintings of *A Midsummer Night's Dream* – it was, according to Croker, a common aspect of fairy appearance – notably in the sinister treatments of Fuseli. *The Times* also noticed that the mixture of fantasy and humour in Croker's elves, which is also evident in the paintings, was present in the Sadler's Wells fairies.

Kean's *Midsummer Night's Dream* at the Princess's the year after Phelps's revival had something of the 'meretricious glitter' that Morley said was entirely absent at Sadler's Wells, and drew from both the Vestris and Phelps productions. It was a great popular success, running 150 nights over two seasons. Kean's biographer, who said that Shakespeare's purpose in writing *A Midsummer Night's Dream* was to produce a fairy play, was only agreeing with current theatrical opinion when he argued that 'if the mortals introduced had been rendered more prominent than the mythological agents, the entire construction and object of the play would have been subverted.'[13] Not long before this it had been considered impossible to render the world of the play on the stage – Hazlitt was of this view – but since Vestris's production and the new interest in fairies critical opinion was revised. Certainly Kean stressed the fairies, whose number he increased principally as a means of spectacle effect. Titania was lulled, rather than sung, to sleep by a ballet of fairies, and Act III ended with a chorus and dance of seventy fairies around a maypole which rose out of the stage, dropping garlands of coloured flowers when it reached its full height – very much a pantomime transformation effect. A panorama was used to indicate changes of scene. The priorities of the *Era* review (9 October 1856) were appropriate to the production, and stated with unconscious irony: 'Having commenced with the "accessories", which on this occasion are the most important part of the play, and which we pronounce to be perfect, it only remains for us briefly to notice the *dramatis personae*.'

Pictorial principles of production were not confined to Shakespeare's so-called fairy plays. They were applied consistently to all of them in the manner of the painter and book illustrator. In speaking at a dinner given in his honour at the close of his Covent Garden management in 1839, Macready declared that his aim in doing Shakespeare had been 'fidelity of illustration' and his endeavour 'to transfer his picture from the poet's mind to the stage complete in its parts and harmoniously arranged as to figure, scene, and action.'[14] Macready's use of pictures in order to achieve his objective was strikingly demonstrated in his 1839 *Henry V*, with three panoramas by Stanfield: the voyage of the English fleet to Harfleur, at the end of which the panorama dissolved into the business of the siege so that the panorama and the stage action seemed to overlap and melt into each other; the French and English camps at Agincourt; and Henry's triumphal return to London. By the time of Irving's Shakespeare at the Lyceum, it was common for critics to spend much of the space in their reviews praising the beautiful pictures in his productions. It was unthinkable to Irving, even though a strong believer in the supremacy of acting over all other aspects of production, that one could give stage life to Shakespeare's characters without realising the places they inhabited. Dismissing the notion that Shakespeare should be played much as he was in his own time, he asked rhetorically if the theatre were to repudiate all progress in stage art, 'to disdain the fruits of historical inquiry, to shun the archaeological and the antiquarian? Would my readers like to banish pictures from their books?'[15] The pictorialism of Shakespeare's imagination had to be made concrete in performance; here, of course, the platform stage of William Poel was no use and could be rejected for this reason alone. Even the poorest pictorial indication of a scene was better than none at all.

One of the best examples of Victorian Shakespeare production conducted along purely pictorial lines was *The Merchant of Venice* at the Prince of Wales's in 1875. The Bancrofts approached Shakespeare in exactly the same spirit as they had Sheridan a few months earlier; there is no indication that they saw much difference in conception between *The Merchant of Venice* and *The School for Scandal*. The latter was staged for the purpose of giving pictorial and archaeological reality to the furnishings, costumes, and manners of drawing-room society in 1777; the former to recreate in a similar fashion sixteenth-century Venice. A visit to Venice with the principal scene painter, drawings taken on the spot, the accurate reproduction of the Sala della Bussola for the Trial scene resolved on, the views of Venice on drop curtains between the acts, archaeological advice received from Godwin – all this was only part of the necessary preparation. Bancroft arranged the play to make it easier to put full pictures on stage of far fewer scenes than in the text. The first and third scenes of Act I followed an opening tableau set under the arches of the Doge's palace, 'the dialogue being welded together by carefully arranged and appropriate pantomimic action from the crowds, who were throughout passing and re-passing.' For this scene Bancroft had made plaster casts of the actual capitals of the pillars of these arches, reproductions of the real thing which were so massive and heavy on the small Prince of Wales's stage that part of a wall had to be cut away to enable the set to be wheeled on and off on trucks. The second scene was set in Belmont and opened with the Prince of Morocco's choice of caskets, followed by the Portia–Nerissa scene of Act I, scene ii, followed again by the Prince of Aragon's choosing the silver casket. The third scene, outside Shylock's house in the evening, concluded with the elopement of Jessica and Lorenzo in Act II, scene vi; the same setting was repeated by daylight and saw Shylock's encounter with Salario, Salarino, and Tubal (III, i). Bancroft's fifth scene was Belmont again and Bassanio's successful choice; the Trial scene and Portia's Garden concluded the play, all else being omitted.[16] Thus Shakespeare's twenty scenes were reduced and rearranged into seven, the kind of external schema the pictorial and spectacular theatre was virtually forced into by the exigencies of its staging.

The production was not helped by the complete failure of Charles Coghlan as Shylock, and except for Ellen Terry, a great success as Portia, the company was generally accused of underacting and being unfitted because of its modern methods to perform the classics. However, the pictures were the chief attraction, and every critic said so. The views of Venice on between-acts drop curtains were of the Campanile, the column of St Mark, the Rialto, and the Grand Canal. Ellen Terry recalled that Paolo Veronese's 'The Marriage at Cana' inspired many of the stage pictures.[17] The failure of the production – it ran only thirty-six nights – led Bancroft to think he was ahead of his time, surprising his audience too much with historical accuracy of costume and with a production which 'looked so unlike a theatre, and so much more like Italian pictures than anything that had been previously shown upon the stage'.[18] Yet, as might be expected, turning Shakespeare into a gallery of old masters did not meet with universal critical favour. Clement Scott, for instance, who lavished praise upon the pictorial recreation of eighteenth-century life in the Bancrofts' *School for Scandal*, objected in this case, quite inconsistently (except that he was reviewing Shakespeare and not Sheridan), that 'the stage is something more than a picture gallery. We go to the theatre to think, as well as to see.' The nature of the Bancrofts' pictorialism is evident from Scott's acidulous description:[19]

It is pleasant enough to be taken under the arches of the Doge's Palace, to admire the carved capitals of the pillars, to watch the picturesque water carriers as they pass, to seem to hear the ripple of the water as the gondolas glide on, and to recall the pleasure of the warm and blue Venetian sky. It is delightful, no doubt, to be introduced to these beautiful Venetian ladies at Belmont, clothed in brocade of blue or robes of peach blossoms, to watch them reclining on soft couches, toying with illuminated volumes, or dreaming under the influence of hidden music. The Prince of Morocco approaches with his splendid train, the heavy curtains of tapestry rise and fall, the caskets are set forth, one procession succeeds another, and each is more magnificent than the last. Lovely enough this Venetian life at Belmont. The scene changes to the lanes at Venice. It is no imaginative picture. We are there. Every brick, every window, the shape of the penthouse, the creeper climbing over it, the melon seller in the projecting building, the posts to which the gondolas are moored – nothing could well be more life-like and admirable. ... The finest passages in the play occur and fall dead upon the audience. We have not come to hear a play tonight, but to see the lanes of Venice. Once more we are taken to the Sala della Bussola. The frescoes on the walls are of rare beauty – every chair, every table, every footstool, has its original in Venice. When the most dramatic scene ever given us in Shakespeare is being enacted it makes no impression. ... What does it matter if an interesting trial is proceeding in the Sala della Bussola, when we look at the magnificent costume of a Doge of Venice, notice that the Venetians use tasselled pocket handkerchiefs, obtain information regarding Venetian halberdiers, and the shape of a Jewish gabardine?

Eight years later, while he had his doubts about the overwhelming richness and colour of Irving's *Romeo and Juliet*, Scott considered that on the whole spectacle served the purpose of poetic beauty and ideal truth. Irving was, in fact, respected for doing just this with his Shakespeare and for valuing the actor above the show. Yet since his views of Shakespeare included pictorialism as an indispensable element of production, it is not surprising to read Fitzgerald's reference to the 'glittering, bewitching pictures' of the Lyceum *Merchant of Venice* and his description of Alfred Thompson's costumes in terms of Venetian art: 'The artist had also called in aid the old gold yellows of the Venetian painters; the patches of crimson, or lake, used in skull-caps, or cuffs; the superb satins; the whole indeed had the effect as though Paul Veronese had been imitated, and suggested the famous feast in the Louvre.'[20] The practice of treating the costumes of *The Merchant of Venice* in the manner of Venetian painters lasted until David Belasco's traditional and strongly pictorial production in New York in 1922, a production noted for splendour of fabrics and reminiscences of Titian, Tintoretto, and Veronese. Like Bancroft, Belasco drastically rearranged the text, and put the choices of casket into three consecutive scenes in Act III.

The use of old masters to supply the costume designer with correct information about colours, cut, and fabric was a well-established practice in the second half of the nineteenth century; the same paintings could also provide useful architectural details. It was thought that managers should be educated in archaeology, costume, and architecture, and possess both a library of appropriate reference books and a collection of prints and engravings of the masters. The application of archaeological principles to the production of Shakespeare was simultaneously seen as the ultimate test and the supreme value of their worth: if archaeology failed to illuminate, illustrate, and bring to life the settings of Shakespeare, it had no real place on the stage. In the 1870s and 1880s, the period of Godwin's outdoor productions and his long series of articles on Shakespearean architecture and costume, the archaeological movement in the theatre was at its peak and its theorists and practitioners at their most confident. An important article on theatrical archaeology in 1886 was clearly written under Godwin's influence. The author at once rejects the view that only the acting in Shakespeare should be a matter of concern. Scenery and costuming are just as significant, because Shakespearean drama is 'eminently picturesque'. Accessories and surroundings are essential aspects of the development of the main idea; for Shakespeare 'externals were all-important'. Aesthetic beauty is a cardinal criterion the archaeologist should never forget, but historical realism must be the main principle of modern Shakespearean production. This is valid, since

it seems reasonable to argue that every play must needs be laid in some country and in some period more unmistakably than any other; and that, having once determined these, the stage manager has next to do his utmost to realise them by every means possible, to spare no pains to make the scenery and surroundings of the action historically harmonious, to look on every detail as an occasion for adding a truth to the verisimilitude of the whole, and to throw himself into the arms of archaeology as his best and surest friend.

The fact that the practice of historical realism and lavish antiquarian display meant long wearisome intervals while heavy sets were changed, and that Shakespeare's text had to be cut and rearranged to make room for all this did not matter, as audiences were quite prepared to accept the penalties for the sake of the benefits, provided that sufficient pomp and splendour attached to the latter. Nevertheless, archaeology must never become pedantry and cannot be applied literally to all Shakespeare's plays. A strict archaeological approach to costume in *Troilus and Cressida*, for example, would disturb an audience comfortably familiar with the theatrical version of the toga, and *The Merry Wives of Windsor* is not a historical play but set in Shakespeare's own time. Archaeological treatment is also unsuitable for a romantic and poetic comedy such as *As You Like It*. The Kendals' *As You Like It* at the St James's in 1884 is criticised for its misconceived archaeology; the characters of the play are not necessarily from the Middle Ages, and Rosalind does not need to step out of an illuminated missal. In this case the dramatist's intentions have been misunderstood; it is Shakespeare's way that must be followed, and followed with caution and respect. However, 'if in any play Shakespeare's purpose was to present as complete a picture as possible of a bygone age, then by all means let us summon the resources of archaeology to do him honour ... it would not matter though we go beyond the utmost limit he ever dreamed of, so only that we are continuing the course on which he started.'[21]

That it was Shakespeare's purpose in many of his plays to present as complete a picture as possible of a bygone age was hardly questioned by the mainstream of Victorian theatrical opinion, whose views on the matter are another striking example of remaking Shakespeare in its own image, first as a seeker after stage spectacle by the most elaborate methods, now as a historical realist and archaeologist. There were dissenting voices. *The Times* reviewer (31 December 1888) of Irving's *Macbeth*, while acknowledging the correctness of the archaeology, asked how all the historical accuracy of costumes and properties could be reconciled with the fact than an eleventh-century Macbeth spoke seventeenth-century blank verse. Such a problem disturbed neither Irving nor any other manager, and archaeological practice in Shakespeare remained unaffected by questions of this kind which queried the whole validity and consistency of the historical method.

Although it is true that archaeological theory and to a lesser extent archaeological controversy were at their height in the last quarter of the nineteenth century, the use of archaeology in Shakespearean production was much older and dates back at least fifty years before that. Like all other important movements in the nineteenth-century theatre, archaeology did not arrive on stage with a sudden bang, but was a long time preparing for its own maturity. Some of William Capon's scenes for Kemble at Drury Lane from 1794 were based on ancient architecture. The archaeological spirit was evident in Elliston's *King Lear* at Drury Lane in 1820, in which, according to the printed Advertisement, the costumes and ornaments were taken from the Saxon period, the decorations being facsimiles of engravings from the best authorities. The virtue of Saxon authenticity was somewhat undercut by another part of the Advertisement, which spoke of stage archaeology in disparaging terms: 'To talk of correctness or incorrectness would be something more than absurd; all that is left is to choose the costume of any period, not too recent, and adhere to it with fidelity, or if any additions are to be made, let them be the products of fancy, and not the fashion of another time.'[22] Clearly Elliston was no Godwin born ahead of his generation, yet archaeology was very much in the air. This was just the time when substantial works of antiquarian research like Stothard's and Meyrick's were appearing in print, and Strutt's two books on historical costume were well-established classics. Elliston's *Lear* was also the one in which Edmund Kean insisted on a storm scene − using the techniques of de Loutherbourg's Eidophusikon − so realistic and spectacular that it quite drowned out his Lear and entirely took away the attention of the audience from the actor; the branches of the trees moved individually in the wind, and each leaf on each tree was a separate rustling entity.

Meyrick, Stothard, and Strutt are among the authorities cited on the playbills of the 1823 *King John* at Covent Garden, whose costumes and properties were designed by the antiquarian-minded J. R. Planché. The bills announced that 'every Character will appear in the precise HABIT OF THE PERIOD, the Dresses and Decorations being executed from indisputable Authorities, such as Monumental Effigies, Seals, Illumined MSS. &c.' Various effigies and seals were mentioned as the originals of costumes, and the British Museum and Bodleian Library listed as scholarly collections consulted. Planché, who had been troubled by the historical inconsistencies of stage costume, recorded the audience reaction to his experiment with some satisfaction, since he had difficulty getting the actors, who thought they would be merely laughed at, to wear his (to them) strange and ugly creations:[23]

When the curtain rose, and discovered *King John* dressed as his effigy appears in Worcester Cathedral, surrounded by his barons sheathed in mail, with cylindrical helmets and correct armorial shields, and his courtiers in the long tunics and mantles of the thirteenth century, there was a roar of approbation, accompanied by four distinct rounds of applause, so general and so hearty, that the actors were astonished. Receipts of from £400 to £600 nightly soon reimbursed the management for the expense of the production, and a complete reformation of dramatic costume became from that moment inevitable upon the English stage.

The 'complete reformation' alluded to took rather longer than Planché implied, but he was at it again in 1824 with a *I Henry IV*, whose playbills made almost the same claims as those for *King John*. Macready's *King John* at Drury Lane in 1842 was also produced with close attention to historical detail as well as spectacular effect. *The Times* (25 October 1842) described the production as 'an animated picture of those Gothic times which are so splendidly illustrated by the drama. The stage is thronged with the stalwart forms of the middle ages.' In his own way Macready was a careful research scholar, writing a series of letters to the antiquary Hamilton Smith asking for correct costume details for a *Romeo and Juliet* set around 1200, a *Merchant of Venice* set around 1300, and a *Two Gentlemen of Verona* around 1500,[24] all of which he produced between 1838 and 1841. Even Shakespeare in the circus ring could be done with authentic period costuming. In 1856 William Cooke recostumed the actors in his equestrian version of *Richard III* at Astley's after designs based on paintings at Hampton Court.[25] Two years earlier Charles Kean had brought out the same play at the Princess's, a production which prompted Kean's biographer to a familiar strain in claiming that the combination of good acting, gorgeous spectacle, and historical accuracy in productions of this kind made the theatre 'a valuable school of antiquarian illustration, and a living lecture on the past'.[26]

To make his theatre just such a school was an object long desired by Kean, whose antiquarian illustration was supported by a great deal of research. To use a production of Shakespeare in order to recreate a past age, to make it 'a living lecture on the past', involved theatre staff in an enormous amount of time and labour unthinkable today, as well as a high standard of historical and archaeological education. An idea of the sort of research required has already been suggested, but it is important to elaborate briefly in order to provide some understanding of the foundation of patient investigation and preparation upon which all historically recreative and archaeologically inclined Shakespeare was built. Such research was impractical with a quick-changing repertory system, and it was not really indulged in on a continuing basis until Macready, Phelps, and Kean. Macready was devoted neither to the long run nor to an entirely reconstructive style of Shakespearean production, and engaged in historical research to a limited extent. Phelps spent less money and less time on these matters than Kean, who significantly of the three came closest to and indeed occasionally achieved long-run Shakespeare. From the business point of view it was only the long run or the hopes of a long run that would bring profits on the investment of so much time and work on the part of so many people, as well as the costly purchase and getting up of appropriate fabrics and materials. Thus when we reach the eighties and nineties, with long runs of single Shakespeare plays regularly recorded, patient and extended antiquarian research for every Shakespearean production became common practice among the major and even some minor managements, both London and provincial. It is from this period, then, that our few examples can be drawn.

As seen in the case of the Bancrofts, old master painters remained an essential source of inspiration and information about costumes and architecture. Lewis Wingfield, in designing the sets and costumes for Mary Anderson's *Romeo and Juliet* at the Lyceum in 1884 and wishing to differ from Irving's dresses for the same play two years previously, followed the architecture and costuming in the famous series of Carpaccio paintings in the Venice Accademia. Working with large photographs of the paintings at his side, Wingfield made his designs, and for materials ransacked curio shops in London and Paris for brocades and damasks of the period.[27] In doing the costumes for Irving's *Henry VIII* in 1892, Seymour Lucas turned to Holbein, state papers, and other contemporary sources. Trips to Belvoir Castle were necessary to study the details of the king's costume in the Holbein there, the Duke of Rutland permitting a copy to be made. The designs for the dresses of pages, heralds, and gentlemen-at-arms were assisted by reference to the Warwick Roll at the College of Heralds. Armour in the Tower was studied, and a judge's robes copied from a monumental effigy carved in the right period. Valuable information on the clothes of ordinary men and women was obtained from the letters home of the Spanish Ambassador to the court of Henry VIII, some of it confirmed by a Holbein at Hampton Court of the embarkation of the king from Dover for the Field of the Cloth of Gold. From many sheets of paper and several notebooks filled with archaeological sketches and commentary, Lucas prepared 138 finished chalk and outline drawings for the use of the costumier.[28]

The research and preparation for another Irving production, *Macbeth*, in 1888, has been fairly well documented. To Charles Cattermole fell the responsibility of designing costumes and properties, and Hawes Craven was the principal scenic artist. Irving's decision to perform *Macbeth* was taken in July, and it came out at the end of December; the eleventh century was chosen as the time of the play. The first month of the intervening five was spent 'searching the British and South Kensington Museums for authority for every article of costume, weapon, furniture, and domestic utensil ... as well as for details of architectural design and decoration.' The vessels in the banquet scene were exact copies of originals in the British Museum, and the patterns for some embroideries came from an eleventh-century cope at South Kensington. Illuminated manuscripts, stained glass windows, the Bayeux Tapestry, and a long list of scholarly authorities provided other information. The making of working drawings followed this initial period of research. For the banquet scene alone such drawings were made for 'swords, helmets, spears, daggers, shields, bucklers, armour (scale and ring), skin cloaks, caps, crowns, bells, musical instruments, wine-cups, ivory-cups, salt-cellars, candlesticks, Anglo-Saxon wine pots, besides cakes in the form of castles, and a host of other articles, dresses with all their manifold details, and furniture with its quaint designs and severe schemes of decoration.' The costumes were all made in workshops attached to the Lyceum, an outside costumier not being employed for *Macbeth*. Cattermole designed 408 dresses altogether, including 165 for soldiers (in groups of ten) and 80 for the traditional Flight of Witches; it took forty skilled workers to execute the designs.[29]

When Irving turned over matters of set design and costume to a man who was in all except name a professional archaeologist and antiquarian as well as a leading artist, the results were the outcome of extraordinarily methodical research. No man more qualified than Alma-Tadema could have been found for *Coriolanus*. Because of the subject matter of his own art, and his own methods of recreating that subject matter, Alma-Tadema was the painter *par excellence* of Roman scenes, entirely familiar with the architecture, materials, implements, utensils, furniture, weapons, and art objects of Roman daily life. He started on *Coriolanus* in 1880, although Irving delayed the production until 1901. In the former year, however, Alma-Tadema was already engaged in drawings, and hired an architect at £5 a week, for several months, to do perspective outlines of Roman columns and buildings. He decided to set the play in the Etruscan period where it historically belonged, rather than the era of classical Rome. In order to reconstruct the exterior and interior architecture of Etruscan public and domestic buildings, he studied Etruscan tomb carvings and Vitruvius on the Etruscan temple; for the scenes in Antium the Lycian tombs of Asia Minor. He even examined the different building materials and methods of the period in order to arrive at set designs. For costume he did a great deal of research on the toga, especially in relation to its texture and folds on ancient statuary and architectural fragments, and found that the conventional stage toga was nothing like the real thing; thus the actors in *Coriolanus* wore Alma-Tadema's restored and historically correct toga.[30]

When the archaeological and historical impulse ceased to dominate the staging of Shakespeare, then of course such massive scholarship and research became unnecessary. Today a Shakespearean producer will do almost anything rather than choose the historical period of the play for his setting, and even though considerable labour may be extended upon selecting another period – the British Raj for *Much Ado About Nothing*, the late Habsburg empire for *King Lear*, Mussolini's Italy for *Julius Caesar* – it does not nearly approach the amount of time involved in the painstaking historical re-creativeness of the archaeological method, not to mention the number of designs necessary to clothe huge casts with period accuracy. Shakespeare no longer needs a local habitation. Even to some contemporary critics, though not commercial managements, this sort of research and effort was tiresome and unnecessary. The last but unrepresentative word on the subject can be left to William Poel, whose notions of performing Shakespeare on a platform stage, in front of curtains, and in Elizabethan costume at least survive on the stage, whereas archaeological reconstruction does not. Poel's ironical advice to Shakespeare producers is as follows:[31]

> Choose your play, and be sure to note carefully in what country the incidents took place. Having done this, send artists to the locality to make sketches of the country, of its streets, its houses, its landscapes, of its people, and of their costumes. Tell your artists that they must accurately reproduce the colouring of the sky, of the foliage, of the evening shadows, of the moonlight, of the men's hair and the women's eyes; for all these details are important to the proper understanding of Shakespeare's play. Send, moreover, your leading actor and actress to spend some weeks in the neighbourhood that they may become acquainted with the manners, the gestures, the emotions of the residents, for these things also are necessary to the proper understanding of the play. Then, when you have collected, at vast expense, labour, and research this interesting information about a country of which Shakespeare was possibly entirely ignorant, thrust all this extraneous knowledge into your representation, whether it fits the context or not; let it justify the rearrangement of your play, the crowding of your stage with supernumeraries, the addition of incidental songs and glees, to say nothing of inappropriateness of costume and misconception of character.

Of all the Victorian theatre managers who practised historical reconstructions of Shakespeare, Charles Kean was the one who made the greatest show of his antiquarian research. Justificatory manifestos with his playbills and scholarly footnotes to his printed texts were directly addressed to a theatregoing and reading public to whom the wholesale archaeologising of Shakespeare was new; they needed convincing by propaganda as well as performance. Since Kean is one of the central figures of nineteenth-century Shakespearean production, he is worth considering here for his skilful combination of spectacle, educational zeal, and historical scholarship. Over a nine-year period at the Princess's, a relatively small theatre unsuited to Kean's style of production, he developed generally excellent standards of preparation, production and administrative operation, which together with the marked favour of Queen Victoria, helped to bring back to the theatre a socially influential middle-class audience that had not been too prominent in theatre attendance over the past generation, except at isolated managerial ventures like Vestris's and Macready's.

Early in his management Kean decided on the course he was to follow with regard to Shakespeare, and kept to it until he vacated the Princess's in 1859. *King John* was his first revival on historical principles in 1852. Then followed *Macbeth* in 1853, set firmly in eleventh-century Scotland, the first of the Shakespearean revivals to be accompanied by a scholarly disquisition included in the playbill. *Henry VIII* in 1855 was Kean's biggest Shakespearean hit to that date, the first Shakespeare to run for 100 consecutive nights. Spectacle always dominated this play in the nineteenth-century theatre, but Kean's printed text also gives a long list of acknowledgments to contemporary documents and drawings and to more recent antiquarians and historians of costume. Kean employed a panorama to depict in Act V the journey of the Lord Mayor and his aldermen on the Thames from London to Greenwich Palace for the christening of Elizabeth. Shown successively on the panorama as it unrolled were the Palace of Bridewell, Fleet Ditch, Blackfriars, St Paul's, London Bridge, the Tower, Limehouse, the 'Great Harry', the state barges of the Mayor and Council, Greenwich Palace and Greenwich Park. The Vision of Katharine was staged with full spectacle effect, Kean using a new and more convincing system, imported from Paris, of flying the angels, and the procession accompanying Kean's Wolsey on his first entrance even outdid in number that of Tree's production in 1910; there were fifty-two of them. For *A Midsummer Night's Dream* in 1856 Kean, although admitting that the play was far from historical, was unable to resist violating his own archaeological principles and localising it in the classical Athens known to the public, since, it was argued, little was known of Athenian architecture in the time of Theseus, when in any case buildings were rude and simple. And not, of course, (though this is not stated) suitable for pictorial and spectacular display. A similar contradiction occurred in *The Tempest* (1857), which Cole described as 'a work exclusively of imagination ... supernatural and imaginative in the highest degree'.[32] To be merely imaginative, however, was not enough for Kean, who because of the occasion presented of introducing a particular style of elegant and picturesque costume, set the play in the thirteenth century, copying his ship from authentic records of the period, classicising the *'strange shapes'* of the banquet as naiads, dryads, and satyrs, and turning the *'divers spirits in the shape of hounds'* who torment Stephano, Trinculo, and Caliban into Furies copied from Etruscan vases. Kean was nothing if not civilised, and to bring order, taste, and aesthetic beauty into Shakespearean performance was one of his principal goals. Spectacle was not neglected: an immensely realistic shipwreck scene, based on Macready's, opened the play, in which the dialogue was inaudible; the masque was produced with elaborate effects.

Preceding both *A Midsummer Night's Dream* and *The Tempest* was *The Winter's Tale* of 1856, one of Kean's more learned productions in the sense of historical and antiquarian scholarship. The text being unfortunately full of chronological contradictions, Kean selected Syracuse as the setting rather than a generalised Sicilia, a Syracuse at the height of its prosperity, since for obvious theatrical reasons (again unstated) the more prosperous the place the greater the justification for display. 'An opportunity is thus afforded', said Kean, 'of reproducing a classical era, and placing before the eyes of the spectator, *tableaux vivants* of the private and public life of the ancient

Greeks.' Kean's urge to localise Shakespeare in conformity with the rules of
geography prompted him to make the substitution, after Hanmer, of Bithynia
for coastless Bohemia, and to adopt from the drawings of George Scharf the
'vegetation peculiar to Bithynia'. On the grounds of 'presenting with closer
accuracy the domestic manners of the period', Leontes and his guests were
shown at a feast in Act I, scene ii. The notes to this scene discuss the use of
herbs and flowers at ancient banquets, the way guests at these affairs reclined
on couches, the Canephorae or female statues supporting the cornice, the
Hymn to Apollo inserted into the scene, and a similarly interpolated Pyrrhic
Dance by thirty-six youths in armour (this last warranted a two-page note) –
all this stage display and all this scholarship, needless to say, expended on the
incidentals of a feast not even mentioned by Shakespeare. The Chorus,
traditionally an old Father Time figure with scythe and hourglass, was
transformed into Cronos, and this became the excuse for an allegorical tableau
bracketing his appearance at the beginning of Act IV: first Luna and the Stars
sinking from the night sky, then Phoebus in the Chariot of the Sun rising,
each figure taken, according to Cole, from the centre of Flaxman's Shield of
Achilles. The blaze of light encircling the chariot was undoubtedly provided
by an electric arc, not long in use on Kean's stage. *The Winter's Tale* was
another resounding success, running for 102 consecutive nights. The *Daily
Telegraph* (29 April 1856) said in its review that Kean was the first manager
'to turn the glitter of spectacle to useful account, and to impart to the most
gorgeous decorations such historical accuracy that, whilst the eye was dazzled
with brilliancy, the spectator was afforded an opportunity of seeing beneath
the surface, and of discovering matter to improve the understanding' – a
claim not allowed by Kean's enemies, such as Lewes and Jerrold. The
reviewer added that the public would no longer be satisfied with merely the
pomp and circumstance of a triumphal procession on stage, but would require
'local colouring, characteristic features and adjuncts true to history and nature
as part and parcel of the show placed before them'. He could not have
foretold the coming of Augustus Harris; the theatregoing public never lost its
taste for a spectacular procession, historically recreative or not.

One of the most spectacular moments in Kean's Shakespeare came in the
procession interpolated into *King Richard II* (1857) of Richard and
Bolingbroke's entry into London, which illustrated York's description of the
event in Act V, scene ii. Typically of Kean, it was also one of his recreative
and archaeological triumphs: mass, colour, sound, movement, and historical
accuracy all came together in the one theatrical event. Kean stated that his
intention was to reproduce the scene as it actually occurred in London 450
years before. The few words spoken in the procession were selected from
contemporary chronicles, and the *'incidental amusements of the crowd'*,
which included acrobats and dancers, from Strutt's *Sports and Pastimes of the
English*. The procession itself contained all the guilds, the Lord Mayor,

minstrels, knights, archers, and many others, to the extent of several hundred supers. Small groups and individuals in the crowd – this was twenty-four years before the visit of the Meininger company – were carefully rehearsed in separate actions and movements which united harmoniously in an immense ensemble. Except that he mistakenly reversed the order of entry of Richard and Bolingbroke (the latter preceding the former), the actor Edward Righton, who played in the mob, caught the atmosphere of the scene in his recollection:[33]

> But what a mob! – made up of historic characters and all sorts and condi-
> tions of people, who contributed to the general effect; the constant move-
> ments and clatter of us green ones, with our well-rehearsed little scenes,
> which were found to dovetail perfectly; the itinerant acrobats and dancers;
> the entrance of Charles Kean as Richard, on horseback, with bowed head;
> and Kate Terry as a boy starting out of the crowd into the procession, and
> flinging a handful of earth at Richard's head, exclaiming 'Behold King
> Richard, who has done so much good for the kingdom of England!' the
> groaning and hooting of the people, not only on the ground, but in
> balconies and at the windows, which changed to shouts of joy and ex-
> clamations of delight at sight of Bolingbroke on a noble prancing steed; the
> attempt of the people to crowd in upon him to press his hand, to hug his
> feet, and even to kiss the tail of his horse (which was actually done by an
> enthusiastic young lady); the showers of flowers which fell at his feet and
> all around him; and then, when the procession was nearing an end, the
> crowding in of the mob upon Bolingbroke, and the soldiers keeping them
> back against immense odds and midst the screaming women and their cries
> for help, while men shouted and children were almost trampled on; the
> clanging of the huge bells, and the sound of the disappearing band, on
> which scene of confusion and general riot the curtain fell.

Quite appropriately, Kean was made a Fellow of the Society of Antiquaries during the run of *Richard II*, an honour of which he was very proud and one not commonly awarded to actors or managers. He exercised his now officially rewarded antiquarian spirit even upon *King Lear* (1858), although it was difficult going. Kean admitted that it would be useless to attempt a representation of a specific historical period for the play, but then did it anyway 'for the sake of securing uniformity of character in the accessories of this great drama'. The Anglo-Saxon eighth century was chosen, and Kean happily enumerated the kinds of sources available to the scholar for theatrical reconstruction, while deploring the disappearance of Anglo-Saxon domestic architecture which should serve the same purpose. Nevertheless, with surviving records it was fortunately possible to 'attain a degree of approximate truth absolutely impossible in the mythical age to which Lear belongs'. Shakespeare's imagination was to be trusted no more than the spectator's historical or dramatic imagination. The facts had to be there for material realisation, and from these facts scholarly footnotes could be made, and everything explained.

At least *The Merchant of Venice*, following a few months after *Lear*, could be set without archaeological lacunae in the Venice of 1600. A visit to Venice to check the location and the authorities preceded the production, and Kean must have been one of the first managers, if not the very first, to travel abroad for the purpose of scenic and archaeological research in advance of an impending production. Kean said in the preface to his own edition that he intended to refresh the memory of the traveller who had seen Venice and exhibit the city to the student who had not; the way to do this was to re-people Venice with the past. The dresses were adopted from Cesare Vecello and sources in the British Museum, and each act in the printed text is followed by extensive historical notes: on the foundations of Venice, on St Mark's Square, on the transfer of the body of the saint to Venice, on the Rialto, on the costume of Venetian Jews, on money-lending. Like the Bancrofts in 1875, Kean combined history with illustration and spectacle in his opening scene, a kind of prologue to the play: '*Various groups of Nobles, Citizens, Merchants, Foreigners, Water-Carriers, Flower Girls &.c. pass and repass. Procession of the Doge, in state, across the square.*'[34]

The last historical revival at the Princess's was *Henry V* in 1859, notable, like Macready's production twenty years earlier, for an attack upon Harfleur – based upon a contemporary account – that vividly illustrated the Chorus's lines, a full-scale battle scene with copies of fifteenth-century artillery, defenders on the walls, a breach made, and hand-to-hand fighting. The major interpolation in the play was the king's triumphant return to London as a spectacular realisation of the Chorus's description in Act V. Kean set this on the Surrey side of London Bridge and based it on the description of an anonymous chronicler. The procession was a further and more elaborate development of the one in *Richard II* and included a Hymn of Thanksgiving sung by a chorus of fifty, 'supposed to be as old as A.D. 1310'. Asking Lady Pollock about her husband's impression of *Henry V*, Macready wrote with regard to Kean's Shakespeare as a whole that it seemed to him 'as if the text allowed to be spoken was more like a running commentary upon the spectacles exhibited, than the scenic arrangements an illustration of the text.'[35] In this view there was much in common between Kean's Shakespeare and the popular giant panoramas of the 1850s accompanied by the spoken commentary of their narrators. Kean's own opinion was of course the opposite. To give him credit he was, with Godwin, the most consistent theoretician of Shakespearean performance in the nineteenth century, although when it came to a choice between archaeology and the imagination in practice his logic occasionally faltered. For Kean and for many Victorians, Shakespeare was a source of such great knowledge and wisdom that he must at all costs be disseminated to a public hungry for education. Where we praise and value Shakespeare for many things, among them knowledge of men, an understanding of human relationships, of the roots and fruit of ambition, pride, greed, power, envy, love, and jealousy, of the workings of political structures and political conflicts, Kean would have added, and perhaps, given his own milieu, made more important than any of these, Shakespeare's understanding of man in history and the use of the past.

Over and over again, as in the preface to his *Henry V*, Kean insisted upon the validity of his own doctrines and their educational importance. Like Addison and Steele in the *Tatler* and *Spectator*, he believed wholeheartedly in instruction mixed with entertainment. His biographer Cole frequently referred to the performances at the Princess's as resuscitations of history, illustrated lectures, texts to lecture on, and so forth, and there was much of the fanatical schoolmaster as well as the dedicated missionary in Kean. At every opportunity he declared that spectacle was an essential though inferior part of his pedagogical method and could not be divorced from it. In a speech from the stage of the Princess's on the last night of his management, he rejected the view that he had been guilty of introducing spectacle for its own sake, a charge frequently levelled at him. He claimed, indeed, that 'in no single instance have I ever permitted historical truth to be sacrificed to mere theatrical effect.'[36] Kean's practice does not always stand the test of the application of his own theories, but in the immense respect he demonstrated for the educational value of Shakespeare in performance he deserves at least our own respect. A strong current of Victorian opinion held that if man could understand history and the past he could understand himself. That opinion was manifested not only in the work of historians and the writing of educationists but also on the stage of Kean's Princess's. It was a strain that ran through theatre, and especially through Shakespeare production, for many more years. When Tree, who believed that the best way to present history truthfully was to show it on the stage, said in 1910 that 'not the least important mission of the modern theatre is to give to the public representations of history which shall be at once an education and a delight',[37] he was speaking with the authentic voice of Charles Kean.

The fact that Kean considered spectacle an integral part of his historical method and educational aims in producing Shakespeare gave it a respectability it might otherwise not have possessed, a respectability also conferred upon Irving's use of spectacle a generation later and upon Samuel Phelps's *Pericles* at Sadler's Wells in 1854, which made some use of the archaeological discoveries of Layard at Nineveh.[38] This was one of Phelps's most spectacular productions, although spectacle was not nearly as common a theatrical technique with Phelps as with the less restrained Kean. The archaeology was beautiful; so was the spectacle. *Pericles* was one of the finer Shakespearean productions of the nineteenth century as well as being admirable spectacle; the latter did not negate its quality but reinforced, even to a large extent created that quality, and certainly could not in any theatrical sense be separated from it. Given his premises, Kean's argument about the inseparability of Shakespearean history and the spectacle method cannot be easily dismissed.

The first person to make consistent use of spectacle for the purposes of historical illustration in Shakespeare was Macready, and it would be well to note what spectacle effects actually looked like on stage, not only historical and archaeological spectacle but also spectacle employed, as it often was with managers of less artistic integrity than Macready and Phelps, for its own sake, Shakespeare himself then being somewhat irrelevant. Macready's *Tempest*, with a fully rigged ship on the stage of Covent Garden veering and heeling according to the wind and the operations of its crew, caused worries about the dominance of scenic spectacle and prompted John Forster to remark, even at that early date, that the production 'carries poetical and pictorial illustration as far as they will go'.[39] The idea that the limits of illustration and spectacle had been attained by the production under review was to be expressed many times in the course of the next seventy years. A few months earlier Forster had reviewed Macready's *Coriolanus* in the *Examiner* (18 March 1838), and in describing the spectacle made of V.iii emphasised its subordination to Shakespeare's intentions:

> The entire Volscian army is shown under the walls of Rome, which are presented, with the proud Capitol still visible above them, in the distance, while we see in various moving towers and battering-rams vivid prepara-tions for a siege. The number of brilliantly equipped soldiers on the stage in this scene is truly startling, and as their serried ranks open for the advance of the suppliants from Rome, we might fancy them thousands instead of hundreds. The appearance – the black apparition rather – of Coriolanus' mother and family with the other Roman matrons, stretching obliquely across the stage, in the midst of these brilliant warrior-files, one long, dreary, sable line of monotonous misery – was in the best and deepest taste.

The difference between Macready's *Coriolanus* and the Irving–Tadema *Coriolanus* in 1901 was a difference in kind as well as degree: in the former spectacle was employed for the purposes of pictorial illustration, in the latter for archaeological display as well. The difference is also partly explainable by the increasingly sophisticated technology of spectacle and the greater importance of costume and colour values. The pictorial principles were, however, the same, and the function of mass identical. Our Lady Corre-spondent in the *Westminster Gazette* (16 April 1901) naturally emphasised female dress in her account, but what strikes the reader is a concentration on colour and costume detail hardly conceivable in Macready's day:

> The curtain goes up on the Forum. Girls carrying great water jars flit across the stage. To the right, beneath the cypress trees, stand a group of

maidens wearing robes of silk of every soft shade of green, brown, and purple, carrying great bunches of yellow lilies. ... We see Volumnia in a magnificent veil of a most wonderful green, thrown over her purple robes, and in her hair a fillet of large turquoises. The stage is crowded with girls carrying palms, men with branches of green trees, children scattering flowers, senators in white and purple, and lictors in brown tunics, wide leather cingula, and large boots of yellow leather. ... We are again in the Forum, which is filled with a rejoicing crowd. There are dancing-girls in beautiful robes of silk or wool; others in white, with black veils on their heads; and Volumnia in a beautiful flame-coloured chiton ... a lovely scene, which changes again to Antium for the death of Coriolanus, which gives opportunity for another brilliant picture, with masses of soldiers in their crimson and gold, with here and there a note of brown.

The beauty of archaeological spectacle was one of the features of the late Victorian stage, and it was particularly marked in Lyceum Shakespeare. Even Irving, who had done the most to cope with the problem, was not immune from the standard complaint of spectacle distracting attention from the actor and the action. In the early scenes of his *Romeo and Juliet* in 1882 Clement Scott found it impossible to concentrate attention on the actors when the background was so beautiful and so constantly changing. The ball at the Capulets was an especially splendid scene, but 'it seemed impossible to get action with all this magnificence. The play was forced to stop, whilst the eye travelled from one detail to another.' The very beauty of the stage pictures dulled the action itself, and Scott singled out Romeo's farewell in Juliet's chamber as an example of what he meant: 'Here we have, if anything, an excess of colour. The golden lattice, the sumptuous surroundings, the foliage in the garden, the sky showing the pinks, and oranges, and purples of a sunrise, and, at last, the golden dawn itself, are all beautiful enough, but they are a trying background for the central figures.'[40] Possibly the most praised of all Irving's Shakespearean stage pictures in his long tenancy of the Lyceum was the church scene in *Much Ado About Nothing*, performed a few months after *Romeo and Juliet* in 1882. There was a smell of incense as the bridal procession moved toward the altar, the plaintive music of the organ and the secular music of the string band attendant on the bride were heard, and contrasts in scenic composition between the religious and the courtly were both interesting and effective. Austin Brereton described the scene thus:[41]

The altar stands at the left hand side of the stage, and the beautifully ornamented roof is supported by massive pillars. These accessories, the massive
pillars, the figured iron gates, the elaborate and costly altar, the carved oak
benches, the burning lights, and the perfume of all incense, all combine to
render this a scene of such richness and grandeur as at first to arrest all
thought of the play and to delight only the eye with the beautiful sight.

This scene so impressed contemporaries that it was virtually copied by George

Alexander at the St James's in 1898. *Henry VIII* in 1892, an even more sumptuous Lyceum production and Irving's most expensive, aroused complaints that the scenery was *too* beautiful. According to one critic, the '*Street in Westminster*' of Act IV, with its old beamed houses, was indeed a re-creation of 'old London':[42]

> At every casement right up to the second floor there are heads of citizens
> and their wives and children peering forth. The road and pathways swarm
> with every grade of society – prentices with their merry faces and
> mischievous ways, beggars, men-at-arms, rufflers, and maidens. In the
> procession of Anne Bullen on her way to her coronation, she is borne aloft
> on men's shoulders in a gorgeous palanquin, and is preceded by bishops,
> priests, officers, and state musicians, pages, heralds, and young girls, who
> strew her path with flowers. And the pity of it is that, seeing how much toil
> of research has been incurred in arriving at the accuracy of these costumes,
> they pass all too quickly and the spectator can but regret that he has not
> more time to profit by the liberal education that might be afforded him as
> to the dress of our ancestors.

The 'liberal education' afforded by Alma-Tadema in *Coriolanus* has already been mentioned; Irving shared with Kean and Tree the educational objectives of historical recreation in Shakespeare production, although with neither the ardour of the former nor the defensive reflexes of the latter.

The question of the relation of the actor to Shakespearean spectacle did come up from time to time in consideration of Irving's Shakespeare, but, since he was on the whole commended for the restraint of his spectacle and its harmonious relation to both play and acting performance, less artistically controlled and more showy producers attracted much more of this kind of criticism. Even the Meininger company, which performed Shakespeare at Drury Lane in 1881 and was famous for its crowd scenes, was reproved for the distracting bustle of its picturesque mob in *Julius Caesar* and the excessive splendour of its scenic illustrations. Another Lyceum *Romeo and Juliet* in 1884, this one by Mary Anderson and Lewis Wingfield, won the admiration of Clement Scott, as mentioned above, for superb mounting and the technical excellence of stage machinery in quick scene changes. It was, however, 'a lovely panorama and little else', to dazzle and delight 'the stupid and unimaginative'. Scott's wrath was chiefly reserved for the quality of the acting and its subordination to spectacle and archaeology:[43]

> The whole of the stage seems to be sacrificed to the harvest of the eye, and
> not to the satisfaction of the senses. Acting is more and more made subor-
> dinate to mere scenic success. There are plenty of people to tell us how
> Juliet went to bed, and what kind of a couch wooed her to sleep; dozens of
> authorities as to where certain pines or orange trees grew in Verona;
> gentlemen with ready pencils who can reproduce bits of Veronese
> architecture; fashioners, modellers, scene-painters, dressers, dressmakers

by the dozen; but apparently not one who can instruct the younger generation how to deliver the Queen Mab speech; not a human being who can persuade a popular actress that the love of Juliet is something superior to that of Mary Jane flirting over the garden wall.

Before Irving took control of the Lyceum in 1878 the quality of Shakespearean acting in London was not high; it was probably much better in the provinces, and had never really recovered from the abolition of the theatrical monopolies in 1843. The managements of Kean and Phelps were like beacons shining in this darkness, but by the 1860s both were out of management, and *The Merchant of Venice* was the Bancrofts' only venture into Shakespeare. Ballets, pageantry, and panoramas were necessary evils in a generation without Shakespearean actors of stature – with one or two exceptions – on the West End stage. If such actors existed, the spectacle might not have seemed so overpowering.

The Drury Lane production of *Antony and Cleopatra* in 1873 can serve as an example of mid-Victorian Shakespearean spectacle of the kind received enthusiastically by audiences but heartily deplored by critics. *Antony and Cleopatra* in the nineteenth century had always been an occasion for scenic display, and this one was very much in the same tradition. Nearly half the text was cut, and the part of Antony much mutilated. Shakespeare's five acts and thirty-eight scenes were reduced to four acts and twelve scenes. Pompey and his associates were eliminated, the second defeat of Antony unmentioned, the death of Enobarbus omitted, the scene between Caesar and Cleopatra not played. Cleopatra's barge appeared on stage, the perfume in the auditorium at that moment caused, according to the programme, 'by means of Rimmel's Persian Ribbon'. A 'Grand Roman Festival' in honour of Antony and Octavia in Act II, scene iii included ballets, choruses, the Processions of Venus, Juno, Diana, and Flora, and a 'Path of Flowers'. James Anderson, the Antony, then a veteran but once a leading actor and manager, said that the performance could not be called a tragedy, since it was 'all made up of scenery, processions, ballet, gaud, and glitter'. It was received 'with maddening demonstrations of approval by the pit and galleries; but the "judicious few" looked coldly on.' He admitted (despite his known powers of vociferation) that he could not make a serious impression on the audience, 'being stunned and cowed by the furious noise of preparation for "heavy sets" behind the scenes that destroyed all power of acting in front'.[44] Thus backstage preparation for a spectacular scene could disturb an actor as badly as the actual onstage spectacle could obliterate his identity.

One does not wish to go on indefinitely describing spectacular scenes in Shakespeare; their character is probably now apparent. They were not, of course, the sole property of the London stage. The provinces possessed two notable first-class managements which produced Shakespeare on a grand metropolitan scale, those of Charles Calvert at the Princess's in Manchester between 1864 and 1875, and of Edward Saker at the Alexandra in Liverpool from 1876 to 1881.[45] North America and the Empire also saw many splendid productions, for the dominant style of Shakespearean production in the bigger urban theatres and with the large touring companies was everywhere pictorial, historical, and archaeological. Two final descriptions are of American productions, and I use them to illustrate the leisured sensual richness and languor, the drowning in colour and light, the sheer hedonistic indulgence of high quality pictorial spectacle in Victorian Shakespeare, the sort of thing that has so utterly vanished from our own Shakespearean stage. The first is of *The Comedy of Errors* at the Star in New York in 1885, and the actual scene shows Antipholus of Ephesus in the villa of the courtesan Phryne:[46]

> Tapestries and skins of the richest hues are scattered over the mosaic floor. Columns of tinted marble support canopies of gaily embroidered and bespangled lace. Palms and brilliant flowers drink in the freshness of fountains of sparkling waters. On tripods burn lamps of perfumed oil. Genuine negroes, selected for their symmetry of outline, and draped in scarlet tunics, perform the part of slaves-in-waiting. In the midst of this voluptuous scene, on sumptuous couches, recline Phryne and her guests, Antipholus and the Jeweller. She calls for her singing slave, and a beautiful black woman appears. As she poses, every movement of her body lending grace to the clinging draperies, and singing of 'Love, love, nothing but love', she looks as though she had just stepped from Makart's canvas, so perfect a blending is she of delicious colouring. The lovely song ended, the singer sinks on a couch, and Cupid enters to herald the dance of the Bacchantes. They troop in, clashing their cymbals, swaying and bending to the rhythm of the music.

The second is of Augustin Daly's *Twelfth Night* at Daly's in London in 1894:[47]

> In the *Countess Olivia's* garden, *Viola* drops upon a bench and falls asleep. Twilight fades into gloomy night. The purple sky grows brighter with stars. The moon rises behind great leafy trees and sheds a silver path across the sea. Soft voices sound, chanting a lover's lullaby. And the lovesick *Duke*, with twenty lovely maidens in his train, steals on to serenade his lady fair, who, oblivious of him and his passion, bends longingly above the sleeping youth. The unfathomable deep blue of the heavens, the silver stars, the shimmering sea, *Viola's* beauty, the gracious lady hovering near, the palely loitering singers in their gossamer gauzes and sumptuous brocades – in short, the sensuous atmosphere of luxury and love, and the wealth of physical loveliness – take one completely captive.

It is hardly necessary to add that neither of these scenes is in the text; each is an elaborate interpolation of the kind so popular with Victorian managers and audiences, an illustration of a line or two or a speech, a realisation of a historical moment, an extension and filling-in of the text – not in any sense a political or satirical commentary upon it, a thematic underlining, or an ironical undercutting of its ostensible meaning. The functioning of the pictorial image in Victorian Shakespeare was entirely different from the way in which it is used – when it is used – today.

Finally, the workings of pictorial spectacle in nineteenth-century Shakespeare required resources of money and manpower quite beyond the economy-conscious theatre of our own time. The Victorian manager certainly operated within financial constraints, those of the box-office receipts which represented virtually his entire revenue, but three factors no longer relevant today helped him survive and, if he were a manager with a sensible popular policy, make a very substantial profit. Labour was cheap and not unionised, although there were agreements on working practices with stage staff; production costs were reasonable; and the break-even point in terms of box-office percentages and seating capacity could be relatively low. Charles Kean had to give up the Princess's after nine seasons because the cost of his Shakespeares – he would sometimes spend over £3,000 on a revival – was such that the small size of the house prevented him from making a commercially appropriate profit. Nevertheless, his company employed 550 people during the run of the bigger revivals; for *The Tempest* Kean printed a handbill asking the indulgence of the audience at early representations because of the complex nature of the stage machinery and scenic effects 'requiring the aid of above 150 operatives nightly'. Estimates of the number of supers on stage in a really spectacular Princess's scene like the entry into London in *Richard II* and the triumphal return of Henry V vary between 300–400 and 500–600. In relation to these figures Phelps's supposed limit of 70 supers was extremely modest; even Macready was reported to have used between 100 and 200 senators in *Coriolanus*, and 300 supers in *King John*. For *Romeo and Juliet* Lewis Wingfield said in an interview that he was drilling 180 supers in groups of six.[48] Late in the century, indeed, the deployment of huge numbers of performers on large stages and the function of scale and mass in human terms were essential aspects of spectacle Shakespeare. The recreation of history seemed to mean a commitment to people those stage civilisations of the past with realisations of society and the life of the street, the marketplace and the public arena. In spectacle melodrama and pantomime human mass and scale had the same pictorial effect, but were used for different ends.

3 · Melodrama and pantomime

To say, as William Archer did, that the poetic drama of the 1880s had taken over the techniques of spectacle from melodrama and pantomime was not only to acknowledge, somewhat after the event, the indisputable connection between Shakespeare on the one hand and these 'illegitimate' forms on the other, but also to recognise what had been obvious to any interested theatrical observer for generations. Melodrama and pantomime embodied spectacle as an essential aspect of their appeal and an integral part of their dramatic structure. Melodrama used spectacle for two main reasons: to imitate social and urban life on a size and scale appropriate to the magnitude of human emotion and the conflict between good and evil at the heart of its being, and to express in striking visual terms the sensationalism inherent in its nature. Pantomime did not pretend to the social verisimilitude of melodrama, although in the Regency harlequinade there was a great deal of social satire. Spectacle in pantomime was directed to the end of fantasy, a fantasy often excessively pretty and ideally beautiful, sometimes darkly grotesque, but employing mass, colour, and light for non-realistic purposes, as opposed to melodrama. As the poetic beauty and archaeological pictorialism and the realistic effects of melodrama followed the path of increasing elaboration, so too did the realisation of the fantasy world of pantomime.

Melodrama was spectacular from its birth. The law itself, decreeing that the spoken dramatic word was the property of the patent theatres, forced early melodrama at the Royal Circus in the 1790s to evolve as dumbshow with extensive musical accompaniment. The presence of mime and wordless physical combat, and the heavy reliance on emotional semiology to carry content and moral point of view meant that from the beginning melodrama was strongly and stereotypically visual; the eye and not the ear was the organ of appeal. When the working of the law permitted the minor theatres to develop melodrama as a spoken form with music, and when Drury Lane and Covent Garden appropriated melodrama for their own bills, the visual fundamentalism altered little but was merely overlaid with dialogue. The restless audiences and bad acoustics of the rebuilt Drury Lane and Covent

Garden early in the century led inevitably to the only possible solution, filling the vast stages and auditoria with spectacle.

The growth to maturity and the main characteristics of both melodrama and pantomime are too well known to require unnecessary retelling here, but the way in which spectacle worked in both forms is important. Because the value and importance of spectacle in melodrama and pantomime had been long established by 1850, the character of this spectacle could only undergo enlargement, elaboration, and the application of a changing technology for the rest of the century. One observer of early nineteenth-century melodrama, writing of the 'necessity of producing great effects', said that 'whatever effect is to be produced, whether terror or pathos, melo-drama depends on the strength of incident. It places characters in striking situations to tell for themselves, and carefully avoids encumbering them with language.'[1] This comment remained valid. The production of great effects and strong incidents could be achieved by strong writing and good actors, but it could also be attained by spectacle.

Before 1850 the frequent use of catastrophe gave melodrama simultaneous sensation and spectacle quite appropriate to its physical and moral extremism: Man is imperilled by natural as well as human forces, fire and flood as well as villainy. The good characters of Samuel Arnold's *The Woodman's Hut* (1814) are tossed upon the river in a violent thunderstorm and then narrowly escape a forest fire set by the villains: '*The whole of the cottage and R. H. of the wood on fire – cracking – wind – rain – clashing of swords, & c. ... The forest is consumed, and as the smoke disperses, the bridge is discovered burning also. The* COUNT, AMELIA, *and* MARIA *escape through the flames over the burning bridge, a part of which falls blazing into the river.*' The explosion that destroys the bandits and their mill at the end of Isaac Pocock's *The Miller and His Men* (1813) is another example of a climactic and spectacular physical sensation, as is the eruption of Vesuvius concluding *Masaniello* (1829), a version by H. M. Milner of the Scribe–Auber opera:

A grand view of the volcano emitting smoke and fire – the lava beginning to flow into the sea ... the eruption has made rapid progress – the crater of the volcano emits torrents of flame and smoke – forked lightnings rend the sky in every direction ... a terrific explosion ensues from the mountain, the lava impetuously flows down its side and extends itself into the sea. The people, awe-struck, bend in submission to the will of heaven and the curtain slowly descends.

In many nautical melodramas the danger is the sea. The *Royal George* sinks at Spithead in C. Z. Barnett's *The Loss of the Royal George* (1835) and sailors are seen swimming in the water; in Edward Stirling's *The Anchor of Hope* (1847) the hero's ship is perceived

beating about in a squall – thunder and lightning – HAL HORSFIELD

and SAILORS seen on deck endeavouring to work the vessel — the mast
breaks with a terrific crash and all is confusion on board — the Rapid *sinks*
— the sea covers the wreck — the moon emerges from the heavy clouds —
green fire is lighted up, and a raft, on which ISABELLA and MAT MERRITON
are seen floating, passes from the extreme corner, and when it reaches the
centre the scene closes.

The shipwreck of *The Tempest* in the productions of both Macready and
Charles Kean was a more elaborate treatment of a scene already familiar in
nautical melodrama. The elemental nature of melodrama is very evident in
the threats that earth, air, fire, and water pose to mankind, and these threats
could only be expressed through spectacle.

Other kinds of spectacle also established themselves early in the
development of melodrama. The use of sensation to shock and horrify is a
necessary part of Gothic melodrama, especially in the appearance of ghosts
and apparitions of every kind, the transformation of hooded figures into
skeletons against a suddenly livid red background, the streaking of
Bluebeard's chamber with blood. More generally, the pictorial treatment of
wild heaths, moors, and churchyards aroused feelings of unease and
foreboding. Nautical spectacle in the famous tank at Sadler's Wells displayed
naval battles between fully rigged model ships for some years after 1804.
Similarly, military engagements were fought in the circus ring at Astley's
(later Sanger's) until the end of the century. Moscow burned and amidst a
desolate winter scene the remnants of the French army were ridden down by
Cossacks in J. H. Amherst's *The Invasion of Russia* (1825); in battles of this
kind the spectators were usually overwhelmed and deafened by the boom of
cannon, the crack of rifles, clouds of smoke, waving banners, the stench of
gunpowder, and the swirl of cavalry charges. Trained studs of horses were a
great attraction at Covent Garden in an equestrianised *Timour the Tartar*
(1811) by Monk Lewis, and in several spectacle melodramas of the 1820s.
One of these was W. T. Moncrieff's *The Cataract of the Ganges* (1823) at
Drury Lane. In addition to the horses there was much oriental spectacle: a
Rajah's palace, a Pavilion of Pleasures, a procession of Brahmin priests, a
grand procession of the Rajah's army, and the interior of the great Brahmin
temple filled with golden images. The pictorial quality of the spectacle is
apparent in the opening stage direction, and the music is also expressively
pictorial:

Field of battle near Ahmedabad by moonlight. Lake and bridge. After
overture descriptive of a battle, the curtain rises and discovers wounded,
dead, and dying Mahomedan and Hindoo soldiers, officers, and horses
stretched confusedly on the earth. ... Music expresses the groans of the
wounded and dying, the retreat of the Mahomedan army at a distance,
and the rallying charge of their Hindoo pursuers: the blue cold light of the
moon glitters on the cannon, arms, and accoutrements of the fallen war-

riors and their horses. The burning ruins of the city are seen smouldering in the distance.

Thus well before the middle of the century processions, lavish display, large numbers of actors (and horses), and catastrophe and conflict by land and sea were already features of spectacle melodrama. Improving technology, increased resources, and a stress in melodramatic writing on the spectacular event led to spectacle scenes becoming the pivot of much staging, the centre or – when sensations and spectacles occurred in each act – centres around which the play was constructed, scenic pegs on which to hang a connecting narrative. The avalanche trapping the hero and heroine in a hut was the big scene in Boucicault's *Pauvrette* (1858), but as a sensation this was far outdone by the most notable stage fire of the century in his *The Poor of New York* (1857), which came to London in 1864 as *The Streets of London*. To destroy vital evidence the villainous banker fires an apartment building but is foiled by his former clerk, Badger. The stage direction is worth reproducing in full, although it neglects to contain the information that a real fire engine with bells ringing dashed onto the stage at the climax:

> *The house is gradually enveloped in fire; a cry outside is heard. 'Fi-er!' 'Fi-er!' It is taken up by other voices more distant. The tocsin sounds – other churches take up the alarm – bells of engines are heard. Enter a crowd of persons. Enter* BADGER, *without coat or hat – he tries the door – finds it fast; seizes a bar of iron and dashes in the ground floor window; the interior is seen in flames.*
> *Enter* DAN.
> DAN. *(Seeing* BADGER *climbing into the window.)*
> Stop! Stop!
> BADGER *leaps in and disappears. Shouts from the mob;* DAN *leaps in – another shout.* DAN *leaps out again, black and burned, staggers forward and seems overcome by the heat and smoke. The shutters of the garret fall and discover* BADGER *in the upper floor. Another cry from the crowd, a loud crash is heard,* BADGER *disappears as if falling with the inside of the building. The shutters of the windows fall away, and the inside of the house is seen, gutted by the fire; a cry of horror is uttered by the mob.* BADGER *drags himself from the ruins, and falls across the sill of the lower window.* DAN *and two of the mob run to help him forward, but recoil before the heat; at length, they succeed in rescuing his body – which lies C. ...* DAN *kneels over* BADGER *and extinguishes the fire which clings to parts of his clothes.*

The technology of stage fire had progressed considerably between *The Woodman's Hut* and *The Poor of New York*. In the earlier piece it would have been a matter of lighting pans of red fire (a chemical compound of strontium, sulphur, potash, and antimony) to cast a light on the scene, igniting lycopodium powder, which produced smoke and flame, pulling down the cutout trees (made in sections and fastened together) from behind, and working the hinge which collapsed the bridge. Fifty years later these things were handled more realistically and more spectacularly, as Percy Fitzgerald noted, for 'now the glaring embers are seen, the walls crack with the heat, the charred rafters tumble down with a crash, the flames roar and blaze, the air is charged with a crimson glow; in fact it is impossible to distinguish the mimic from the real conflagration, so perfect is the imitation.' Fitzgerald went on to explain that it was mostly done with light, and lighting of a kind unavailable in the theatre at the time of *The Woodman's Hut*. His comment actually refers to a spectacular stage fire in Paris that alarmed the audience with its realism, but the techniques were now universal:[2]

> The ordinary limelight turned on to the full suffused the stage in a flood of light, while crimson glasses were used, which imparted a fierce glow of the same tint. Any vapour of the whitest kind moving in such a medium would at once give the notion of volumes of livid smoke. Accordingly, a few braziers filled with a powder known as 'lycopodium' are placed at the wings, each fitted with a sort of forge bellows, each blast producing a sheet of flame and smoke. The lights in front being lowered, rows of little jets, duly screened, are made to follow the lines of the beams, rafters, &.C., and thus make these edges stand out against the fierce blaze.

In a real sense melodrama and pantomime were creatures of technology. The very existence of new materials, new stage machinery, and new methods of lighting impelled them into a dramatic structure which in part existed to display the ingenuity of machinist, gasman, head carpenter, costume designer, and stage manager. This is more obviously true of pantomime than melodrama, but when we consider the long series of Drury Lane autumn dramas produced by Augustus Harris and then Arthur Collins, it is clear that much of the content of these plays as well as of the pantomimes was determined by what could be done technically on the stage of Drury Lane and how large numbers of actors and quantities of expensive fabrics could best be deployed. Nor was melodrama unaffected by pictorialism and archaeological theory and practice. The panorama was widely used; there was one in Milner's *Mazeppa* (1831) showing the scenery which the wild horse bearing Mazeppa passes through as it runs for days from the Dnieper River to Tartary, the horse galloping on a treadmill in the stage as the panorama unrolled the other way. Boucicault was supposed to have been inspired to write *The Colleen Bawn* (1860) through purchasing a set of steel engravings of the Lakes of Killarney. The story may be apocryphal, but there is no doubt that the strong pictorialism of many exterior and some interior scenes in his Irish dramas derives from a well-established scenic tradition of the sublime and picturesque in the staging of melodramas with Irish settings. This tradition was in turn indebted to pictorial conceptions of Ireland, especially Killarney and the West, disseminated in illustrated books about Irish scenery popular from the 1820s.[3] Harris's production of *The Armada*, by himself and Henry Hamilton, at Drury Lane in 1888, realised Seymour Lucas's painting 'The Armada in Sight' and the railway station in Cecil Raleigh's *The Flood Tide* (1903), also at Drury Lane, was seen as a partial realisation of Frith's famous painting.

Seymour Lucas, as will be remembered from the previous chapter, was the costume designer and historical adviser for Irving's *Henry VIII*; he performed the same archaeological function for *The Armada*, one of whose notable scenes, in addition to the sea fight between the English and Spanish ships and the attack of the English fire-ships, was the processional thanksgiving visit of Queen Elizabeth to St Paul's with much historical pageantry and archaeological accuracy of costume. Archaeology and spectacle in melodrama, or at least melodramatic tragedy, were truly married in Kean's productions of *Sardanapalus* and Sheridan's *Pizarro* (1856) at the Princess's. Encouraged by the success of his historically recreative Shakespeare, Kean applied the same principles to *Pizarro*, selecting it, as he said in the preface, 'for the purpose of exemplifying the customs, ceremonies and religion of Peru at the time of the Spanish invasion'. Since Sheridan was somewhat deficient as an archaeologist, Kean chose Cuzco as a setting instead of Quito because more was known about it, and added to the text at the end of Act III a Grand Festival of Raymi, which, with its procession, warriors' dance, banquet, and '*Rising of the Sun. Outburst of National Enthusiasm and Ceremonial of Adoration*', happily lent itself to both archaeology and spectacle. Another spectacle not in Sheridan was the incorporation of Rolla's funeral procession into a new final scene set in the '*Interior of the Temple of the Sun*'. The addition of the Festival of Raymi prompted a lengthy historical note in the text, and there are other notes of a similar nature.

One of the best examples in the century of the combination of spectacle, archaeology, and pictorialism in melodrama was the production of W. G. Wills's *Claudian* at the Princess's by Wilson Barrett in 1883. *Claudian* was a rather daring replacement for the long-running and entirely different melodrama *The Silver King*; in the event it proved almost as popular, with a run of 248 performances. The play is set in Asia Minor in AD 362 and 462, and tells the story of a profligate and sacrilegious pagan nobleman cursed by a dying Christian holy man, whom he has murdered, with eternal youth and the visitation of death or blight upon anyone whom he should love or favour. He is unable to die until redeemed by love and capable of true self-sacrifice. The *Daily Telegraph* (7 December 1883) thought that Alma-Tadema might have painted the Prologue, a slave market in Byzantium, 'a city of white marble overlooking a sea of waveless blue. Slaves of every variety and tint of beauty are crouching in the market-place of an old world city ... with its marble seats and stately terraces; nature with her sunshine, blue skies, and bluer seas; affectation with its various conceits in dress and masses of vivid colour ... it is a living picture.' The *Daily News* (7 December) said that it was the aim of the production 'to bring before the eyes of the spectators the ancient city of Byzantium as it may be imagined to have appeared immediately after the death of the Emperor Constantine'. The temples, columns, baths, palaces, and humbler dwellings,

> with here and there the spires of dark cypresses rising in little groups are seen sloping gently down to the shores of the Bosphorus. Beyond the blue unrippled sea the outline of distant hills bound the horizon beneath which dim indications are discernible of the town of Chalcedon and its aqueducts with villas basking in the brilliant sunshine along the Asian shore.

The stage was soon filled with people, and

> as the crowds of Greeks, Romans, Gaulish, and Dacian slaves, and men of Egyptian and of Nubian race, here watch the wrestlings and the games of boys, there passes from time to time a peasant girl bearing upon her head an earthen jar just filled from the fountain, or a proud dame in rich saffron-hued robes protected from the sun's rays by the skiadeion, held aloft by female attendants as seen in some of the bas reliefs brought from Persepolis.

After the business of the slave market had been transacted, and Claudian duly cursed for his crimes, the first scene showed a vineyard near Charydos, with the blue sea in the background; peasants carry harvest produce on their heads and drag a loaded wagon across the stage. This scene, reminiscent of Tadema or Frederick Leighton, was deemed almost as beautiful as the Prologue; 'purple clusters of grapes hang from vines supported on the branches of trees. Snow-clad mountains fill the distance, and a pastoral valley leads down to the sea. The whole tableau is pastoral and idyllic, and presently the stage becomes filled with a crowd of vintagers proceeding to a festival.'[4]

The pictorial beauty of Claudian was matched by a fine sensation at the end of Act II, an earthquake which destroys Claudian's palace, leaving him, because of the curse, a solitary survivor. This scene was also beautiful in the presentation of the architecture of an imposing classical palace with gigantic columns of granite, and dances and festivities interrupted by the divinely sent earthquake (for no mortal happiness must come to Claudian), preceded by a sudden darkness, a flash of fire and a roll of thunder; 'walls fall in, columns lie in awful confusion, and ruin and desolation take the place of light and beauty.'[5] Unfortunately, there is no precise account of what actually happened on stage during the earthquake, or any surviving technical information as to how the earthquake was managed. It did, however, take over eighty carpenters to work, and the production was delayed for a week in order to get it right. The earthquake was universally accounted an immensely impressive stage effect, although Our Captious Critic of the *Illustrated Sporting and Dramatic News* (22 December), in a suitably captious vein, thought it would have been even more impressive if the palace had been built

of real marble. The earthquake was not quite the end of the play. Another
scene followed in the ruins, with moonlight shining through them and a calm
sea behind, a scene of quiet picturesque beauty.

All critics united in praising the spectacle and pictorial beauty of *Claudian*,
but many of them noted a contrast between magnificence of scenery,
costumes, and effects and paucity of content, a point made much more
forcibly, and over a long period, of the Drury Lane autumn dramas under
Harris and Collins. The archaeology of *Claudian* also struck critics
favourably, and since Barrett's archaeological adviser was Godwin, it is not
surprising that there was a lot of it. Godwin supplied drawings to the scenic
artists, the costumiers, and the property master, predicating his designs upon
the base of an obelisk of Theodosius II, the disc of Theodosius the Great, the
statues and coins of Julian the Apostate, the paintings in the Catacombs, the
Bassus mosaics, and the consular diptychs ranging from AD 391 to 430.
Godwin explained that wherever possible he had 'gone to the objects
preserved in our museum cases belonging to the period; *e.g.* swords, spears,
shields, axes, personal ornaments of gold, silver, bronze, precious stones,
cameos, & c.' As an example of his method, Godwin took the floor of
Claudian's palace from an ancient specimen of decoration 'showing that
combination of tesserae and slips of marble which became quite a fashion in
the middle of the fifth century'.[6] Luckily the play was set in a period when,
according to Godwin, the inhabitants of towns loved gorgeous display, which
could then be authentically archaeological. Nevertheless, Godwin worried
about the accuracy of the costumes, since there was an absence of full
archaeological information for the period, and he had trouble with Wilson
Barrett, who declined to make his first entrance carried on in an exact copy of
a Roman litter (from photographs supplied by the National Museum in
Naples); he also refused, on the grounds of garishness, to wear the authentic
tunic intended for him in the Prologue, one with a broad purple stripe down
the centre. He did, however, consent to put on the gilded high boots or
cothurni reserved for distinguished personages; Our Captious Critic was not
sure whether Godwin found them in the British Museum or the Burlington
Arcade. Among all the footwear necessary, the amount of archaeological detail
indulged in − carefully combined with historically correct display − just for the
sandals is staggering. They were made from Godwin's designs, and a
description survives:[7]

> Those to be worn by Mr. Coote, Mr. De Salla, and Mr. Girth were truly
> the most magnificent sandals we have ever seen. They were jewelled more
> or less all over with imitation pearls, rubies, emeralds, cameos, amethysts,
> &.c. all set in elegantly wrought gilt work, on a foundation of scarlet or
> crimson leather. Then there were the sandals for 'A lady', almost equally
> splendid in their embroidery of gilt and small pearls. Then the deep-red
> plain leather ones for Mr. Polhill's wear; the cinnamon-pink ones for the

slaves, the amber ones, adorned with jewels and silver crescents, for another 'Lady', and lastly the somewhat complicated mass of interlaced bands to cover the feet of Miss Ormsby.

Claudian is a not unusual example of a melodrama masquerading as a high-toned poetic tragedy, or at the very least a serious romantic drama of literary and archaeological pretensions. Basically, however, it uses sensation and spectacle in much the same way as the common run of spectacular drama everywhere, especially on the large and well-equipped stages of big theatres like the Standard in the East End and Drury Lane in the West. A brief survey of spectacle melodrama of the latter variety should provide sufficient information about their character and visual quality.

One could just as well choose the Standard for this purpose as Drury Lane, for the spectacle at the former was much of the same kind as and occasionally superior to that of the latter, and all the elements of spectacle were used in just the same way. However, since Drury Lane autumn drama for so many years encapsulated the whole of late Victorian melodrama and was, like Drury Lane pantomime, virtually a national institution, it would be appropriate to choose that theatre rather than any other. Yet a word about the Standard is in order, if only to get away from too much concentration on the West End; there was, indeed, a great deal of spectacular melodrama and pantomime staged in other East End theatres beside the Standard, and in the bigger provincial theatres as well. The peak of spectacle at the Standard was reached in the 1880s under the management of John Douglass, the author of many of the plays. In *The Ruling Passion* (1882), a real balloon inflated with gas, containing the heroine, an escaped lunatic and his keeper, rose from a crowded fete at the Crystal Palace and eventually descended into a stormy Channel, its occupants rescued at the last moment by an eight-man lifeboat. *Glad Tidings* (1883) exhibited Rotten Row with fashionable riders cantering up and down, and the wreck of a Thames excursion steamer based on the *Princess Alice* disaster in 1878. In *Daybreak* (1884) the Derby was put on stage for the first time with real horses, well ahead of Drury Lane. The race itself necessitated the use of a huge scene dock on one side of the stage, a raking piece leading from the dock to the street, and a large open space on the other side of the theatre. The horses started from the scene dock, cantered into the street round to the other side, tore through the open yard, and emerged onto the stage at full gallop, to be pulled up with difficulty in the street again. The street was also used for another scene representing the road home from the Derby, in which a long procession of cabs, wagonettes, and carts crowded with racegoers streamed across the stage. *Our Silver Wedding* (1886) put 250 children on stage in a Sunday-school excursion to Epping Forest; they arrived in a dozen wagonettes each drawn by two horses. A huge and newly installed water-tank on stage stretching well into the wings was used for the sensation scene in which a garrison in Burma escaped on rafts down the Irrawaddy River. In *A*

Dark Secret (1886) the tank was utilised for the Thames at Henley the day before the Regatta, with real swans, houseboats, steam launches, wherries, and a storm with real rain.[8]

Both the realism and the spectacle were duplicated at Drury Lane, whose audiences may have been more middle class but still possessed about the same tastes in melodrama as the audiences of the Standard. Harris himself, pointing out the losses he had incurred on English Shakespeare companies and the visit of the Meininger company to Drury Lane, said that to be successful modern drama must be realistic. 'The requirements of an average Drury Lane audience are sufficiently clear. They demand a performance which must be, above all things, dramatic, full of life, novelty, and movement, treating, as a rule, of the age in which we live, dealing with characters they can sympathise with and written in a language they can easily understand.'[9] Reviewing the success of Harris's early productions, one critic in 1882 explained the kind of play that worked at Drury Lane:[10]

The great success achieved at Drury Lane by 'The World' and 'Youth' certainly justifies Mr. Harris in his strong opinion that at a theatre so large as his action is vastly more important than dialogue, and situation infinitely preferable to sentiment. The proof of the pudding is in the eating, and as a rule the playgoers of to-day want to see and not to think. A facile stage workman who understands dramatic effect is nowadays of far greater value to a manager than a man of letters who has a capacity of writing for the stage. ... The dramatist has to give the company a sketch or outline, and the artists fill it up.

Commenting on the 1881 autumn drama, Dutton Cook stated that although the story was weak, the language puerile, and the play generally absurd and trashy, 'there are yet scenic exhibitions in "Youth" such as a large section of the public regards with fond admiration. It is thoroughly understood that the plays at Drury Lane are things to be looked at than listened to.'[11]

Youth itself, by Harris and Paul Meritt, is an excellent example of the overblown Drury Lane spectacle style. The splendid rooms of the hero, 'as luxurious as an Eastern seraglio', observed the *Era* (13 August 1881), were furnished by Messrs Gillow in the Oriental fashion and boasted 'rich curtains and hangings, an exquisite conservatory with a fountain sending up a jet of real water, lovely flowers, gorgeous paintings, costly and luxurious carpets upon which the footstep falls unheard'. All this was thought a bit too elaborate for the son of a country vicar, but that was Harris's way of doing things. Other striking scenes were a panorama of the upper reaches of the Thames, the embarkation of troops at Portsmouth, and a fierce engagement near the Khyber Pass, for which real Gatling guns and rifles were supplied by the Birmingham Small Arms Co. The battle was joined when the tribesmen attacked the barricades:[12]

The besiegers are met with a withering fire from Martini-Henry rifles, whilst the murderous Gatlings bellow forth ever and anon. Eventually the combatants are completely enveloped in smoke amidst which are discerned the spurts of fire from the weapons of the assailed, and the huge sheets of flame which belch forth repeatedly from the mitrailleuses. Then the Afghans with their broad, heavy swords, rush in, and a hand to hand *melée* occurs, in which scimitars and bayonets clash together, the din of the strife being added to by the sharp detonations of the officers' revolvers and the deep bass voices of the troops as they cheer each other on to the fray.

Of this battle Dutton Cook observed that the lavish use of blank cartridges by the British force 'so filled the house with noises, fumes, and odours, that by the more sedate spectators the victory of our arms was strongly felt to be dearly purchased'.[13]

The next year's spectacle, *Pluck*, by Harris and Henry Pettitt, wearied critics with seven long acts and interminable waits, despite a scene with two train wrecks, a snowstorm in Piccadilly Circus, a mob breaking real glass bank windows, and a burning building. Opening nights at Drury Lane, both for melodrama and pantomime, tended to be very long indeed; as soon as they were over, the cutting began. The spectacle was praised, but there was always too much of it. One critic defended the leisured and often unnecessary dialogue of front scenes in the dramas on the grounds that 'if the public will take delight in big stage pictures, it must not grumble at these expanded conversations, which are necessary to give the carpenters what time they need. The slowness of pictorial plays between the pictures is the Drama's revenge upon us for subordinating plot and action to canvas, limelight, and costume.'[14] Clement Scott pointed out of *Human Nature* (1885), also by Harris and Pettitt, with its scene of the Guards returning from the Sudan marching past Charing Cross and the crowds kept back by real policemen borrowed from Bow Street station, that 'if we cannot get Julius Caesar at Drury-Lane and no actors are forthcoming to do justice to Brutus or Antony, we must be content with crowds at Charing Cross. It cannot be helped; let us at least acknowledge that the manager does his very best with the material at hand.'[15]

The problem of acting in the Drury Lane spectacle dramas was one to which the critics constantly recurred. Of *The Armada* the *Illustrated London News* (29 September 1888) was restating general opinion when it declared that at Drury Lane acting was an art subordinated to pageantry and scenic splendour. 'All its subtlety and refinement are lost on a stage peopled with an army of supernumeraries and dedicated to din. It would require lungs of leather to shout louder than the din of carpenters and scene-shifters.' A deficiency in acting technique was supposed to be one reason for the inability of some performers to make themselves heard in Drury Lane, but others managed to overcome both space and largeness of spectacle, such as Mrs John Wood in Raleigh and Hamilton's *The Great Ruby* (1898), whom J. T. Grein praised for mastering such difficulties; 'to act in such a piece is no small matter, it requires physical strength, a powerful voice, and a thorough knowledge of the stage.'[16] Joseph Knight, however, objected to the waste of the actor in *Pluck*, whose slow and laborious progress 'is not to be interrupted while any actor, no matter who, gesticulates or makes faces. ... A series of tableaux having to be exhibited, the object of all concerned was to make way for them. ... Upon the well-drilled stage of Drury Lane, no actor is so ill-advised as to seek to interfere with the scenery.'[17] Although the problem of finding a suitable acting style for spectacle was more extreme in melodrama than in Shakespeare, it was of course not unique to Harris's Drury Lane. Similar comments can be found much earlier than the 1880s. A striking one is Planché's recollection of Alfred Bunn's staging of Beaumont and Fletcher's *Bonduca* under the title of *Caractacus* at Drury Lane in 1837. In a rough sort of way Bunn was the Augustus Harris of his day, devoted to spectacle, and willing to do anything for an elaborate procession. For *Caractacus* Bunn added a final scene of a Roman triumph which was a disaster; 'the actors, poor as they were, had not the slightest chance allowed them. Everything was neglected for the procession, of which he undertook the whole arrangement and responsibility. Day after day the stage was occupied by crowds of supers, horses, goats, and other animals, and eventually the piece was produced positively without one complete rehearsal.'[18]

Harris's actors, in melodrama and pantomime alike, were at least splendidly attired. *A Run of Luck* in 1886 (by Harris and Pettitt again) was the first of his autumn dramas in which the ladies' dresses, on the lawn at Goodwood, were provided by Worth of Paris. It was also the first in a long line of sporting dramas, with a hunt as well as the climactic scene at the track with a dozen horses thundering past at the back of a stage crowded with people. Goodwood, the Derby, Newmarket, the Grand National, Longchamp, Hurlingham, Lord's – these were among the sporting locations and events that appeared on the stage of Drury Lane and provided an opportunity not only for the spectacle of sport itself but also for large and colourful crowds of supers, numbers of them elegantly and expensively dressed as befitted the elevated social tone of many Drury Lane settings. Campaigns in which British troops had recently been involved continued to be fought on stage: the Sudan, the Burmese War, the Matabele War, and the Boer War. In Harris and Pettitt's *A Million of Money* (1890), the chief spectacle interest, apart from military pomp (the departure of the Guards from Wellington Barracks) and a shipwreck, was centred on the interior of Squander Mansion; here, as far as possible, was an absolute replication of luxurious domestic reality. Harris turned over the job of designing and furnishing this scene to a well-known antiquarian, Litchfield. The drawing-room set was decorated in Louis Seize style, with recesses, alcoves, an ante-room, and stairs with a Nubian figure holding a lamp on each side. The furnishings aroused the most comment:[19]

The furniture and accessories were, if we omit the trifling item of artificial flowers, entirely real; there was not a single 'property' article of any kind. The piano on which Mr. Harry Nicholls nightly played was made by Mr. Litchfield from the Adams' designs, it being a replica of the one which received the gold medal at an exhibition of musical instruments a few years ago. The table at which baccarat was played by Stella's guests, was an old Louis XV writing table, and two of the gilt chaces are historical from having been contents of Fontainbleau *Chateau*. Knick-knack tables, cabinets and other trifles, were either good reproductions or genuine old specimens. The silk curtains alone cost upwards of £100, and were trimmed and lined as if for a drawing-room in Belgravia.

One result of this realism was that some complained that the set lacked stage effect, an objection which once again raised the question, mooted by Fitzgerald, Shaw, and others, of the essential unreality in the theatre of articles and furnishings from real life.

After the death of Harris in 1896, Arthur Collins maintained the policy of autumn drama, sensation, and spectacle. His first production of this kind was *The White Heather* (1897), by Hamilton and Raleigh, in which the scenic attractions of the interior of the Stock Exchange paled into triviality beside the under-water fight to the death (gauzes, not real water) between the hero and villain in diving-suits. An Alpine avalanche swept the villain to his death in the same authors' *Hearts Are Trumps* (1899), which also contained a Royal Academy exhibition and the stage and auditorium of a popular music hall. A full House of Commons set in Raleigh's *The Price of Peace* (1900) and a motor smash in his *The Great Millionaire* (1901) preceded the importation of *Ben-Hur* in 1902 from New York, where it had been first performed in 1899. In this production could be seen a panorama of Jerusalem, and the interior of a Roman galley packed with slaves chained to their oars. *The Times* (4 April 1902) thought that the drama was so tedious that 'the best plan would really be to dispense with dialogue altogether, and to give it as a series of *tableaux vivants* with a little dumb-show action in between.' The chief scenic attraction was the chariot race in the arena at Antioch. Here twenty-two horses were used instead of the twelve in New York, although only four chariots could actually race together side by side. The *Tatler* (26 March 1902) explained the mechanics of the race:

> The scene consists of four great cradles, 20 ft. in length and 14 ft. wide, which are moveable back and front on railways supported by a bridge structure capable of supporting twenty tons. The tops of the cradles are 2 in. below the stage level. Each cradle bears four horses and a chariot. On each are four treadmills covered with rubber 12 ft. long and $2^1/_2$ ft. wide, and on these the horses are secured by invisible steel cable traces, which serve to hold the animals in their places. As the horse gallops the treadmill revolves under his feet, thereby eliminating the forward pressure created

by the impact of his hoofs, which would force him ahead on an immovable surface. The wheels of the chariot are worked by rubber rollers, operated on by electrical motors. An impression of great speed is created by the presence of a panoramic background, 35 ft. high, representing the walls of the arena, with numbers of spectators seated in their places. This is made to revolve rapidly in a direction opposite to that in which the chariots are going.

After *Ben-Hur* the run of Drury Lane autumn dramas continued until the outbreak of war, with occasional interruptions; there would be little point in recounting several years more of sensation and spectacle. One more description will suffice. In 1903 Raleigh's *The Flood Tide*, intended partly as a parody of Drury Lane drama, contained the usual set of scenes which were taken seriously enough by the technical staff, among them the lounge of the new Hotel Metropole in Brighton, the paddock at Kempton Park, the departure of a boat train from a London station, and the saloon deck of a steamer. The sensation scene was the bursting of a dam in Cumberland and the ensuing flood. The actor Weedon Grossmith, who was engaged to play the comic man, his first time in a Drury Lane autumn drama, described the backstage activity just before the big scene and the flood itself. His account is well worth quoting; its length can be excused by its interest and detail:[20]

Scene III, Act III, was what is termed a front scene. It was very dark, and a couple of dozen men dressed as workmen, with lanterns in their hands and pickaxes, were discussing the seriousness of the continuance of wet weather. It was difficult to hear all they said, for dozens of men were knocking and hammering behind, getting ready the big sensational scene. After this, Lady Tree was heard bribing Norman McKinnell, an Italian scoundrel, to murder the lunatic millionaire, played by Charles Somerset to slow music.

When they had departed the workmen re-entered; some had struck work, fearing a great accident, and the chief of the gang, who shouted, and he had to shout loudly to give the 'music cue', informed his mates at the top of his voice, 'Things can't go on much longer, lads. The masonry is giving already. We have had three months of continuous rain, and with another night of this cursed deluge the great dam which-has-taken-seven-years-to-build-will *be in Blackmere Lake* by – the – *morning*!!!'

The stage suddenly 'blackened out'. We are all in total darkness, black gauzes are lowered. There are shouts from the stage manager. 'Strike!! Lower your borders!' Stage hands rush in every direction, carrying something, or pushing something.

'Mind your backs!' they shout. 'You jump aside!' The safest place is close to the curtain, down by the footlights. ...

'Get on your blues! Down with the borders! Take care! Who's working the lifts? Then why the devil don't you do it? Come on! Look out!

Get your cloth down above there. Now then, boys', etc.

'No. 3 is too low! Do you hear? *Too low*. Get your props. D—n it, mind the batten! Why the tum, tum, fum rum, don't you do what you're told?' etc. The front row of the stalls frequently complain of the loudness of the band, particularly the brass, and wonder why it is not remedied, but James Glover, the conductor, knows why!

'Look out for your calls!' Then a boy with an electric torch leads you through rocks, rivers, spars of iron, and cautions you against an open trap, and conducts you to your place. The band is still crashing and booming, an electric sign to the orchestra, and the music changes to the tremolo and mysterious. The gauzes rise slowly, opening on the big sensational scene. The gallery is noisy with shouts of 'Down in front! Order, please! Take off your 'at', 'Lay down!' etc.

I shall never forget that first night, when the flood commenced. Tons of rice and spangles poured from the side to indicate the bursting of the dam. Children floated by, clinging to barrels and floating trees, screaming and yelling, especially as some of them got frightened and tipping sideways fell down the trap, to be caught by the men underneath. Then the boat-house, with myself hanging outside from the roof, commenced to wobble, and then the whole structure toppled over, and a huge floating tree – with a well-concealed mattress – passed by, and Somerset and myself jumped on to it and were supposed to be saved as the curtain descended slowly.

The whole point of spectacle melodrama like *The Flood Tide* – aside, of course, from making money at the box office – was the reproduction of emotional, physical, and social sensation and the painting of a highly selective, highly coloured portrait of modern society and modern urban life in as 'realistic' a way as possible. This 'realism' was conceived not as naturalism but as a verisimilitude expressed in terms of surface detail, mass, scale, conflict, and disaster. In Victorian pantomime, on the other hand, the means of spectacle were directed to the ends of fantasy, to a delight not only in the reproduction of a fairy and transcendental world generously conceived in terms of space and magnitude, but also in theatrical effects of light, colour, costume, and pictorial beauty. Since its inception in the eighteenth century English pantomime had always been a mixture of fantasy, low comedy, trick effects, and spectacle. Until the form of late-eighteenth-century and Regency pantomime was fixed at a short verse 'opening' of one to four scenes and a longer dumbshow harlequinade to follow, scenes of classical legend alternated with the exploits of Harlequin. The Regency harlequinade was dominated by Clown, whose greed, selfishness, social alienation, insecurity, and criminal propensities dictated the nature of the entertainment. The activities of its players – transformed by the good spirit or fairy from the characters of the opening – themselves constituted a grotesque, physical, and topically satiric social and urban fantasy. The fairy element was then strictly confined to the opening and to the final scene of the restoration of order and love set in a landscape transformed from the streets of London to a celestial and radiant hall or bower of harmony and bliss. It is no coincidence that the opening lengthened, the fairy element strengthened, and the harlequinade shortened as the interest in fairy culture grew and intensified in the 1830s and 1840s. Just at the time when the fairy boom was at its height and fairy painting much practised in the late forties and early fifties, pantomime appropriated the transformation scene from the fairy extravaganza popular since the thirties, a transformation now of place rather than person. This scene concluded the opening but no longer introduced the harlequinade, which still remained in truncated form – two to four scenes only – but had no connection with the opening. The opening became all-inclusive, embracing the grotesque, the topical, the ideal, the satirical, low comedy, and fairyland fantasy in the same entertainment, as well as panoramas, minstrel and music-hall songs and dances, ballets, performing animals, jugglers, magicians, and speciality acts of all kinds. Toward the end of the century the harlequinade had virtually disappeared in the West End, and a late Victorian pantomime there was almost entirely concerned with the scenic grandeurs, low comedy, and fairy-tale narrative of the opening.

Texts for pantomimes hardly exist in the conventional sense. The pantomime author, or 'arranger' as he was known in earlier days, had nothing to do with the harlequinade, which was devised by the Clown in consultation with the machinists of the trick-work and the ballet master, sometimes the Harlequin, who supervised the dances. The author's responsibility was to fit in somewhere with the manager, stage manager, machinists, lighting men, and scene painters, make room in his script for their ideas, provide suitable material for songs and music-hall artists, and accept a great deal of cutting and hacking about of his work, not only by the manager and his assistants, but also by the low comedians. E. L. Blanchard was always complaining in his later years how his scripts for Harris were almost unrecognisable on stage, and *Truth* (10 January 1884) recommended, apropos his *Cinderella*, that the public never go near a pantomime until it had been running for about a week:

> By that time the whole of the author's text is forgotten; new songs and new verses are added, and the comedians, who understand the art of amusing far better than authors and managers, have full liberty to do what they please, and in their own fashion. I purchased a book of the words of the Drury Lane pantomime, intending to follow it as well as I could. But I soon flung it away, for I found that scarcely a word of the text was delivered from the stage. The pantomime had been virtually re-written by the performers since the first night.

A script or libretto did not always receive such drastic treatment, but it is impossible to speak in any meaningful way of the relationship between performance and an established text in pantomime. A collaboration in which the author could be a relatively unimportant partner was also true to some extent of the composition of spectacle melodrama, but it was a marked feature of pantomime.

The success of the Christmas pantomime was absolutely crucial to the financial health of the unsubsidised Victorian theatre, and preparations were carefully made long in advance. The subject was often considered and the principal artists engaged while the previous year's pantomime was still in progress, and production meetings between manager, stage manager, author, principal scenic artist, wardrobe mistress, property master, and ballet master could begin in the middle of the summer, when the general plot and the chief features of the spectacle would be decided. Work in earnest started from that date, and intensified in the three months before Boxing Day; in the days before Christmas stage and costume work went on nearly twenty-four hours a day. Separate music rehearsals for chorus, the ballet, and the principals were held for several hours a day until the time came to merge all groups together in general music rehearsals and then dress rehearsals. Augustus Harris has left an interesting account of how he lived during the early stages of preparation for *Mother Goose* in 1880:[21]

> How can I put down all that has to be done – of my hundred daily inter-views with property men, costumiers, scenic artists, ironsmiths, musicians, with clowns, shoemakers, acting managers and advertisers, with drapers, carpenters, ropemakers, and supers; how everything has to be ordered, everyone to be drilled? ... Constantly besieged from morning till night, at least twenty people always waiting to see me, each one on different busi-ness. Rushing, for forty-eight hours at a time, to Newcastle, Birmingham, and Paris, driving from one place to another, ordering goods worth thou-sands of pounds, returning to the hotel only to find a score of telegrams calling for my immediate return to London, where on arriving besieged as before by acrobats, chorus, money-takers, columbines, and more people than I can remember. And to think that this life was led for ten weeks, without one moment's peace, without time for eating, drinking, or even sleeping.

The final pantomime rehearsals at a big theatre like Drury Lane would be huge and exhausting affairs, particularly in the management of the spectacle element. In *Sindbad the Sailor* (1882) the procession of thirty-six kings and queens of England and their attendants necessitated the marshalling on stage and orderly processing of 650 people, according to Harris,[22] who organised the participants in each reign separately and marched alongside them. Every sovereign and his forces had individual and group business to perform, King John's barons, for example, demanding the Magna Charta from him, and every person in the procession was given a number to facilitate grouping and sequence of movement. Harris had been known, stopwatch in hand at dress rehearsal, to cut out a procession on which £3,000 had been spent because of overrunning, although this seems to have been a rare exercise of temporal economy during the rehearsal period. From the stalls, when he lost his voice – a frequent occurrence – an aide next to him would shout his instructions at the performers through a pasteboard trumpet, sometimes complete with bad language. But it was Harris's feverish activities on stage that his contemporaries most remembered. One described his part in a Christmas Eve dress rehearsal of *Aladdin* in 1885:[23]

> With his cloak floating loosely about him, and giving him the semblance of a pantomime demon, he darts from one end of the stage to the other like a globule of quicksilver. ... He is, indeed, ubiquitous, and not content with directing everything and everybody, acts and attitudinises every part played. Now he is instructing a principal as to his entry, and going through it for his edification with emphatic gesticulation. Now he interrupts a leading lady with 'No, my dear, that's not it', and proceeds to illustrate how the words are to be uttered and the action performed that is to accompany them. Now he takes another by the hand, and leads her along, and postures her and poses her till she acquits herself to his satisfaction. Now he is demonstrating to an attendant the right use of her fan, or to a guard that of his weapon. Now with a bound he pounces on a member of a procession and leads him along in the way in which he should go. Now he indicates to a pantomimist that he must get through his work higher up or lower down the stage. Now he comes to the rescue of Mr. Barrett with 'That will not do at all' and insists on words being sung out and music kept time to. Now he is turning over the pages of a bundle of papers which he carries in his hand, and rapidly scoring alterations thereon. Now he is hastily scribbling messages and instructions on scraps of paper, rumpling these up into balls, and flinging them at some satellite in the stalls. Anon he is in the stalls themselves studying the effect of a coloured light or of a grouping from the front, and hoarsely issuing instructions for its modification. Anon he flops for a moment as though exhausted, into an armchair, placed with a table at one of the wings, but only to spring up again like Antaeus five seconds later. Occasionally he soliloquises somewhat forcibly on the stupidity of the human race in general, and of Drury Lane supers in particular.

Almost at the last moment came the scenic, or what we would call the technical, rehearsal, an almost equally tiring affair. This kind of rehearsal was not, except for the technicalities of the transformation scene, unique to pantomime. It was standard procedure for any major production, Shakespeare, pantomime, or melodrama, so that Harris's description of it here is relevant not only to this chapter:[24]

> You sit with the scenic artists in the stalls or the circles – sometimes in one, sometimes in the other – to judge of the artistic effect, and to dispose the lighting of the various sets or pictures. The fly-men (that is, the carpenters

up aloft), the cellar men (those below the stage), and the stage-carpenters have never yet worked together; and it appears almost marvellous, looking at the crowded cloths and borders, wings and ground-pieces, with the complicated ropes and pulleys above, and cuts and bridges in the stage, not to mention the traps and sliders, gas-battens and ladders, how a series of fifteen or sixteen scenes, besides the elaborate transformation scene, which, perhaps, demands the united skill of fifty or sixty men to work its marvels and develop its mysterious beauties, can even be worked with such systematic regularity and unerring correctness. A good master-carpenter is a general, and all his men depend on his head in time of action. Then there are the gas-men, who have to raise or subdue the floats or footlights, the ground-rows, the wing-ladders, the battens or border-lights, and the bunch-lights or portable suns, which are required to give one effect to a brilliant tropical landscape or a bewilderingly luxurious palace. The limelights also have their special guardians. Each head of a department makes his special list of effects and changes, and notes the alterations or in-dications made at rehearsals.

Spectacle in pantomime did not of course emerge fully matured in the year 1850. Pantomime had been growing more elaborate scenically before that date, and some of its ostentatiousness was borrowed from the fairy-tale extravaganza of Planché and his contemporaries in the 1830s and 1840s, who were in their turn influenced by earlier English pantomime and the French *folie féerie*. The combination of extravaganza and *féerie* attained the peak of splendour in 1872 with Boucicault's *Babil and Bijou* at Covent Garden, a transposition to the English stage of the immensely elaborate *féerie* currently popular in Paris. *Babil and Bijou* lacked only a harlequinade to make it a pantomime in the strict sense, and is worth mentioning here for the way in which it used all the resources of spectacle to express the purest fairy-tale fantasy on stage. The plot was hard to follow and it was difficult to hear 'the necessarily feeble voices of the performers, who struggled on the vast stage amidst such a sea of accessories',[25] but in five acts and eighteen scenes the piece narrated the search of Babil and Bijou for the Regalia of Fairyland. Their search took them to the bottom of the sea in a diving-bell and to the moon in a balloon. In the sea they encountered oysters, crabs, cockles, seals, sea horses, sharks, alligators, swordfish, lobsters, and starfish, among other marine creatures, and half-way through the play came the revolt of the vegetables and fruits against the tyranny of the Court of Flowers and their allies the bees and insects. The stage in Act IV was occupied by a beautiful Garden of the Four Seasons, changing according to the time of year, and the action consisted of a ballet of the seasons which lasted nearly an hour. One of the most admired scenes was the march of the Amazons of the Silver City in the Mountains of the Moon; 'such a glitter of gold and burnished armour, such tossing of plumes and jewelled head-dresses, such tunics of brown and blue, and black and scarlet, such lavish wealth, such fringe of bullion, such lances and swords gleaming in the lime-light, such drummers and bandsmen in Royal apparel, such comely faces, and such superb specimens of womanhood, have never surely yet been combined with grand effect.'[26] The admiration of the *Observer* (1 September 1872) was as great, but with a qualification common in reaction to later pantomime, especially at Drury Lane. If anything, this scene was 'too gorgeous, too golden, too overlaid with glitter, limelight, and jewels; in fact to be so bright that it is painful to behold such brilliance.' The artistic beauty, delicacy, and grace of the costumes and visual effects so praised in the production must have been enhanced by another feature of mid- and late Victorian pantomime, the vast preponderance of young women in the cast and the mass transvestism of processions and large groups gathered for any purpose. The female physique, and the feminine domination of fairyland were linked in a sexual, pictorial, and spectacular combination of ideal purity and handsome flesh. Another highly commended scene in *Babil and Bijou* was interestingly topical, a presentation of evolution in the 'River of Life' that concluded with a huge review of man's ancestors back to the ape, an ape in fact occupying the summit of the scene between two ascending staircases. Percy Fitzgerald described it.[27]

> At a particular crisis the genii or leading fairy called up from the past figures belonging to every age from the beginning, in their respective costumes, a man and woman of each era. Gradually the stage filled with the enormous heterogeneous crowd of every generation. As all arrived, down to our day, they ascended a sort of sloping platform at the back that reached nearly to the top of the scene, forming an inclined plane, particoloured and of the most bizarre combinations. Then all descended and entered on a kind of fantastic promenade, crossing and recrossing – people of the early centuries finding partners in those of a later age. It was half a dream, half a nightmare. The conception was new and carried out perfectly. This spectacle took but a few minutes, yet it may be conceived what an outlay in time, labour, and money must have been requisite.

This scene was praised for archaeological accuracy of costume and educational value; the *Morning Post* (30 August) said that the critic 'is delighted to hail a spectacle by which the eye is educated while it is pleased. ... It is no small triumph for Mr. Boucicault to have made one of the most popular forms of English entertainment, pantomime, subserve the needs of education.'

Naturally, the preparations for *Babil and Bijou* were extensive, and the number of people involved very large. The scenery was prepared on the paint-frames of twelve different theatres; seventy seamstresses were installed in a house in Bloomsbury to make up Alfred Thompson's costume designs, and the property department was put into a house in Goodge Street. The ballet master's staff numbered five, and they were rehearsing 100 dancers. The production included four complete ballets and four marches with 200 girls in each march. Apart from supers, dancers, and children, the other performers numbered nearly 100, and the stage during final rehearsals was occupied day and night by 500 people.[28] Although *Babil and Bijou* ran for six months, losses were rumoured to be anything up to £30,000; the properties alone were supposed to have cost £17,000. It must have been one of the heaviest and most expensive productions of the nineteenth century; it was certainly one of the most spectacular.

The transformation scene at the end of *Babil and Bijou* was the 'Ascension of the Fairy Court', and the transformation itself, taken over from extravaganza and more specifically from William Beverley's conclusion to Planché's *The Island of Jewels* (1849), in which the leaves of a palm tree fell away revealing fairies holding up a coronet of jewels, was a notable feature of pantomime spectacle. The effects of a transformation, which might take twenty minutes to unfold, were dependent upon a combination of machinery, lighting, changing scenic pieces and gauzes, and the display of a large number of beautifully costumed women, some floating high above the stage. More than half the machinery for a transformation scene was worked from beneath the stage, and basically what happened was that a large platform suspended by ropes and counterweights rose through an opening in the stage created by removing that section of the stage floor during the preceding scene. On this platform were about twenty fairies, mermaids, water-nymphs, angels, or the like standing or reclining on the various pedestals of a device of French origin called a *parallèle*, which resembled a central pedestal or cylinder with lesser pedestals attached to it by arms. As the platform slowly rose the *parallèle* opened, rather like an umbrella opening upside down, the weight of the figures causing their platforms to sink in conjunction with a man operating a windlass connected to all the ropes binding the arms of the lesser pedestals to the central cylinder.[29] The centre pedestal, higher than the rest, always held the brightest and most glittering being, the presiding spirit or fairy queen. The pedestals and their arms were draped with materials to look like clouds, water, bowers, jewels, or stars, and so on, and no hint of mechanical origin could be seen. Another way of doing it was to strap each fairy to a long iron which extended like a lever through a trap in the stage floor to machinery beneath.

While this was going on the lighting intensified, gauzes were raised, scenery changed, the orchestra played, other performers appeared on stage, and the transformation moved in a leisurely way toward a climax. The ever-useful Fitzgerald explained the procedure in some detail:[30]

All will recall in some elaborate transformation scene how quietly and gradually it is evolved. First the 'gauzes' lift slowly one behind the other – perhaps the most pleasing of all scenic effects – giving glimpses of 'the Realms of Bliss,' seen beyond in a tantalising fashion. Then is revealed a kind of half-glorified country, clouds and banks, evidently concealing much. Always a sort of pathetic and at the same time exultant strain rises, and is repeated as the changes go on. Now we hear the faint tinkle – signal to those aloft on 'bridges' to open more glories. Now some of the banks begin to part slowly, showing realms of light, with a few divine beings – fairies – rising slowly here and there. More breaks beyond and fairies rising, with a pyramid of these ladies beginning to mount slowly in the centre. Thus it goes on, the lights streaming on full, in every colour and from every quarter, in the richest effulgence. In some of the more daring efforts, the *'femmes suspendues'* seem to float in the air or rest on the frail support of sprays or branches of trees. While, finally, perhaps, at the back of all, the most glorious paradise of all will open, revealing the pure empyrean itself, and some fair spirit aloft in a cloud among the stars, the apex of all. Then all motion ceases; the work is complete; the fumes of crimson, green, and blue fire begin to rise at the wings; the music bursts into a crash of exultation; and possibly to the general disenchantment, a burly man in a black frock steps out from the side and bows awkwardly. Then to shrill whistle the first scene of the harlequinade closes in, and shuts out the brilliant vision.

Such scenes were thoroughly expressive of the fantasy world of Victorian pantomime, a microcosm of it meaningful only in terms of spectacle, existing only because of the techniques of spectacle. They could, however, be trying on the eye. Clement Scott noted that the transformation in the Drury Lane *Aladdin* of 1885 ('Aladdin's Golden Dream'), was 'such a gleaming, flashing, glowing, and glittering of intensified lights and burnished metals, diamonds, emeralds, and rubies that the eyes almost ached with its redundancy of splendour.'[31]

The transformation scene would have been impossible without the developments in technology and materials alluded to in the first chapter, and pantomime is the best example in the nineteenth century of a dramatic genre virtually defined by a new technology. The impact of new kinds of lighting or new kinds of fabric, paint, and scenic materials immeasurably widened the bounds of stage effect. For instance, spectacle in Victorian pantomime would have been much the poorer, indeed would not have developed as it did without technical improvements in gas lighting and the evolution of limelight. Albert Douglass recalled that the gaslight effects in pantomime at the Standard were so elaborate that they required months of preparation. The fairies of the 'Valley of Jewels' scene in *Harlequin and Sindbad the Sailor* (1881) carried white wands each surmounted by a capital letter in copper spelling out the names of jewels in words of blazing light, such as RUBIES, EMERALDS, and TOPAZES, each group of fairies being dressed in the colour of its jewel. The words were made of gaspipe plunged into sockets, and Douglass explained the technicalities of the effect:[32]

It would be comparatively easy to gain such an effect with electricity – but in those days it meant miles of gaspiping beneath the stage, a thousand holes punched in every letter, with care to ensure each tiny gas jet containing a roll of paper percussion caps (similar to those used today in toy revolvers) to ignite the gas, and the whole 'prop' covered with non-inflammable leaves to prevent the letter being distinguished before being illuminated.

Two years later the transformation scene in the Drury Lane *Cinderella* was lit by twenty limes and twenty pans of green and red fire, the use of the latter instead of coloured mediums on the limes being justified at the time by the more vivid colour and greater brilliance possible through the combination of coloured fire and untinted limelight.[33]

Late-nineteenth-century pantomime, its technicians as well as its audiences, was utterly fascinated with the effects of electric light on glass, since by 1900 very few homes, and those only of the wealthy, were electrically illuminated. Glass alone was interesting enough, and for years had been in great demand as a scenic material. In *Little Bo-Peep, Little Red Riding Hood and Hop o' My Thumb* (1892) at Drury Lane, a clever arrangement of enormous mirrors reflected and re-reflected principals and attendants in a procession of the characters of twenty-nine fairy-tales, so that the great Hall of the scene seemed endless and the stage peopled with thousands. However, it was the aesthetic uses of electric light and the combination of electricity and glass that proved irresistible. Scores of little electric lights twinkled from the petals of the lilies and convolvuluses with which the dancers in the finale of the Drury Lane *Humpty-Dumpty* (1891) were laden, and the wedding scene of *Dick Whittington* (1894) at the same theatre was reputed to have been decorated with more than 4,000 lamps. One of the great effects of Collins's *Sleeping Beauty and the Beast* in 1900 was a fairy palace of crystal and a crystal fountain, the palace alone being made of 35,000 pieces of Venetian glass costing £2,000, assembled by Italian workmen and glowing with the light of about 2,500 electric lamps, which, constantly changing colour, turned the waters of the fountain into flaming, many-hued cascades. A favourite pantomime for electric light was *Cinderella*. In the 1895 Drury Lane version Cinderella went to the ball in a motor carriage encrusted with jewels while a large electric wheel blazing with light rotated in the background. This effect was outdone by the Hippodrome *Cinderella* of 1900, a one-hour pantomime coming at the end of a variety bill. Cinderella's coach was built entirely of glass and fitted with 1,000 light bulbs; small lamps interwoven with flower designs shone from the dancers' head-dresses. When Cinderella, in a white and silver satin ball-gown studded with light-refracting diamonds, arrived at the ball in a replica of the Lord Mayor's Coach drawn by six black ponies caparisoned in red morocco and gilt harnesses, the whole coach, including the wheels and spokes, was outlined in electric light and the costumes of her retinue were picked out in myriads of tiny lights. The final scene in the Palace of Lustres, where 200 ball guests arrived costumed as flowers, naturally shone with light and light through glass. The scene was lavishly decorated with roses, festoons of them stretching from the pillars of the circle to a great crown over the centre of the ring. At a single light cue roses, crown, and the whole front of the circle blazed with electric light, 10,000 additional lamps being used to outline the auditorium.

This lavish outpouring of light (the electric bill for the Hippodrome *Cinderella* was £90 a week) and the special refulgence of glass and crystal was well matched by marvellous costume effects, a proliferation of elegant small properties, beautiful scene painting, and imposing groupings of hundreds of handsome young women. All the glare and glitter could be redeemed by delicate touches of artistry such as Wilhelm's costumes for the ball scene of the Lyceum *Cinderella* in 1893, with colours of[34]

the palest primrose ranging to citron and bronze; mahogany, paling into apricot tones; symphonies of orange and lemon, maize colour, cinnamon, ivory – all were pressed into service. Tiger lilies and Gloire de Dijon roses, sunflowers and narcissus; faun and leopard skins; leather, and the sheen of gold, copper, and brass ... the costumes of the leading characters being carefully chosen in heliotrope, faint sea green and vieux rose, no jarring note was present.

Some critics were not pleased by spectacular pantomime effects; much of their criticism was directed at Augustus Harris but other London and provincial pantomimes did not escape. Pantomimes were thought to have too much spectacle and too little fun; their stages were crammed with so many people that they scarcely had room to turn around. The lights were too bright, the evening too long, the cumulative effect of all the spectacle too tiring. These criticisms were heard repeatedly, from the very same critics who heaped praises on individual effects and individual spectacle scenes. Harris's obsession with processions could wear down the sensitive; of the 1885 *Aladdin* Scott complained that 'procession follows procession, each more dazzling than the last; the eye is almost fatigued with the contemplation of all the splendour'[35] – a complaint so familiar that it could have been graven on Harris's tomb. *The Times* (28 December 1885), reviewing this *Aladdin* and noting a 'magnificent sameness about the whole thing', asked wearily: 'Who can say that if the same pantomime was given year after year, with only a change of name, it would not, like some sermons, escape detection?' Nevertheless, it admired the steam cranes at work on the realistic building-site for the palace, the hosts of building labourers represented by young boys, and the ballet danced by the little girls who played their wives.

George Bernard Shaw certainly did not admire Drury Lane pantomime. He would not perhaps have been impressed, had he seen them, by the sets for the procession of Greek and Roman divinities in *Jack and the Beanstalk*

(1889), which imitated Alma-Tadema's painting, 'Sappho', or by the spirit of archaeological inquiry manifested in the 1882 *Sindbad the Sailor*, in which every detail of the costumes for the procession of the kings and queens of England was copied from books and drawings in the British Museum, or by the archaeological recreation of a medieval Lord Mayor's Show in *Dick Whittington* (1884). All this archaeology, although it illustrates the pervasive influence of the science and of historical recreation on even the lightest forms of nineteenth-century theatre, was at Drury Lane a matter of lip-service and primarily a technique for further display. Shaw probably did not believe Harris's repeated and seemingly sincere wish to make high art of pantomime and thereby elevate the taste of the public. He did not care for display in pantomime for its own sake, and said so after a visit to the 1897 *Babes in the Wood*. Although Shaw praised some of the costumes in the ballet of flowers – based on Walter Crane's flower designs in *Flora's Feast* (1889) – as rising 'above mere theatrical prettiness to the highest class of decorative art available for fantastic stage purposes', he hated what he judged the waste of artistic talent in a morass of purposeless spending: 'The modern pantomime, as purveyed by the late Sir Augustus Harris, is neither visible nor audible. It is a glittering, noisy void, horribly wearisome and enervating like all performances which worry the physical senses without any recreative appeal to the emotions and through them to the intellect.'[36] This was an extreme expression of the critical and intellectual hostility felt not only toward spectacle in pantomime but also to the place of spectacle in all forms of Victorian theatre. Pantomime endured the greatest wrath because it had neither Shakespeare nor even W. G. Wills to write the book. There were, of course, other sorts of pantomime. Shaw much enjoyed a visit to the Britannia in 1898, and the Grecian under the Conquests from 1851 to 1879 specialised (like other East End theatres) in original scripts which did not use the conventional fairy tales but ones that afforded opportunities for an extraordinary series of grotesque demons and monsters and thrilling aerial combats by means of counterweighted traps, springs, and trapezes. Such theatres and provincial pantomimes retained the harlequinade after it nearly disappeared in the West End. Yet it is to Drury Lane that we must turn to examine the fullest display of spectacle in Victorian pantomime; there is no escaping that, despite a minority of critics. And these critics were not the public, who except for staying away from one or two failures received the long line of lavish Drury Lane pantomimes with an enthusiasm approaching rapture.

Such lavishness was costly, but over the years the annual investment paid off in terms of box office; otherwise Harris would have had to give up Drury Lane. Unfortunately the accounts for his tenure of the theatre either do not survive or have not been found. There are, however, some statistics, since Harris was fond of giving them to the press and tended to boast of the number of people on his payroll and the amount of money he spent on pantomime. A brief consideration of these figures is necessary, since the ability to stage spectacle was, after all, a function of income and one needs to be reminded of that fact. It is also helpful to know what reserves of money and manpower were necessary to stage a spectacle like the Drury Lane pantomime. Since we do not know what total box-office receipts were from the Christmas pantomimes, we can look at the figures – money spent and people employed – as indicative of the vast resources of labour and cash required to mount spectacle of this type. To translate these figures into today's values is almost impossible. In the last quarter of the nineteenth century retail prices fell and wages rose, prices beginning to climb again in the late 1880s. On the whole money held its value remarkably well from 1850 to 1910 and there were no inflationary periods. In 1910 prices in real terms had just got back to the levels of 1850, while industrial wages were considerably higher. At the very roughest calculations £1 on a hypothetical retail price index in 1900 – although this index did not actually exist in 1900 – was worth about ten to twelve times as much as it is today, but this is not quite the same thing as the equivalent value of a pound in the pocket.[37]

Although reliable figures over a range of theatrical occupations for earlier periods in the nineteenth century are hard to come by, theatrical wages at the end of the century are well documented by two studies a decade apart.[38] Harris also supplied additional figures for Drury Lane.[39] In 1892 at a theatre like Drury Lane a member of the ballet would be paid between 10s and 35s a week, with an average of 30s, depending on whether she appeared in the first, second, or third row, but a top solo dancer might earn between £30 and £50. A super would receive between 1s 6d and 2s a night, a child super 6d to 1s, a child actor 12s to £2 a week. Scene-shifters and limelight men were paid 2s a night, a head stage carpenter £4 to £5 a week, and a journeyman carpenter 25s to 30s. A male member of the chorus received between 30s and £2 a week, less for women, and the average orchestra musician 21s to 42s. Adult supers, journeymen carpenters and lighting men usually had other jobs during the day, and many performers were paid extra for matinees, although only for the last week or fortnight of rehearsal. Harris paid a good principal boy £60 to £100 a week, a troupe of acrobats £70 or more as a group, a clown £30 to £40. Ten years later there was little difference in these salaries, except that a super's wage had gone up by a shilling a night and that first-class low comedians and music-hall artists asked and received considerably more.

At Christmas time the size of the Drury Lane company, including all staff of whatever description, would be at least double the number employed at any other time of the year except during the autumn drama. Even in 1865, in the pre-Harris years, it was estimated that the total theatre staff for *Little King Pipkin* was nearly 900, including 200 children, 60 in the ballet, 48 seamstresses and wardrobe ladies, 45 dressers, and 17 gasmen.[40] Another set of figures is available for Drury Lane in 1881, probably relating to the

Mother Goose of the previous year. The orchestra then numbered 40, the chorus 20, the ballet and extra dancers 100, supers 100, carpenters 50, property men and assistants 30, gasmen 15, limelight men 18, dressers 20, scene painters and assistants 12, firemen 10. In the front of the house were 8 policemen and 20 money- and ticket-takers.[41] These figures were only partial. During the run of the 1881 *Robinson Crusoe*, a more lavish production than *Mother Goose*, a comparable set of figures estimated the orchestra at 30, the ballet and extra dancers at 150, children and supers at 260; the total theatre staff was put at 700 or 800.[42]

At the beginning of his tenure of Drury Lane Harris was spending £5,000 to £8,000 on the production of a pantomime; *Mother Goose* cost £6,000.[43] As for running expenses and box-office income, it would seem that about £250 a performance would then have represented average running costs; good receipts would average about £500 to £600 a performance.[44] After the Christmas school holidays were over, the box office dropped off and matinee performances were reduced, but nevertheless some long and profitable runs were recorded. *The Forty Thieves* (1886), for instance, ran until 23 April for 155 performances, and *The Babes in the Wood* (1888) closed on 27 April after 176 performances. By the end of the eighties and in the early nineties Harris was estimating his production costs at between £16,000 and £20,000, and running costs at £290 a performance.[45] Since he could spend £5,000 on a single procession – that in *Sindbad the Sailor* used 300 different costume designs – and was given to the advance purchase of thousands of yards of brocades and silks, some of which he never used, this increase in costs is not surprising. The Christmas pantomime production budget figures for 1826, summarised in *The Times* (1 January 1827), look absolutely puny by comparison, ranging for five London theatres from £100 for the West London and Sadler's Wells to £1,000 for Covent Garden and Drury Lane. Harris may have been a prodigal spender in comparison to other managers who did not talk about their finances, but the truth is that whoever the manager was spectacular pantomime on a large scale was a very expensive business, the most costly of all forms of Victorian theatre.

The difficulties of reconstructing performances of late-century Drury Lane pantomime are considerable. The promptbooks are missing; the book of words sold in the theatre sometimes bore little relationship to what actually happened on stage and tells us almost nothing about business and effects; the copies submitted to the Examiner of Plays can contain fuller stage directions but obviously were never intended to convey vital information about ballets, processions, transformation scenes, speciality acts, the acting of low comedians, and the visual nature of spectacle. One has to fall back on press reviews, which can be most helpful but repetitive, and too often unspecific. Something of the style and character of spectacle pantomime has already emerged in this chapter, but to conclude with, a descriptive impression of some aspects of two Drury Lane pantomimes will concentrate this approach more specifically on two performances, those of *The Forty Thieves* in 1886 and *The Sleeping Beauty and the Beast* in 1900.

There were two principal spectacle scenes in *The Forty Thieves*, scene iii of the robbers' cave, and the final scenes of Queen Victoria's Jubilee; both were processional. The pantomime was shorn of a transformation scene, a novelty evoking much comment, but apart from the two processions other scenes were lavish enough to satisfy the most gluttonous of visual gourmands: a magnificent interior of the Forty Thieves Club in Tehran; an opening scene of a Muhammadan Paradise, populated in part by a large number of characters from *The Arabian Nights*, where beautiful houris waited on the heavenly faithful who were entertained by exquisitely dressed dancing-girls; a scene in a Turkish dormitory featuring a pillow-fight ballet by three dozen children in white silk nightgowns revealed after they doffed fezzes, embroidered slippers, and other accoutrements of Turkish costume preparatory to going to bed; and a dance of monkeys in a forest given by the same children, who came from Katie Lanners's National Training School for Dancing, which appeared at Drury Lane every Christmas for some years.

The opening night began at 7.30 in the customary way with an overture containing the themes of current popular and patriotic songs, to which the gallery sang the words, 'Rule Britannia', and then the National Anthem, on the first bars of which the house rose to its feet, the gallery cheering and waving caps and handkerchiefs. The opening performance did not end, however, until nearly 1 a.m. This was typical of the first nights of Drury Lane pantomimes. Some went on even longer: *The White Cat* (1904), for instance, lasted six hours, until 1.30. Within a week an hour and a quarter had been chopped off *The Forty Thieves*, with more cuts evidently to come. It was such a luxurious production that estimates of its cost were put at between £15,000 and £20,000; it certainly outdid all its Drury Lane predecessors in show and expense. Harris was rebuked in the usual way by critics who praised the spectacle but deplored the absence of ogres, giants, good fairies, evil demons, a decent harlequinade, and the sacrifice of spirited fun to ostentatious display which fatigued the eye.

The most greatly admired aspect of *The Forty Thieves* was the splendour, beauty, and variety of the costumes; one would have to go back to reviews of *Babil and Bijou* to find a comparable chorus of praise, but it is clear that at least in the wardrobe department Harris and Wilhelm excelled Boucicault and Thompson. The *Daily Telegraph* (18 December 1886) declared that 'it is the Jubilee Year, and an attempt has been made to show what the effect of gorgeous material is when massed on stage.' The greatest displays of costume occurred in the Thieves' Cave and the Jubilee pageant, and the brief comments that follow should be read in conjunction with the Appendix of *Era* articles detailing the costumes of both scenes. Since the business of the Jubilee finale is made fairly clear in the *Era*, it is necessary to add only that Harris was cleverly cashing in on the interest aroused by the Colonial Exhibition held earlier in 1886 at the South Kensington Museum, and that the last and grandest of the three scenes was presided over by a statue of Queen Victoria (played by an actress) clad in a golden mantle and standing upstage on a pedestal at the end of a long vista behind which was a view filled with shipping; the procession streamed downstage to be welcomed to the Temple of Fame by Britannia. By the end of the scene all the marchers were spread out in a massed fan shape facing the audience; the pantomime ended with the singing of a new song, 'Victoria, Queen of a Nation'.

The business of the Cave scene needs a little more explanation, as the *Era* description concentrates entirely on the costumes, which the *Telegraph* reviewer said would be 'infinitely admired by those who consider that mere costliness is the essential aim of effect in dramatic art'. The cave itself was built up high at the back with the magic door in the centre; a zigzag path on each side wound down the rock to the stage floor. When the right word was spoken the door flew open, a full moon shining through it into the cave. The Forty Thieves were each given a band of followers whose costumes were carefully related to those of their leader, and they all poured down both sides of the rock in their hundreds. Estimates of the total number in the procession varied between 200 and 500, but if the *Era* is correct in stating that each of the forty leaders was accompanied by a retinue of at least twelve, then the figure must have been close to 500; a knowledge of Harris's taste in processions would support that. The entire entrance was made to a bold march tune from the orchestra and took over fifteen minutes to complete. When this multitude had marched and countermarched and were assembled on the stage floor, and when the stage glittered with armour and danced with plumes, a chorus of welcome was sung to the robber chief. On the first night, at least, a storm of applause broke out when the tableau was complete, and Harris stepped out from the prompt side and bowed his acknowledgment. Almost all critics agreed that nothing so splendid as *The Forty Thieves* had ever been seen on the stage; the *Echo* (28 December) thought that every scene 'is a beautiful work of pictorial art'. Our Captious Critic of the *Illustrated Sporting and Dramatic News* (8 January 1887) was sufficiently enthusiastic to write his review in passable heroic couplets, from which a section on the Cave scene may be quoted as conveying the sense impressions received by the audience:

> By living rainbows now the stage is spanned,
> As in succession file on, band by band,
> The Amazons, in astral arms arrayed,
> Shimm'ring in satin, blooming in brocade;
> The dazzled eyeballs grow with gazing dim

As now before them in confusion swim
The sheen of silver and the glow of gold,
The rich-toned velvet draped in mossy fold,
The floating wealth of silk of every tint,
The buckler's glitter and lance's glint,
The spangled kirtles and the gleaming vests,
The nodding plumage and the radiant crests,
The jewelled weapons and the curaissed breasts,
Whilst ladies, who with awe this sight regard,
Whisper, 'I'm sure it costs four pounds a yard.'

The concluding couplet is a typical piece of undercutting, but nevertheless draws attention to what must have been a matter of compelling interest for a sizeable proportion of the Drury Lane pantomime audience.

By 1900 and *The Sleeping Beauty and the Beast* Drury Lane had undergone some alteration. Apart from the redecoration of 1897, when the auditorium had been more lightly treated in cream and gold, the stage floor was in 1898 divided into six large sections each 40 feet by 7 feet 6 inches, independently movable by electrically powered lifts. Each section could be raised 12 feet or lowered 8 feet, and took one minute to move up or down the full 20 feet; it could also be tilted to right or left. Since the outside walls were raised 10 feet in 1908 to improve the height of the flying space to 70 feet, the grid in 1900 must have been 60 feet above the stage floor.[46] Estimates of audience capacity vary; it seems that by 1900 Drury Lane could seat about 2,600 but crowd in considerably more. The *Graphic* (5 January 1901) put the figure as high as 3,800 and the *Daily News* (27 December 1900) at 4,000; both of them occur in reviews of *The Sleeping Beauty and the Beast*, but they may be exaggerated.

A show like *The Sleeping Beauty and the Beast*, according to the *Echo* (27 December 1900), 'has got to fill the stage of Drury Lane in the eye of the pit and topmost gallery, is forced to satisfy a taste that insists on great and accumulated masses of colour, winding processions, and blinding electrical illuminations.' In an interesting and hostile criticism that aptly characterises the vast pot-pourri that was Drury Lane pantomime, the *Star* (27 December) took the piece as thoroughly representative:

The Drury Lane pantomime, that national institution, is a symbol of our
Empire. It is the biggest thing of the kind in the world, it is prodigal of
money, of invention, of splendour, of men and women; but it is without
the sense of beauty or the restraining influence of taste. It is impossible to
sit in the theatre for five hours without being filled with weary admiration.
Only a great nation could have done such a thing; only an undisciplined
nation would have done it. The monstrous, glittering thing of pomp and
humour is without order or design; it is a hotch-potch of everything that

has been seen on any stage; we have the Fairy Prince and the Sleeping
Beauty and the quite different legend of Beauty and the Beast, we have
President Kruger and the President of the French Republic hinted at in
the same figure, we have Yvette Guilbert's gloves and Marianne's hair, we
have the motor car, the twopenny tube, and the flying machine, we have a
transformation and a harlequinade, we have a coon dance, music-hall
songs, ballets, processions, sentimental songs, and occasionally even a
good joke. And we have all this over and over again, for five hours, always
with fresh foolery and fresh glitter, in a real crescendo of effects.

The reviewer could also have added a dancing puppet; a juggler; a magician;
a palace and fountain of crystal; orchestral music from Mendelssohn,
Wagner, Tchaikovsky, and the music hall; a burlesque on Inaudi, the
mathematical wizard of the Hippodrome; another burlesque on Marianne in
Stephen Phillips's *Herod*, currently at Her Majesty's, and Dan Leno on his
first entrance dressed as if he had stepped right out of a Gainsborough
portrait. The spectacle was as splendid as ever. A scene in the Presidential
palace was populated by hundreds of courtiers, all women dressed in white
satin eighteenth-century costumes and wearing powdered wigs. A
transformation scene showed Beauty's Wedding Gifts mostly of pearl and
diamonds, the scene developing as each gift was added to the collection; the
Star preferred 'the monstrous ripening of the gold and silver vegetables,
which come to life with a slow, sprawling expansion of themselves, like the
vegetation of an opium dream'. The palace of crystal and its fountain, shining
with multi-coloured electric light, has already been mentioned. Around the
fountain flitted the Grigolati Troupe, moths in black and gold with elaborate
wings that shimmered with colour, and fairies danced in and out of the palace,
their dresses also gleaming iridescently with changing light. There was also a
witch's wine cellar in which grinning faces of fire appeared on the walls and
barrels, and a Royal Aviary in which a huge gilded birdcage occupied half the
stage. Dan Leno as the Queen and Herbert Campbell as the King, Beauty's
mother and father, carried the low comedy, their funniest scene taking place
when a stalled motor car fell to pieces under their inexpert attention.[47]

Objections had been made to the complete absence of pastoral beauty or
any touch of the English countryside in *The Forty Thieves*. In *The Sleeping
Beauty and the Beast* this deficiency was more than remedied, since the most
beautiful and spectacular scene of all was a series of tableaux of the seasons at
the end of the first part of the pantomime, immediately before Beauty is
woken by a kiss from the Prince.[48] The two previous scenes, set with a
background of the ruined and cobweb-festooned palace, had been comic, but
these could not have given sufficient time for the preparation of the four
seasons sequence since it was necessary to bring on a juggler directly
afterward who did an entertaining but quite irrelevant and prolonged act in
which he smashed articles in disgust when his tricks 'failed'. Then in a very

brief scene, no doubt a front cloth, of the 'Interior of the Palace of Sleep', the Fairy Queen uttered a few graceful couplets reminding the audience of the constant rhythm of the seasons while Beauty has been asleep and telling them that they are about to see what she wishes to show Beauty in a dream. The tableaux of the seasons that followed were a combination of procession and ballet, Collins not having Harris's single-minded devotion to monster processions but not excluding them as a means of spectacle.

In a pastoral landscape Spring entered, escorted by graceful children as Cupids, each armed with bow and arrow, and attended by guards as Valentines; then occurred a Valentine ballet. As tableau succeeded tableau each backcloth was raised to allow a progressively augmented stage depth in which to accommodate the steady arrival of the newcomers. These remained on stage when their business was finished, taking up positions at the sides after reaching the footlights and leaving free for those coming next a central space increasingly confined by the press of numbers. The second tableau opened with the entry of the shamrocks of St Patrick's Day and then a gravely dignified allegorical figure of Easter with youths and maidens in its train bearing palms, others representing variously decorated Easter eggs and bird-nesters. April Fool's Day was portrayed by an entry of traditionally garbed fools, and primroses in dresses of delicate pale yellow. The revellers of May Day, attired as daisies, laburnum, wisteria, and white and pink hawthorn, performed a dance around a gaily adorned maypole. Apple and almond blossoms accompanied a litter bearing the May Queen. The blossom trees and sheep of the May Day backcloth, behind an arch of hawthorn blossom, gave way to a Summer backcloth, a painting of hayfields with a river winding through them. Summer was a brighter and more colourful affair than Spring; in fact there were complaints that some colours in the summer tableau were too vivid and not in harmony with the scene-painting behind. Summer consisted exclusively of pretty roses in shades of pink, white, and red. The fourth main tableau, Autumn, contained a group of gleaners with golden sickles, and girls as scarlet poppies scattered among girls as ripe golden corn. A Harvest ballet was followed by a Shooting ballet, as the stage filled with tinted autumn leaves and participants in a stag hunt and a fox hunt. The last tableau was Winter. In front of a snow-covered landscape appeared 'a host of coryphees, dressed in lovely white draperies, sewn with snowflakes of swansdown, touched with silver frost and finished with charming head-wreaths of holly, with its shining red berries, presently to be delicately illuminated with electric light.'[49] The girls dressed as snow were complemented by girls dressed in red and green as holly, and a Holly and Mistletoe ballet was danced. Over the group in white standing out from the bright colours all around them, and over the assembled company hovered the Grigolati Troupe as swallows or magpies (the reviewers were not sure which), clad in black and white feather waistcoats and large white muffs. At the back of the scene the landscape cloths gradually made way for a view of Beauty on a high platform lying asleep; the Prince, holding a sprig of mistletoe, broke through a thicket of holly to kiss her. A combined ballet of rejoicing with dancers representing all four seasons followed downstage, while to music from the *Nutcracker* the Prince, Beauty, and the Fairy Queen sang a trio of thanksgiving, the Grigolatis still swooping gracefully overhead.

Late Victorian pantomime was the most purely visual, pictorial, and lavish of nineteenth-century theatrical arts and the most spectacular form of theatre in English stage history. Spectacle existed for its own sake more than in any other sort of theatre, feeding upon itself, growing bigger and bigger, greedily consuming all the resources of technology, money, and manpower it was given. Yet pantomime spectacle was a close relation of other kinds and other uses of spectacle. The sumptuous Drury Lane *Aladdin* and Irving's *Faust* opened within a week of each other in 1885; the two productions and the point of view of the two managers were worlds apart. However, they shared the same methods and utilised the same techniques. Mass, light, colour, costume, pictures, and effects employed in special combinations are the essence of spectacle. In *Faust* Irving tried his best to use spectacle for the ends of serious art. To make pantomime a high art was also Harris's professed aim, although fewer people believed him than they did Irving, and considered that Harris used spectacle to benefit his box office (like Irving) and for its own sake (unlike Irving). Nevertheless, *Faust* and *Aladdin* are blood-brothers beneath different skins. More evidence exists for the reconstruction of a performance of *Faust* than any late-nineteenth-century pantomime; the Lyceum was written about more seriously and more frequently than Drury Lane, and every Irving production was carefully examined and thoroughly discussed. For the historian's purposes, *Faust* also has the advantage over, say, *The Sleeping Beauty and the Beast*, of having two strong central acting performances as the object of much critical attention; far less space was devoted to the acting of Leno and Campbell, despite their great popularity. Irving's Mephistopheles, at least, fitted into the spectacle style like a hand into a glove, and that is another reason to attempt a recreation of *Faust*, to consider precisely how an actor solved, or attempted to solve, the peculiar and enduring problems of performing in spectacle. Lastly, despite Goethe and despite W. G. Wills's pretensions to poetic tragedy, *Faust* is fundamentally a romantic melodrama in disguise; to consider it will also enable us to consider an extended example of the function of spectacle in large-scale melodrama.

4 · Henry Irving's *Faust*, Lyceum Theatre, 1885

By 1885 Henry Irving had been manager of the Lyceum for seven years and had already established himself as London's leading actor-manager. In those years his managerial policy had become clearly defined and was to stay relatively unchanged for the remainder of his management: the building up of a loyal and stable company, meticulous repertory planning, thorough rehearsing, productions with high artistic and (where relevant) archaeological standards, himself as star attraction and a distinguished leading lady, Ellen Terry, secured from the beginning faultless social respectability and professional integrity. The plays themselves were mostly a mixture of romantic melodrama, sometimes commissioned from living dramatists, and Shakespeare. Irving was financially successful, socially popular, and internationally famous. The Lyceum Company had already done two tours of North America, the first of eight altogether, and Irving's work was becoming widely known in Europe. Controversy still attended his acting, which retained its enemies, but the quality of his productions always commanded respect if by no means unanimous critical acclaim.

The theatre Irving had taken over in 1878, and in which he had been acting with the Bateman company since 1871, was built in 1834. Some improvements were made immediately, more in 1881. In the summer of 1885 the theatre architect C. J. Phipps supervised structural alterations and further redecoration. At the time of *Faust* the stage had a 33 foot 5 inch proscenium opening and a depth of 40 feet, with a rake of half an inch to the foot. The major structural change was the raising of the stage roof 20 feet to avoid wear and tear and inconvenience caused by rolling up the painted backcloths and the doubling up of scenery; such pieces could now be flown straight up. The lower portion of the main cornice around the ceiling was removed, thus improving sight lines from the gallery. The space freed by the disappearance of four of the six private boxes level with the stage was given over to stalls seats; thus widened, the stalls also offered greater leg-room with a simultaneous reduction in the number of rows from eleven to ten. Even then overcrowding was a problem, as it was in all London theatres of the time when they were full. One writer noted that 'the stalls are placed nearer together than is the rule at most theatres; and the popularity of the Lyceum is such that there is seldom a vacant stall.'[1] This overcrowding was necessary from the box-office point of view. In 1878 the financial capacity of the Lyceum was only £228. This was raised in 1881, and by the opening of *Faust* the house could hold possibly 1,700–1,800 people and about £420 – more on special occasions such as important benefits. Seat prices then were 10s 6d for stalls, 6s 6d in the dress circle, 4s in the upper circle, 2s 6d in the amphitheatre, 2s in the pit, 1s in the gallery, with private boxes 2 to 4 guineas.

The redecorations of 1881 greatly improved the front-of-house area, and after that date anyone entering the Lyceum for a performance would have noticed Arabian and Persian design motifs in the entrance hall, and, if he were going to the dress circle, would have passed between two massive gilt candelabra on high majolica plinths to mount a 20 foot wide grand staircase carpeted in ruby-coloured Axminster with a broad border of amber and black. A plush portière of old gold divided the head of the staircase from the vestibule, around which were palm trees and potted plants. The vestibule was lit by Moorish-looking candelabra, gasoliers, and hanging oil lanterns, all with ruby glasses. Inside the softly lit auditorium the spectator seeing any performance in the 1885–6 season found himself looking at a green baize curtain; above it and over the proscenium arch groups of boys personifying music, acting, and dancing were depicted against a background of blue sky and fleecy clouds. Above him was a ceiling with medallions of classical poets and dramatists painted to match the new gracefully curved white box-fronts panelled with gold mouldings, each panel containing a painting in the Italian-master style. The old Italian pattern was repeated in shades of green and blue on the walls, which were also decorated by rich amber hangings lined with cerise.[2] All this created a distinctive and unique atmosphere, remarked by many who saw it. H. A. Saintsbury, for example,[3] said that once one was inside the auditorium,

> the spirit gripped you; it had enveloped you before you took your seat,
> gas-lit candles in their wine-coloured shades glowed softly on the myrtle-
> green and cream and purple with its gilt mouldings and frescoes and
> medallions by Bartolozzi [preserved from the days of the Vestris manage-
> ment], the green baize in a diffused bluish mist; the music that did not start
> but insinuated itself upon you till the baize melted and you were in the pic-
> ture, beholding, yet part of it.

Percy Fitzgerald had the same feeling: 'As the curtain draws up and reveals the mellowed and harmonious colouring of Mr. Hawes Craven's scenery, the spaces in front and behind the footlights seem to blend, the scenic world to become rich and solid, that of prose to join the airy brilliance of the scene.'[4]

Such architectural and ornamental information is not retailed for its own sake, but to show how a late Victorian actor-manager like Irving conceived of entrance-hall, staircase, vestibule, and auditorium as entertainment, how the social ritual of entering the theatre and seating oneself to watch a play was, in terms of unity of design and harmony of visual effects, of richness, luxury, and the spectacle of interior decoration, a real part of the performance. Irving's Lyceum was a perfect stylistic marriage between audience space and performance space, a marriage made in many Victorian and Edwardian theatres. It is rare these days, except sometimes at Covent Garden, the Coliseum, the Garrick, Wyndham's, the Albery, and a few provincial theatres, for such a harmony to be achieved in the same formal and decorative way, although the environmental theatre movement has the same visual and architectural objectives as Irving, to create an audience space exactly appropriate to the production given. Such a formality and sense of visual grandeur would have been heightened at the Lyceum by the impeccable evening clothes of stalls and dress circle spectators – as it would also at Tree's His Majesty's, an even more resplendent theatre. The *de rigueur* formal dress of these spectators gave the theatre of the period a sense of sartorial pomp and magnificence, entirely suited to the elaborate spectacle on stage, vanished from today's theatre.

The Lyceum was fashionable as well as popular, and possessed considerable social distinction. Irving himself frequently entertained the representatives of culture and aristocracy at banquets on stage after performances or in the Beefsteak Room; his knighthood in 1895 was a mark of social achievement as well as theatrical merit. A complimentary stall or dress circle seat on a Lyceum first night was an esteemed social as well as theatrical privilege, conferred only on men of public or artistic worth. A Lyceum first night, commented the *Pall Mall Budget* reviewer (24 December 1885), 'is a theatrical court, and gives much the same *cachet* in the world artistic, literary, and theatrical as a presentation in Court in other circles.' Describing the first night of *Faust*, he observed Princess Louise watching from the front and the Prince of Wales, officially in mourning, looking on from behind the scenes. 'The Strand is lined with carriages; Wellington-street is blocked. ... The pillared entrance to the theatre is blocked again by crowds of onlookers, each pressing forward to see the arrivals. ... The circles were brilliant with pretty women in ravishing toilettes, the stalls like a parterre of flowers.' First nights were special occasions, however, and Lyceum audiences not always so fashionable. Pit, gallery, and upper circle were occupied by the humbler middle class, students, and a sprinkling of working class. Provincial visitors attended regularly, as did considerable numbers of clergymen – a sign of the Lyceum's great social and cultural respectability. That respectability was a matter of comment in the press. The run of *Faust* was barely three weeks old when W. H. Hudson declared, in the *Dramatic Review* (9 January 1886), that 'men and women are found in the Lyceum to-day who, a few years ago, would have been shocked at the thought of being seen in a theatre. Paterfamilias even consents to take his daughters "just to see Mr. Irving"; and in that society where the doings of the dramatic world in general are still ostracised subjects, *Faust* receives no small share of attention.' Hudson complained that this public showed too much favour to Irving at the expense of other managements; 'as a consequence the Lyceum pit is nightly visited by those who would be unwilling to enter any other London theatre.'

By the 1880s the scenery at the Lyceum was a mixture of new-style built-up sets with the old system of painted flats, cloths, and borders. Some idea of the size of the older type of scenery may be obtained from Bram Stoker's statement that the rolled-up cloths were 42 feet long and when framed 30 feet wide.[5] Many pieces were architecturally and ornamentally modelled in moulded cardboard to imitate brick and stone, such as pillars, statues, and the cathedral door in *Faust*, rather than presented as flat painted surfaces in cut-out profile. For *Faust*, built-up scenery predominated. Irving's scenic mechanisms were effective and appropriate but not especially original. The technical glory of the Lyceum was its stage lighting, and this was largely Irving's personal creation. In 1885 the stage lighting at the Lyceum was entirely by gas and limelight; the limelights were independently operated but all the gas was under the control of a single operator at the gas plate on the prompt side of the stage. The system was a fairly conventional one – a combination of footlights, battens, lengths, standards, and ground rows[6] – but it was Irving's experiments in colour and light intensity that produced the effects for which the Lyceum became a byword for artistry and taste. Such effects will be exemplified in the examination of *Faust*, but one can say in general that early in his management Irving sharply reduced the level of house lighting during scenes – evidently almost a new practice – and extinguished them entirely during scene changes carried out with the curtain up; it is quite possible that at a later period in his management the house lights were out during the performance. Without a bright auditorium subtler lighting was feasible and the level of stage lighting could be reduced accordingly. Unless he wanted a blaze of light Irving did not subject audiences to the merciless glare complained of on other stages, and tended on the whole to subdued lighting that avoided showing up every little detail, and a rich, deep colour scheme that did not distract attention from the actor. Irving's sense of colour was highly aesthetic, and produced many beautiful scenes with gaslight and limelight that lived long in the memory of those who saw them, but his experiments were mainly concerned with developing a variety of coloured lacquers for limelights and later for the bulbs of the electric lighting introduced at the Lyceum in the 1890s.

The lighting staff at the Lyceum was large in comparison to most other London theatres, and as has been suggested in the first chapter the combination of labour-intensive scene changing and the technical operation, cheap labour relative to box-office potential, and the very nature of contemporary production meant that to do his kind of work Irving needed and maintained a veritable legion of offstage and backstage personnel, in addition to the acting resources necessary for a spectacle like *Faust*. Interviewed at the start of *Faust*'s second season in 1886, Irving said that in the production 'we have over 350 men and women, including myself, constantly employed on the stage and behind the scenes, not including those in the orchestra.'[7] The orchestra was vitally important as a dramatic element in production. Its director, Meredith Ball, wrote music for Lyceum performances, as did specially commissioned composers such as Sullivan. The role of the orchestra's work can best be summed up by a description of its impact in America: 'The continuous music of the Irving plays, now suggesting the emotions of the situation, now intensifying the effects of the acting, now dominating the scene, now almost unheard in the excitement of the dramatic incident, was unknown. People said of Irving's first productions, "Why, they are like grand opera!"'[8] The comparison with opera is valid for spectacle drama, although it must be pointed out that almost continuous musical accompaniment had been a traditional feature of melodrama and pantomime, no matter how small the orchestra or how unspectacular the performance.

The Lyceum orchestra was especially augmented for *Faust*, but normally it numbered about thirty. According to Irving's notes in the *Faust* preparation book, it may have totalled thirty-five or thirty-seven: fifteen wind instruments (two flutes, two oboes, two bassoons, two clarinets, two horns, two trumpets, one or three trombones) and twenty-one strings (ten violins, four violas, three cellos, three basses, one harp); there was also a tympanum. The chorus was large: eight sopranos, six altos, six tenors, and five basses. However, H. J. Loveday told the *New York Tribune* (19 November 1887) that the chorus for the Brocken scene numbered forty-three. Percy Fitzgerald said that the backstage staff during a revival of *The Corsican Brothers* in 1881 comprised fifteen property men, thirty gasmen, and ninety stage carpenters,[9] and Alan Hughes put the total staff for *Robespierre* in 1899 at 639, divided into 355 performers and orchestra members, 236 backstage and technical, and 48 administrative.[10] Irving regularly used eight limelight men, who were rehearsed with the greatest care. Once the inevitable difficulties of a first night had been overcome, the highly trained, smoothly operating technical staff could achieve marvels. Fitzgerald described with wonder the way in which a full supper party set in *The Corsican Brothers* — 'two handsomely furnished rooms, Aubusson carpets, piano-forte, nearly twenty chairs, sofas, tables, clocks, and a supper-table covered with delicacies, champagne bottles, flowers, & c.' — was changed to the wintry Forest of Fontainebleau in thirty-eight seconds.[11]

Of this well organised and sizeable theatrical army Henry Irving was the undisputed generalissimo. It was not merely a matter of adminstrative power and responsibility, but also of artistic policy. Irving alone decided what pieces should be performed, how long they should be rehearsed, what part each actor should take, what music should be played, what scene design should be adopted, what lighting arrangements made, what costumes worn. From long experience as actor, stage manager, and manager, he was a master of every theatrical department; he not only knew what he wanted but how to get it. Many stories demonstrate the truth of this, from his rejecting Alfred Thompson's designs for the 1882 *Romeo and Juliet* and choosing the materials, colours, and costumes to be used, to declining to use some incidental music Sullivan had written for *Macbeth* in 1888 and being able, though quite unmusical himself, to give the right ideas to the composer. Of his knowledge of lighting Stoker said, 'Let it be clearly understood that the lighting of the Lyceum plays was all done on Irving's initiation and under his supervision. He thought of it, invented it, arranged it, and had the entire thing worked out to his preconceived ideas under his immediate and personal observation.'[12] When asked during the run of *Faust* if he concerned himself with all the details of production Irving replied, 'Certainly. In everything. We build up the whole play scene by scene, in order to produce a perfect work of art. ... Each scene is like his picture to a painter. You have to combine colours, group figures, and arrange the mountings.'[13] Finances and play selection aside, spectacle production was at its best when under the control of a single manager with an iron will, great executive ability, the respect and admiration of his staff, immense theatrical knowledge, and a consistent policy. Charles Kean, Irving, and Augustus Harris are the men who immediately come to mind and who dominated spectacle in the Victorian period.

The fact that Irving defined his function as producer in terms of pictorial art is significant, and his remarks give us the opportunity to examine briefly to what extent the productions of one manager, working in and further developing the pictorial traditions of theatre discussed generally in the first chapter, were conceived of as stage paintings. Irving himself was always willing to sacrifice archaeological details to artistic effect, and told the *Pall Mall Gazette* that 'the first duty of any one who mounts a piece is to produce a beautiful and pleasing effect'; in this respect 'archaeology must give way to beauty'. No painter would disfigure a canvas with an ugly dress because the dress was historically correct; the same applied to his own use of costume.[14] The familiar equation between painting and the stage is interesting to us, but so ordinary in its own times as to be unremarked. What *was* admired was the quality of pictorial art at the Lyceum; it was generally believed that such art had there been brought to the limits of stage perfection. Reviewing the first years of Irving's management, William Archer noted his technical realism of detail, comparable to Alma-Tadema's, his mastery of artistic invention:[15]

As one thinks of the past five years at the Lyceum there rises to the mind's eye a whole gallery of scenic pictures, each as worthy of minute study as any canvas of the most learned archaeological painter. ... He works over every inch of his canvas, leaves no corner without its little illustrative or merely decorative touch. ... The smallest hint in the text is made the germ of some picturesque conceit, and if the text affords no hint, why, Mr. Irving's brain is fertile to the point of spontaneous generation.

Many scenes from Lyceum productions looked to spectators like oil paintings, and Irving as an artist was praised for his sense of colour, composition, harmony, line, architectural detail, and contrasts of light and shade.

The production of *Faust* was in particular considered a notable artistic achievement as well as a theatrical success. Several articles were published, two or three of them in specialist art journals, examining the scenery, costumes, and staging from the point of view of pictorial composition. The scene painting of Hawes Craven and William Telbin was thought worthy, in its design phase, of a place on the walls of the Royal Academy. At least two critics compared the return of the soldiers in Act III with Rembrandt's 'Night Watch'; the Brocken scene evoked comparison with Callot, Retsch, John Martin and Gustave Doré; Margaret's chamber with Whistler; the scenes in Faust's study and the streets of Nuremberg with Dürer. One writer commented that 'the flavour of mediaeval German art pervades and dominates all these settings, which may well have been arranged, studied, and painted under the influence and the inspiration of the old German painters.'[16] In writing of the study scene, the artists Joseph and Elizabeth Pennell thought that Irving's purpose was as much artistic as dramatic: 'Mr. Irving sees himself and Mr. Alexander [Faust] not only as the chief characters in the tragedy, but as the principal figures in a picture rich in colour, vigorous in composition. Their every pose is a subject for a painter, and the result of long and careful study.'[17] The question of Irving's acting in relation to pictorial composition will be touched on below, but clearly critics as well as manager saw *Faust* as art and theatre simultaneously. At times, indeed, an unknowing reader could be forgiven for thinking that Irving was a painter rather than an actor or manager. Joseph Hatton described the scene in Martha's Garden entirely in terms of art, concluding, 'In itself here is a stage picture that might be successfully transferred to canvas. It is earnest and interesting in composition, pleasing in colour, tells its story, has good lines in it, is well grouped, and might be criticised from the standpoint of a cabinet painting.'[18] That Irving thought of his theatre as a temple of Art as well as Drama is obvious, and the artistic opportunities in presenting *Faust* on stage must have been a powerful incentive to doing the play.

This incentive was recognised by the author, a painter himself, as well as the manager. In defending himself against those critics inclined to judge his work by the achievements of Goethe, William Gorman Wills said that the motive of the substitution of Nuremberg for Goethe's Leipzig 'was, of course, the opportunity given for such beautiful scenery, characteristic of Germany, as might furnish an elevating aid to the public mind.'[19] A sense of place is almost irrelevant in Goethe but of the greatest consequence for Wills and Irving. Goethe's settings must be localised, pictorialised, made archaeologically correct and aesthetically beautiful; no less was expected of the Lyceum. The medieval picturesqueness of the result was widely praised, whatever was thought of Wills's adaptation; the beauties of the former were held to remedy the deficiencies of the latter. Setting philosophy and tragedy aside, Wills had at least provided a most satisfactory spectacle, a splendid part for Irving, a reasonable one for Ellen Terry, and a romantic, melodramatic realisation of the love of Faust and Margaret in a series of vivid and realistic stage pictures. So ran the consensus of opinion, which discounted the fury of Goethe purists by agreeing that as it stood Goethe's poem was unstageable and that comparisons between it and Wills's script were pointless.

Wills, in private and public life a somewhat eccentric bohemian with odd methods of work, had already written several plays for Irving, of which *Charles the First* (1872) was the most successful. The Irving–Terry partnership in a revival of *Olivia*, Wills's adaptation of *The Vicar of Wakefield* first written for the Court Theatre in 1878, proved enduringly popular. Many versions of *Faust* had reached the English stage, the three most notable being Charles Kean's production of Boucicault's *Faust and Margaret* (1854), Gounod's opera, first performed in London in 1863, and W. S. Gilbert's *Gretchen* (1879). Like other adaptors, Wills was concerned only with Goethe's Part I. He started writing this version in Paris in the summer of 1880, and it took him several years to finish. The Lyceum financial records show an item of £300 for the January–July 1882 season on the Production and Preliminary account which looks very like a lump-sum payment to the author, probably an advance. Since Wills received from Irving £600 for *Don Quixote* in 1887 and £800 each for an unused *Rienzi* and a discarded *King Arthur*, £300 in total would seem low. However, Wills did not receive royalties or nightly fees for *Faust*, and no other payment to him is recorded separately in the accounts. Undoubtedly he received another instalment, perhaps £300, included in all the other expenditure on *Faust* in the 1885–6 season; he did ask for 'another payment' in an undated letter to Irving. The script itself was written in close collaboration with the manager; Wills knew how to tailor his play to Irving's acting strengths and scenic requirements. He also supplied fresh dialogue during the rehearsal period, when many minor deletions and adjustments were made.

Wills's play took two or three years to reach the stage after its completion, and Irving told a reporter that he had been thinking and dreaming of staging *Faust* 'many years' before its production.[20] As was his wont, Irving occupied the interval with planning and research. To his library he added all kinds of scholarly tomes that would help him reconstruct medieval Nuremberg and the costumes of its inhabitants: books on costume, painting, architecture, military and religious life, furniture, arms and armour, sculpture, and decorations. Standard reference works such as Shaw's *Dresses and Decorations of the Middle Ages* and Planché's *Cyclopedia of Costume* were joined by Hirth's six-volume *Kulturgeschichtes Bilderbuch aus drei Jahrhunderten* and Ephrussi's *Dürer et ses Dessins*. Irving also bought at least six different translations of *Faust*.[21] Money was spent on the Production and Preliminary account for *Faust* in 1882 and 1883, but real preparations began about six months before the first night. After the Lyceum season closed at the end of July 1885, Irving and a party of friends and colleagues, including Ellen Terry and joined later by Hawes Craven, spent a fortnight in Nuremberg and Rothenberg, soaking up atmosphere, observing and recording scenes and architectural details, and buying authentic antique properties and costume material, shipped in great box-loads back to the Lyceum. Characteristically, the single-minded Irving saw everything on his holiday in terms of his forthcoming production; after he returned, according to Hatton, his rooms in Grafton Street were 'crowded with the sketches of Telbin, Craven, Burgkmair, Cranach, and others; with relics of Nuremberg and the Goethe country; with textiles ancient and modern; with studies by Albert Dürer; with folios of costume; and with many editions of *Faust*.'[22]

Irving had hoped to open *Faust* early in the new season, but technical problems and the immense amount of preparation necessary caused a postponement until December. An electric organ was especially installed for the cathedral scenes, and a peal of bells cast for £400. In rehearsal Irving was even more the great despot, usually kind and extremely patient, sometimes ruthless, always the autocrat. He knew exactly what he wanted to achieve in every line and with every scene, and would go to infinite lengths of trouble in order to obtain it; as J. B. Booth said, 'He had passed the whole production through his mind before the first rehearsal.'[23] Irving's rehearsals were a model of discipline, order and calm – in total contrast to Tree's – but because of his methods of endless repetition with the actors and because he also had to spend much time on matters of scenery, stage carpentry, lighting, and music, they could be very long and tedious. Edwin Booth, who played *Othello* with Irving in 1881, noted that 'as he is very exact as to every detail, and requires its elaboration to a nicety, you can readily imagine that the scene does not quickly reach perfection.'[24] Irving usually fitted in his own part in the latter stages of rehearsal, and to others never seemed to spend any time rehearsing himself. Nevertheless his conception of his own role was as clear as his conception of everything else, and he always knew in advance precisely how his figure and costume would become a distinctive and vital part of stage groupings and gain particular emphasis from lighting. Violet Vanbrugh, who joined the Lyceum company in 1891, said that rehearsals for a big production commonly lasted eight or ten weeks, initially for four or five hours a day and then as everything came together toward the end, from 10 a.m. to 3 or 4 the following morning.[25] Some indication of the kind of pressure Irving experienced in the last rehearsals is given in a letter from him to Ellen Terry, inscribed by her ' 3 nights before "Faust" ', and telling her that she need not rehearse that day:[26]

Tonight at seven dress.
Last night was a desperate affair from seven till five this morning.
Then only to end of 3rd act.
I left at one. . . .
It was quite amusing last night – the absolute fog of some of 'em.
It will be all right – of course – but it is a stern business.
Between ourselves I think tonight we may struggle through 3 acts –
    perhaps.

After a run of *Olivia* and six performances of *Louis XI*, final rehearsals were held while the theatre was closed for a week. *Faust* opened on 19 December 1885, in a Prologue and five acts (later reduced to five acts in total); there were eleven scenes altogether. The scenery was all by Hawes Craven and Telbin, who worked with three assistants. Incidental music was specially composed by Meredith Ball and Hamilton Clarke, and also adapted from Beethoven, Berlioz, and Lassen. The curtain went up on the first performance at 8 p.m. and did not fall until nearly midnight, Irving coming forward at the end to apologise for delays and technical hitches. Many reviewers said the play needed cutting, and indeed Irving made several changes during the long run. When the production had overcome its initial difficulties and some cuts had been made, the running time was about three hours, even with the addition of the Witch's Kitchen scene.

This reconstruction of the production of *Faust* comes from many sources. The promptbook itself has disappeared, but there is a printed translation of Goethe by John Anster, possibly prepared for production on Wills's behalf, possibly by a German scholar, with many unsuitable scenes and passages omitted. This early preparation book also contains the notes by Irving relating to the size of the orchestra and chorus. The Irving papers in the Theatre Museum contain at least seventeen letters from Wills to Irving about his play; only one is dated. The corrected copyright edition of December 1885, privately printed by the Chiswick Press and incorporating amendments, deletions, and additions made to a previous proof copy, is the principal source for the text, supplemented by two rehearsal copies annotated by Ellen Terry corresponding to the two states of the copyright edition. It was often Irving's practice to have his texts printed and distributed to his casts for rehearsal purposes; these were not for general sale. The Witch's Kitchen scene, a later addition to the production, was printed and corrected in the same way. I have seen no production photographs, but there are several studio portraits of Ellen

Terry as Margaret, and many drawings and caricatures in illustrated newspapers and magazines. The Lyceum souvenir-book of *Faust*, written by Joseph Hatton and reprinted from the *Art Journal*, is illustrated with drawings by Helen Hatton, W. H. Margetson, Hawes Craven, Telbin and Bernard Partridge. A long series of programmes supplies factual information, and weekly summaries of the Lyceum accounts give a continuous record of income and expenditure throughout the whole run, as well as for all revivals except the last in 1902. A great number of newspaper reviews from London, the provinces, and America are available, and articles also appeared in the intellectual monthlies and quarterlies, in addition to accounts in memoirs and theatrical works. The amount of space and attention an important new London production could command in the press in the late Victorian and Edwardian period must be a source of envy to theatre critics and artistic directors today. A production like *Faust* or Tree's *Henry VIII* was a national event of major cultural significance; the *Saturday Review*, for instance, printed three long reviews of *Faust* in the first seven months of its run, and American state newspapers reviewed *Henry VIII* in New York.

Wills had eliminated Goethe's theatre prelude and heavenly prologue and begun his version with the scene in Faust's study, a high narrow Gothic chamber with the elderly, grey-bearded doctor in cap and long fur-lined gown seated at a massive reading-desk, heaped with old volumes and manuscripts, a globe and a retort by his side, a skull and hour-glass on the desk; above it, suspended from the ceiling, the dried carcass of an alligator, against the wall shelves of books and a case of skulls, more retorts and vials, a skeleton hanging from the wall – the whole breathing the very spirit of musty Gothicism, a thoroughly authentic and atmospheric period set. The lighting was dim: a weak lamp on the desk and moonlight from a window. This was the first of the many lighting effects to win universal praise. 'The moonlight does not come in through the window in a great square splotch so that you know an electric moon is at work, but falls softly across the floor and touches, with pale silver light, the table near which Faust sits.'[27] As in Goethe, Faust is saved from drinking poison by the sound of bells and the Easter hymn, but Wills cut out the appearance of the Spirit, Wagner, and the whole scene outside the city gates, jumping straight to Faust's exorcism and the manifestation of Mephistopheles in a mist, which formed in the dark upstage shadows by the stove. This mysterious mist was one of the experimental devices developed to suggest the supernatural powers of Mephistopheles, and was produced by the following method:[28]

> A gas heated boiler supplies steam at 60 lb. per square inch pressure, which is led by 1 in. pipes to a valve near the point of escape, from which the pipe is enlarged to 4 in., and on it funnel-shaped openings, also provided with taps, look upwards. This effect, as well as every other stage device, is controlled by the prompter by means of a 'pull' or signal string,

to which a small weight is attached. On the prepare-for-steam signal the stop-cock is opened, the contents of the small pipe are allowed to expand into the larger one, and, on the second pull, other assistants open the several cocks which control the admission to the stage. Nothing can be simpler or more effective, yet the easy method of overcoming the noise was only arrived at after many experiments.

The first appearance of Mephistopheles in the mist was a striking effect. The lurid red glare of the stove cast a weird light on the shadows of the study, while the mist materialised only a white and ghastly face, with bloodless lips and lidless eyes, conveying a sense of foreboding and evil with a single visual image. In the *World* (23 December 1885), William Archer objected that the steam on the first night was not thick enough, and that he could see Mephistopheles enter by the door. However, this fault must have been speedily corrected. Gradually the vapours cleared to reveal Mephistopheles in the dress of a travelling scholar; he soon reappeared *in propria persona* in a scarlet costume, a rapier at his side, a yard-long cock's feather in his cap, with a pronounced limp to match his inner malignancy, but looking for all the world like a high-spirited, fashionable, though somewhat seedy rake. The canvas of the first scene was now complete; as the Pennells pointed out, 'The dim Gothic chamber ... is but a background for the red *Mephistopheles* who is ever the highest light and the center of interest, and for the somber *Faust* who is in such strong contrast to him.'[29] Throughout the production, indeed, Irving simultaneously emphasised his own character (not to mention his role as star) and filled in the stage painting with the dominant colour of Mephistopheles's costume, which stood out even more powerfully in the predominantly dim lighting, Irving himself being always well lit. We shall see in the reconstruction of *Henry VIII* how Tree, also a star actor-manager, dominated the stage of His Majesty's in exactly the same way, through costume and lighting – acting entirely apart. Shortly before his reappearance Mephistopheles tempted Faust with an upstage vision of Margaret at her spinning-wheel, which on the first night failed to appear. Later in the run this was replaced by a more immediately sensual vision of voluptuous and scantily dressed young women. A short exchange, much reduced from Goethe, between Mephistopheles and a bewildered visiting student, was criticised as irrelevant and soon eliminated from the performance, although Ellen Terry and Walter Pollock greatly admired it. The scene was concluded by Faust signing a compact with Mephistopheles in his own blood, to the accompaniment of mysterious and romantic music from the orchestra. The book in which he signed shone with a strange light (produced, the *Engineer* tells us prosaically, by a 50-cell Grove battery); 'the features of the tempter relax, and there passes over them a gleam of fiendish joy.'[30] The scene ended as in Goethe, with Mephistopheles enveloping Faust in his cloak and flying away with him (somewhat jerkily on the first night) as thunder rolled. There was a great deal of thunder in *Faust*, and it was caused by cannonballs of different sizes dropping 8 feet from several hoppers simultaneously on to a 1-inch boiler plate, from which they were released down an inclined chute by slides, either singly or together, depending on the strength and kind of thunder required.

The second scene of the Prologue was originally the St Lorenz Platz, but for the 244th performance on 15 November 1886, a new Witch's Kitchen scene, written by Wills and closely following Goethe, was inserted between Faust's study and the St Lorenz Platz scenes. When Wills was earlier criticised for not including this scene, he replied, 'I cannot believe that a thoughtful English critic would miss a scene which before the footlights would degenerate into burlesque.'[31] In his curtain speech on the first night, however, Irving promised to consider including in the production both the Witch's Kitchen and the drinking scene in Auerbach's Cellar. The latter never reached the Lyceum stage but the former did, no doubt because of the opportunities it provided for further spectacular and supernatural effects. On a simple plot level it also enabled the audience to see the transformation of Faust from age to youth after he drank the magic potion instead of this occurring somewhat obscurely offstage after the first scene.

The curtain did not come down on scene i, but after Mephistopheles and Faust had vanished a series of thick gauzes were lowered, obliterating Faust's study from sight. Behind them could be seen flickering points of flame, and when the gauzes were taken up a dark rocky cavern became visible, with a smoky and fiery cauldron downstage right from which sparks mounted to the roof; *'household goods of witches all about'* is the stage direction. Crouched near the cauldron, dimly seen in the fitful light, were five monkeys, one of them skimming the brew. Mephistopheles and Faust entered, and the fiend watched the monkeys hissing, chattering, and rolling a large globe about the floor. Seated on a settle with a whisk in his hand, he tolerantly observed these antics and their dancing, while Faust was enchanted with another vision of a female form, beckoning enticingly, which appeared in a bright light against a previously dark wall of rock. The neglected cauldron boiled over, and the Witch herself, astride a broom, came down through the flames that streamed upward, screaming and cursing horribly, wearing worn and ragged garments to which blue mould clung. The colour scheme of the scene was again a painter's:[32]

> The dark, damp, underground cave, a subdued brown in colour, the grey garments of the old witch, worn and worm-eaten, and seemingly heavy with a dank grave-mould, the flashes of red light from the bubbling cauldron, from the lamps that form the circle of incantation, and from the nimbus in which *Mephistopheles* seems to move, make a picture that is as grand in its well-balanced consistency as it is fascinating in its terrible weirdness.

Mephistopheles, irritated at not being recognised with due obeisance, smashed up the crockery and then seized the disrespectful but soon cowering Witch by the throat and ordered the potion prepared for Faust. The Witch's incantation was strongly declaimed by Tom Mead, a veteran Lyceum actor, in a circle ringed by candles and scattered with tokens of evil such as dead snakes and lizards. According to Hatton in the *Faust* souvenir-book, Irving in preparation for this scene did as much research on the literature of wizardry as he did for all other aspects of the production. At the end of the incantation, read from a book resting on the back of a monkey while the other monkeys crouched inside the circle holding torches, the magic brew was offered to Faust; as he hesitated to drink a flame rose from the cup. After he had drunk it the transformation of an old man into a young one began; a youthful face was seen but the hair was still white. Mephistopheles hurried Faust off at the end of the scene as the Kitchen grew dim and the gauzes came down again. The business of the Witch's Kitchen, as several observers noted, came very close to the grotesqueness of pantomime,[33] but Irving's grim earnestness and sense of a power both evil and awe-inspiring reduced the comic aspects of the scene to minor proportions. The grotesque remained chillingly grotesque, rather than ludicrous; it was a fine line that the production was perilously to tread more than once.

Goethe had placed the scene in Auerbach's Cellar before the Witch's Kitchen. In adding the latter to his production Irving reversed the order and brought the drinking scene out of doors as the opening section of his original scene ii, the St Lorenz Platz. Before the Witch's Kitchen was included, the curtain fell on Faust's study and rose again after a twelve-minute interval; afterwards, the cloud-like gauzes concealed the vast scene change going on behind, for the Kitchen occupied the entire depth of the stage and the St Lorenz Platz was a full and very heavy set. H. J. Loveday, the Lyceum stage manager, told an American journalist that it took nearly 100 carpenters, fly-men, property men, and lighting men to effect the change:[34]

> In order to lose no time the different heavy parts of the scene which represent the statuary, archway, market cross, & c. have to be kept ready slung in the flies, and are immediately lowered by signal on to the framework, which is quickly fitted together. There is no noise or bustle on the drop curtain descending, the scene-shifters, who all wear indiarubber shoes, fall into their respective places much like men-of-war's men at station drill, all doing their allotted work at the word of command, which is given by signs.[35]

The St Lorenz Platz was a much-admired spectacle scene, and because of the relative brightness of its beginning was greeted with relief by those who found two consecutive dimly lit scenes trying. The scene was the square in front of the cathedral, whose elaborate carved doorway with flanking statues of saints was on stage left; on the right a wine shop, with a bush hanging from a wrought-iron sign, a scroll above the door, a table and seats outside, and men inside drinking. Upstage of the table was a tree, upstage of that again the statue of a saint. Streets lined with quaint gabled houses led out of the square; 'the perspective is effectively managed, so that the eye is led away gradually into the distance, and is not brought up sharply against the back drop.'[36] Percy Fitzgerald was at pains to explain that the cathedral was one of those modelled architectural pieces for which the Lyceum was noted, 'wrought in pasteboard; that is the design was moulded in plaster, and sheets of paper were pasted over it until the desired thickness was reached. Thus was ingeniously secured all the effects of stone – in a material excessively light and portable – and enduring any amount of "knocking about".'[37] Many reviewers were impressed with the medievalism and pictorial realism of the whole, and felt as if they were actually looking from a near-by window onto the old stone buildings of a medieval German city.

What gave the scene its spectacular nature was not just the set, however, solid and beautiful as that was, but also the tide of townsfolk washing into the square as the bells rang for service and the organ played softly within the cathedral. Of all the critics who recorded the scene, the Pennells were the most detailed and informative, and their description will serve better than any synthesis of mine:[38]

> In the crowd there are great ladies in shining brocades, and peasant women in bodices and gay-colored aprons; knights in velvet and plush, swaggering soldiers in armor, and peasants in plain hose and jerkin; little girls in stiff brocades and broad-brimmed hats, and little girls in dark woolen gowns like the child in Rembrandt's picture of 'Christ Blessing the Little Ones'; pages in silk attire, and a beggar in picturesque rags with pipes under his arm; brown-cowled monks in solemn procession, and white-veiled nuns who linger to talk to the women and children just beneath the shrine at the church door, where there is a blue Madonna with flowers at her feet.

The costumes had a feeling of wear, and some were none too clean. The soldiers, off to the wars, were having last-minute adjustments to their armour. Clement Scott noticed that pages carried the trains of grand ladies; burgomasters, soldiers, and everybody, he thought, 'might have stepped out of panes of old German glass'.[39] Irving had composed his stage crowd in colour patterns and broken them up in groups to form a series of pictures. In the earlier stages of the run Faust and Mephistopheles entered together, the former now entirely youthful and sporting a light brown beard. Later Irving devised new business for himself and entered amongst the women, trying to kiss a girl and propitiating a mother by noticing her child; all shrank from him in revulsion. He was now even more resplendent in a short silk cape, tight silk hose and doublet, jewelled girdle round his waist, rapier with a red scabbard, and the inevitable long feather in his red cap. The crowd soon went up the steps and into the cathedral, a single file of monks among them. The drinkers left the tavern and Mephistopheles began his sport with them, which included producing from a table wine that spurted fire when spilled on the ground. The fire was caused by the lighted gas in a funnel-shaped pipe, covered by paper and held immediately under a stage grating, being turned up by the prompter; the realism of the magic was aided by the burning particles of paper.

After this bit of fun and the exit of the muddled drinkers, the worshippers left the cathedral following the service – Fitzgerald objecting to the swelling and booming of the organ, which 'made all quiver'; from the outside, he claimed, it should sound only faintly,[40] as it evidently did at the beginning of the scene. Among the departing congregation was Margaret – Ellen Terry in a yellow dress, golden hair in braids to her waist, highly nervous as usual on the first night and greeted then by a long burst of applause which she was forced to acknowledge, thus interrupting the action to the annoyance of some critics. Upon Faust accosting Margaret and offering to escort her home, the actress's rehearsal copy note is 'Taken aback – a little frightened – look straight in his eyes – be simple – not as if she were *used* to being spoken to – surprised thinks he's making fun of her.' It took Ellen Terry only a moment to establish the innocence and simplicity which were to be later developed as key aspects of her character and her appeal to the audience. With the same two-line reply spoken in Goethe, Wills's Margaret rejected Faust's offer and passed on. The text gives her first appearance as '*Enter* MARGARET, *dogged by* MEPHISTOPHELES', but none of the reviews mentions that he followed her out of the cathedral, and Irving would certainly not have wished to spoil his co-star's first entrance by sharing it with her. One illustration of this moment shows him watching and lurking behind the statue, evidently expressing in dumbshow a malevolent mockery.

The scene concluded with emphasis on Mephistopheles rather than the love-stricken Faust, who left the stage having commanded 'some lustrous present to enchant her'. Three cowled monks came from the cathedral laughing heartily at some joke; Mephistopheles smiled at the sight; the monks went off, the bells rang out once more, and the fiend grew much troubled by the sound, crouching in torment against the tree. One reviewer said that 'with a skinny finger thrust in each ear, and his form quivering with fear, he slinks out of reach of their sweet sounds';[41] another that 'the spirit of evil is seized with dread and apprehension which display themselves in all kinds of grotesque and horrible writhings of the body.'[42] With this impressive and strange mime the act ended and the drop curtain fell. There had been little opportunity for Irving to impose himself on the scene after fooling the drinkers; his way of taking command here was by giving a physical demonstration of fear, evil, and the grotesque – three things Irving was always good at – and, once again, by colour. The picture of the deserted square and the quiet grey stone, the dull red of the tiled roofs, was made complete by the single touch of bright colour in it, Mephistopheles's costume.[43]

The scene in the St Lorenz Platz concluded the Prologue, and the drop curtain remained down for several minutes before rising on Act I and Margaret's chamber at twilight, a scene that left Ellen Terry in solitary possession of the stage for most of its duration. The set was compared to a painting of Whistler's by more than one critic. The *Pall Mall Budget* (24 December 1885) said that it was 'what Mr. Whistler would call an arrangement in French grey, against which Margaret's white bedgear stands out in relief'. The chamber was simply furnished. Aside from the bed, built into a recess of the back wall, there was a table upon which stood a crucifix (at which Mephistopheles recoiled slightly), a carved oak chest, a chair, and a small mirror. The setting sun shone through the panes of a small leaded window. The simplicity and clean lines of the room formed an effective contrast with the crowded townscape of the previous scene, and obviously represented the naive innocence of its occupant. The whiteness of that innocence, in terms of set and costume, was soon to be darkened by the redness of the devil; Mephistopheles and Faust made a brief entrance to conceal the casket of jewels. Margaret entered, crossed herself at a little statue of the Virgin, and began to take off her frock, singing Wills's version – much altered by the actress – of Goethe's 'Es war ein König in Thule' to the music of Lassen. She discovered the casket in the chest and opened it. Amazement and then a long laugh of delight succeeded surprise as she tried on a necklace. Ellen Terry's rehearsal note is 'Coquette – *No*! Pleased and shy blushing', and the reviewer for the *New York Morning Journal* (8 November 1887), one of the very few to find her too old for the part – she was thirty-seven when *Faust* opened – nevertheless praised this moment: 'The abandon, artlessness, and joy of the scene are past describing. It was all wonderfully natural and bubbling, sparkling and true.' Calling Ellen Terry a 'picturesque and beautiful figure', Lyman Weeks selected as especially admirable the pose in which she half-reclined in her chair after discovering the jewels from 'a hundred other poses that are assumed with equal grace and charming *naïveté*'.[44] Such pictorial acting was a necessary complement to Irving's, but it was also at the heart of the Victorian actor's style.

The scene closed with a change of Margaret's mood to apprehension as she wonders if she will meet Faust again and whether her simple life will ever be disturbed. The answer had already been ironically given by the sight of Mephistopheles, peeping through the window, spying on her as she opened the casket. Music came up under her last few lines as the lights went slowly down and the drop curtain fell.

The second scene of Act I, 'Nuremberg: the City Wall', was a front scene with one of Hawes Craven's most praised backcloths representing an elevated view of the whole city from the rampart on which Faust and Mephistopheles stood. The time was evening, with the red roofs of the city bathed in the golden and then reddish light of the setting sun. The action is of little consequence, part of it adapting Goethe's scene 'A Walk', and the rest concerned with the exposition of Mephistopheles's plan to acquaint himself with Martha by bringing her news of her husband's death. The figure of the devil against the blood-red setting gave the scene a remarkable quality of menace, as if Mephistopheles himself had created that light and darkened it with his own colour.

The next scene, in Martha's cottage, can also be passed over quickly, as together with the City Wall scene it is only a narrative link with the scene in Martha's garden where Faust and Margaret talk. Wearing her yellow dress with an embroidered black and white apron and a chatelaine at her waist, Margaret showed the second casket of jewels to Martha, who was seated with her work. Mrs Stirling, then seventy, played Martha in a broadly comic way, and several reviewers thought she was much too old for the part of a flirtatious widow. Ellen Terry relates the story of how Mrs Stirling, whose sight was none too good, invariably dropped part of her work near the door when Mephistopheles knocked so that by picking it up she could find her way back to her seat after letting him in.[45] The scene closely follows Goethe, and ends with Mephistopheles promising to introduce Faust as a witness to his story of the death of Martha's husband.

The ensuing scene in Martha's garden had a much more elaborate set, one of the most beautiful in the production. On the backcloth rose the spires of Nuremberg, below it a garden whose footpaths were edged with roses in bloom. From the point of view of design, grouping, and colour it is worth quoting Hatton's description:[46]

> Quiet red-brick garden walls with climbing roses; an old moss-grown
> apple-tree with an ancient bench; a rustic cottage porch; a background of
> city towers; the whole a characteristic town garden. As to the placing of the
> figures, if they pause, during the action of the story, they pause near the
> tree, forming a foreground group. Margaret is in a dress of pale yellow and
> white brightened by a slight touch of black; then Faust in a costume of
> rich brown, a connecting link of colour, leading up to Mephistopheles, the
> antithesis of Margaret; forming as it were a second focus of colour in the
> picture, the splendour of it relieved by the sombre tones of the gateway
> against which it is massed. Over all there is a rich glow of summer evening
> colour deepening towards twilight.

The time was sunset, and the lighting changes as the scene progressed were sensitively done. The contrast in the scene was between the courtly but sarcastic wooing of Martha by the bored Mephistopheles and the ardent exchanges between Faust and Margaret, each relationship claiming the foreground as each pair of lovers came forward round the winding footpaths or paused by the apple tree. The keynote of Ellen Terry's acting here, judging by her rehearsal notes, was a happiness carefully graded in stages of surprised pleasure mingled with shyness, contented satisfaction, and overwhelming feeling in which agitation and the ecstasy of love played equal parts. Her note at the beginning of the scene is 'Timidly Happy'; when Faust kisses her hand after seven lines it is 'Startled! a little ashamed – happy.' In telling Faust her life story she is 'in the *domestic* speeches losing thought of who it is she is speaking to until Faust kisses her hand.' Soon she is 'brimming over happiness', a mood soon tinged with wonder and then fear, on 'And yet too soon – too soon. I know thee not.' Faust reassures her; she playfully picks the petals from a daisy to prove whether he loves her or not. Here the note expresses, to put it mildly, extravagant emotion surging under the playfulness: 'Discovery! Awful fearful throbbing – Heavenly discovery – Mad Happiness – Care-less Happy – Certain Happy', and the word 'Happy' is scrawled in large letters five more times down the margin. Such emotion has little expression in the text except for the repetition of 'He loves me – he loves me not' over the daisy, the exit line 'I tremble – let me be silent' after the renewed declaration of Faust's love, and the stage direction *'she suddenly presses his hand convulsively, then exits hurriedly.'* All this time Mephistopheles, seemingly absorbed with the flattering Martha, was throwing keen side-glances at the young lovers. There was much comedy in Irving's performance, especially in this scene, and his lines after Martha's exit,

> Where will she go to, by and by,
> I wonder? I won't have her.

never failed to bring down the house. The scene and act ended with his mocking echo of Margaret's rapturous exclamation to Faust, 'Oh, thou King of all the World!'

The first interval, which must have been a long time coming, was after this act, and by the end of January 1886 was reduced to only six minutes. It was followed by a brief 'Trees and Mountains' scene, another front cloth painted by Telbin: an immense and precipitous cliff on its right-hand side, trees, rocks, and distant mountains in the foreground and on the left. The scene was a link between Martha's garden and Margaret's garden, both of which required full sets and more than six minutes to effect the change. Faust's long philosophical speech in Goethe is cut down by Wills to eleven lines. (Ellen Terry observed of Conway's Faust in rehearsals that 'this is blank verse & he must preserve the lines.') Mephistopheles suggests a night visit to Margaret and a harmless opiate to make sure that her mother sleeps soundly; the whole scene is much reduced in length from Goethe.

Audiences saw Margaret at her spinning-wheel when the lights next went up; the scene was laid in her garden, again at evening, and she was seated stage left by the porch of her cottage. The Pennells praised the realism of the set in comparison to the same thing as usually seen in productions of

Gounod's opera, 'a pretty green space shut in with high brick walls, with near and distant gables and spires and towers showing above it, instead of the conventional scene, with its characterless house, and single tree and flowers from the nearest florist's. In just such gabled cottages, with latticed windows and projecting upper stories, would people of *Martha's* and *Margaret's* rank have lived.'[47] Wills's scene is a fusion of two of Goethe's and opens with Margaret singing sadly of her heaviness and lost peace; 'she sh^d be a drooping girl', wrote Ellen Terry, who changed several lines to suit herself. Paradoxically, however, Margaret is still happy and very much in love, though anxious and bewildered, as the marginal notes show. Mephistopheles's appearance provided a strong dramatic confrontation between malignant evil and innocent goodness, although after Margaret's initial shudder at his entrance he spoke to her in a soothing, fatherly and persuasive way as she continued working (Ellen Terry had taught herself to spin for the part): 'Honest Iago' is the actress's note here. Seeing a cross on her breast, Mephistopheles started to edge away. Perceiving this, Margaret, frightened though she was, raised it in front of him; the direction in the text is *'he cowers away out of the* [garden] *door, looking devilishly behind'*, as appropriate music played. '*Strong* so much depends on the music' is the comment in the rehearsal copy. After his exit Margaret cries, 'He's gone! He's gone! It is some fiend disguised' − 'difficult' is the observation on this line − and evidently cowered against the upstage wall before running down to Faust, who did not see her upon his entrance and then had to parry, confusedly, her desperately earnest pleading for marriage. Mephistopheles's unnoticed re-entrance at this point prompted the *Pall Mall Budget* (24 December 1885) to remark on the relationship between costume and lighting, with 'the whole garden suffused by the moonlight, casting weird shadows upon the remote corners ... and lighting up the tendrils which climb the porch of Margaret's house. The garden door opens and Mephistopheles appears ... one cannot fail to be. struck by the remarkable ingenuity of arrangement of colours, the scarlet of Mephistopheles standing out in vivid relief against the silvery sheen of the moonlight.' Margaret frantically urges Faust to part from Mephistopheles; Faust innocently gives the deadly phial as a sleeping-draught for her mother, and she leaves to administer it.

Faust was now alone with a Mephistopheles in his most mocking and sneering mood. In rehearsal Ellen Terry praised Irving's comedy at the beginning of this dialogue and exclaimed admiringly, if vaguely, 'How he will do it!' The cynical banter changes rapidly to rage when Faust informs him that he wishes to marry Margaret − a desire not expressed by Goethe's Faust and much objected to by many critics, who must have forgotten the innate morality of the Victorian stage, Goethe or no Goethe. This moment was probably the highlight of Irving's performance. 'Change to fiend − NOT light' is Ellen Terry's note opposite

Then in good time I'm here.
Thou shalt not wed this maid, nor dally with her
After this night.

Mephistopheles's answer to Faust's 'By what pretence canst thou forbid me, fiend?' is accompanied by her marginal comment, 'Like a Thunder god.' Irving must have been impressive enough in rehearsal for her to remark, 'H. sh^d do this his grandest – not *frighteningly*, but *awfully*.' The speech is as follows:

Thou answer'st me
As if I were some credulous, dull mate.
I am a spirit, and I know thy thought.
You think you may be fenced round by-and-by
With sprinkled holy water, lifted cross –
While you and your pale saint might hold a siege
Against the scapegoat – 'gainst the devil here.
Ere that should be I'll tear thee limb from limb,
Thy blood I'd dash upon the wind like rain,
And all the gobbets of thy mangled flesh
I'd scatter to the dogs, that none should say
This carrion once was Faust!
Yon cottage would I snatch up in a whirlwind,
At dead midnight, like pebble in a sling,
And hurl it leagues away, a crumbled mass,
With its crushed quivering tenant under it.
Dost know me now?

Increasing his pace as he went, Irving spoke with a terrible and withering calm, deliberately playing against the extravagant and horrific vocabulary. The dreadful force of the passage made the blood of the Glasgow *Evening Citizen* reviewer (6 September 1887) run cold: 'His figure, as he waxes in wrath, seems to fill the stage; the tone of concentrated and contemptuous malice with which he addresses his cowering companion, strikes awe into every listener; the cruel, unhuman, expression of his eyes is of the kind which haunts the beholder, returning to the memory again and again, like the recollection of a fearsome and evil dream.' Perhaps Scottish audiences were particularly affected; in Edinburgh the speech 'was followed by a dead silence only broken by a burst of shuddering applause'.[48] The *Echo* (21 December 1885) noticed the stage effects accompanying Mephistopheles's threats: 'As he stood there in the darkened garden with Faust half seen in the gloom, and all around shadowy and mystic, by a most ingenious piece of management the scarlet-clothed Fiend is made to glow like a red-hot cinder, and his eyes literally flashed with light.' It was the only time in the play when Irving allowed the potential of demonic fury in his part to be visible to the audience, even more effective through being strictly controlled.

Faust could only collapse before this onslaught with a weak 'Fiend, I obey.' Margaret then came out of her cottage and led Faust in by the hand, Mephistopheles watching this from the garden gate and giving a final ironical laugh as he stood alone on the stage. Act II thus ended on a note of utter dominance by Mephistopheles. It was almost universally felt that one of the weakest aspects of Wills's text was the reduction of Goethe's Faust to a romantic but uninteresting and spineless nonentity. Neither H. J. Conway, who failed in the part, nor his successor, George Alexander, promoted from Valentine, could make much of the role, and of course with the relationship between Faust and Mephistopheles so unbalanced in favour of the latter Irving acted both of them off the stage.

The second interval, of twelve minutes, now occurred before the only scene in Act III, 'Street by Church'. Despite the thirty-eight seconds it took the Lyceum stage staff to change from one big set to a forest scene in *The Corsican Brothers*, they needed at least the twelve minutes provided by the intervals before Act III and Act V (the dungeon) to set up a big scene in *Faust*, which however used a great deal more built-up scenery and was a much heavier show. The six-minute interval between Act I and Act II was followed by the 'Trees and Mountains' front scene which must have taken at least that time to play, and the change to the massive Brocken set of Act IV was preceded by a fifteen-minute interval. The changeover from Faust's study to the St Lorenz Platz was covered by a wait of twelve minutes. All these interval times are listed on programmes from the end of January 1886, and had been slightly reduced in length from times listed on earlier programmes.

Wills's Act III is a conflation of four consecutive scenes in Goethe, 'At the Well', 'A Shrine in the Ramparts', 'Night', and 'Cathedral Nave'. The scene showed the cathedral occupying much of stage left, one window shining with light. A well with a canopy was near the side of the cathedral and a statue of the Virgin upstage centre. Girls were gossiping by the well about the fall from purity of one of their friends. Margaret, in a grey dress, a 'fearful burden of grief upon her', according to Ellen Terry's note, listened with sympathy and growing horror; a further note is a reminder to 'realise before going on'. After the girls, laughing maliciously, had departed with their buckets of water, Margaret addressed a heartfelt appeal for pity and aid to the statue of the Virgin. A sketch in the second rehearsal book shows a figure standing a little down right of the shrine with arms uplifted and outstretched towards it, and the speech is well annotated. The beginning was subdued with grief, and the apostrophe in the second line − 'Thou through whose anguished heart the sword hath pierced' − was to be broken up. The voice then dropped to a whisper as Margaret described how terror 'ever follows/My footsteps as my shadow.' At some point she knelt, possibly after laying flowers at the feet of the Virgin. *Blackwood's* objected that the flowers were shabbily artificial, and that for only ninepence a day Ellen Terry could be supplied with fresh flowers that would bring a touch of spring and of nature to the scene.[49] The ensuing speech, which represents Wills's blank verse at its best, ends as follows:

> These flowers I bring are watered by my tears.
> Oh, heal this bleeding heart – oh, rescue me
> From death and shame! Mother of many saviours!
> Have pity, oh, have pity – turn to me!

For the second of these four lines the note is 'More passion then burst out more passionately.' 'Mother of many saviours!' is to be said 'with loving entreaty', and at the end is written the general instruction, 'Voice must be under cool control – must SING all this.' Margaret then went to her house; the note is 'Drag myself of[f].' Clement Scott in the *Daily Telegraph* (21 December 1885) declared that the absolute truth of Ellen Terry's acting here 'brought tears into the eyes of the most hardened in the audience', and was himself much moved by 'her deep pleading voice – that wonderful voice of hers – half-choked with sobs that poured forth the pitiable lamentation.'

Night was falling as Margaret addressed the shrine; after she had entered her house, soldiers returning from the wars, accompanied by townspeople, crossed the stage. This was another highly praised crowd scene. The soldiers did not march in, but hurried quickly across the stage in small irregular groups, carrying flaring torches, drums beating and banners waving, welcomed by the women and children. The Pennells as usual observed with an artistic eye, paying particular attention to the lighting at the beginning of the scene:[50]

> When the curtain goes up, there is still a faint color in the sky at the end of the long twisting street to the left, but it quickly fades. The church rises, a great dark mass away above the stage, and you see only the heavy buttresses and one large window. The rest is in shadow, save in one corner where a lamp burns before a shrine. From out the gathering gloom and to the sound of distant drumming come the soldiers home from the wars, – wives, children, and sweethearts hanging to their arms, the halberds wreathed with green, and torches and cressets borne aloft. Each separate group is a study in itself.

The fatal wounding of Valentine through Mephistopheles's interposition in the duel with Faust followed Mephistopheles's hideous serenade on the mandolin to Martha, and the duel itself was made more exciting by a device emphasising the supernatural quality of his victory. Two iron plates were screwed into the floor of the stage, to which two wires from the 50-cell Grove battery were attached. Faust and Valentine each wore a metal sole in the right boot, and insulated wires were run up the clothing of both men to an indiarubber glove in whose palm was a metal plate. When each duellist had the correct foot on the plate in the stage, a 90-volt intermittent current was generated and an eerie blue fire flowed from small saw-teeth on the sword blades when they clashed. Playing Valentine, Alexander received a nasty shock on the first night when he grasped an uninsulated part of the sword hilt.

To enhance the supernatural atmosphere Mephistopheles may have had an electric light on the tip of his sword, so that as he pointed contemptuously with the sword at the dying Valentine a light from an apparently inexplicable and other-worldly source would have fallen on the latter's face. This may not have happened, however, as the information comes from only one source,[51] and none of the reviews mentions this effect. From several sources comes the knowledge of another ingenious lighting effect: Irving carried three different battery-operated coloured lights in his cap, by means of which he could illuminate his face as he chose. This would have explained the 'nimbus' around his head referred to by Lyman Weeks and the flashing eyes remarked by the *Echo*. The *New York Times* (8 November 1887) said of this lighting that 'sometimes it is red, and at other times its rays lend to his leering features a death-like aspect' – suggesting that one of the other colours was white; blue or green would have been a logical choice for the third. For some years it had been possible to generate electricity on the person of the actor by means of storage batteries, bulky though they still were, most notably for the fairies in the finale of *Iolanthe* in 1881.[52] Pantomime quickly adopted the method. However, the electric sword-fight in *Faust* was entirely original, and the other uses of portable electric light sources experimentally ingenious.

From the point when Valentine fell by the well to a venomous laugh from Mephistopheles the pace of the scene quickened considerably. Faust and his companion left the stage and a crowd gathered around Valentine; its grouping and lighting in relation to the dying soldier evoked considerable admiration, and Rembrandt was again mentioned. Some of the crowd, citizens and soldiers alike, carried torches, the half-light of their flames flickering on excited and shocked faces. Margaret came out of her house wearing a cloak and knelt by her brother. Valentine's face was lit by the torch of the man supporting him; his sister knelt in a symbolic mass of dark shadow. Valentine cursed her and died, telling her with his last breath that her lover was responsible for his death. With a cry Margaret staggered back; with murmurs of execration the crowd advanced menacingly upon her, but dispersed without more threat. One of the girls returned to kiss her sympathetically; Margaret then stumbled into the cathedral. Faust rushed on, determined to find her, but Mephistopheles cast a spell on him and caused him to vanish in a cloud of mist – the same faithful steam first visible in Faust's study and regularly used for any sudden Mephistophelean manifestation or disappearance not managed through the more conventional channels of entrance and exit. Skirting along the side wall and shrugging his shoulders at the blood on the ground, Mephistopheles resolved to enter the cathedral and tempt Margaret further.

By the *coup de théâtre* of instantly removing the cathedral wall and illuminating the interior, it was unnecessary to set a new scene or move any scenery at all: 'we see the interior of the church, with its stately pillars and fretted arches, its carved altars and painted windows, the whole filled with a mellowed light, the organ pealing, the choir singing.'[53] For this to happen without even flying a cloth, the cathedral wall must have been painted on gauze, with lights coming up behind the gauze in combination with the extinction or drastic lowering of all lights on the audience side of the gauze. Priests and a congregation could be seen at the high altar upstage and Margaret facing front at prayer with Mephistopheles standing behind her. Several critics wondered why, if Mephistopheles could be so disturbed by the sound of church bells and the sight of a cross, he was quite at home in the middle of a church service. The logic of a devil's behaviour was, however, no part of Irving's desire for a strong scene. As in Goethe the choir sings the 'Dies Irae', and the kneeling woman, half enveloped in the red cape of the presumably invisible tempter which he held between her and the altar, began with a desperate plea to the Virgin:

Oh, who but thou canst know my agony?
I have no refuge now but thee!

The actress's note is to dwell on 'agony', sing 'I have no refuge now', and '*press* out' the word 'thee'. The prayer is counterpointed with verses from the chorus and Mephistopheles's dreadful reminders of her fallen state and her responsibility for the death of her mother and brother. Margaret's last lines,

The massy pillars seem to totter over me!
The vaulted arches crush me!

are annotated 'quicker, *fiercer* − terror', and Mephistopheles's suggestion that she should murder her child was greeted by a faint, Ellen Terry rejecting the textual direction '*shrieks*' with the comment, 'I'm SURE she sh^d make no sound.' However, she seems to have compromised with a long moan. The chorus sang its last verse; Mephistopheles smiled horribly, and the interior of the cathedral suddenly vanished. All that could be seen was the solitary figure of Mephistopheles stealing down the dark and deserted street − an extraordinarily powerful yet austere visual coda to the emotional and visual riches of the two preceding scenes. The act curtain fell.

After the fifteen-minute interval the curtain went up again on *Faust*'s great spectacle scene, the Brocken, a visual realisation of Goethe's Walpurgis Night scene. The music for it was entirely composed by Hamilton Clarke, and for this scene alone, to aid in the grouping and dancing, Irving had the assistance of Carlo Coppi of La Scala, Milan, a ballet master who also worked in London. Almost all reviews of any length devoted considerable space to an account of the scene, and there is a mass of often rapturous but sometimes precise descriptive material to sift through in order to find out what actually happened. In terms of set, lighting, and the mass of performers the Brocken scene was very heavy. The setting itself, the summit of a mountain and the slopes leading up to it, was a huge timber framework rising at an angle of 20 degrees from the first grooves near the front of the stage to the fourth grooves near the back, where it sank and then rose again. It was overlaid with rocks of pasteboard and pine trees 20 feet high, also of pasteboard, planted by stagehands in between the rocks. On stage left was a flat timber framework which served as the peak of the summit rock. On this set 250 performers rushed about and danced, many of them witches, the remainder – in addition to the principals – imps, goblins, demons, and other species of unpleasant supernatural being. Ellen Terry said that on tour in America the company took with it six 'leading' witches for this scene and recruited the forty others necessary from local talent; 'their general direction was to throw up their arms and look fierce at certain music cues.'[54]

When the lights went up audiences first saw a snow-covered mountain-top bathed in a dim half-light, huge rocks and blasted trees conveying an atmosphere of grim desolation. On the left was the flat rock, on the right the trees, in between a wasteland of tumbled rock and snow, in the background a louring sky of cloud and mist, and, vaguely perceived, a great cliff rising in the distance. Throughout the scene, Loveday told the *New York Tribune* (19 November 1887), the backcloths were frequently changed, 'but this is done so noiselessly and invisibly that only the effect is observed.' The colouring of the scene was black, white, and grey; the whole effect was of unutterable coldness and bleakness. Lightning flickered and thunder rolled, and the air was full of groans and cries and strange inhuman sounds in chorus. Soon, emerging from a cleft in the rocks, came the form of Mephistopheles, Faust clinging to him in fear. Lightning flashed again; though used often in the scene it was not electric in origin but caused by lycopodium flares and gas burners turned up and down at frequent intervals. The glare of this lightning was softened behind a transparency hung in front of the backcloth, since an open display would have been too bright for the scene and the rest of the lighting. The entrance of Faust and Mephistopheles was the signal for all hell to break loose, as it were. A flight of witches on broomsticks crossed the yellow disc of a hazy, watery moon; 'a flock of owls flap their solemn wings through the stormy night. Strange nameless beings and goblin spectres, half men, half beasts, chattering imps, and winged fiends swarm out of the mountain sides with unearthly shrieks and cries and deep grave chaunts and songs.'[55] Mephistopheles made his way toward the summit rock while one old witch, again played by Tom Mead, complained querulously that she had been climbing for 300 years and never reached the top. Mephistopheles thrust her aside contemptuously but she resumed her upward struggle as two choruses of witches and wizards, previously separate, joined voices in celebration of the revels. These began as Mephistopheles seated himself on the flat rock, from which electric sparks flashed. Several reviewers at this point compared him to Milton's Satan reviewing his Hellish host, a comparison that was to be made again at the end of the scene and also include some references to John Martin,

1 Military spectacle, *The Battle of the Alma*, Astley's, 1855

2 Painted actors to swell a crowd. Stock Exchange setting, *The White Heather*, Drury Lane, 1897

3 Elegance in costume. Violet Vanbrugh
in *Hearts Are Trumps*, Drury Lane,
1899

4 The sinking yacht, *The Price of Peace*,
Drury Lane, 1899. From the *Graphic*

5 Photograph of the set for the same scene, showing the electric bridges tilting and sinking

6 Stables at the Horse Show, *The Whip*, Drury Lane, 1909

7 The Great Hall, Falconhurst, *The Whip*

8 The flies at Drury Lane, *Cinderella*, 1883. From the *Illustrated Sporting and Dramatic News*

9 The Cave scene, *The Forty Thieves*, Drury Lane, 1886. From the *Illustrated London News*

10 The Jubilee scene, *The Forty Thieves*. From the *Illustrated London News*

11 The Court scene, *Puss in Boots*, Drury Lane, 1887. From the *Illustrated Sporting and Dramatic News*

12 Dress rehearsal of *Cinderella*, Drury Lane, 1895. Arthur Collins standing behind the seated Augustus Harris. From the *Illustrated London News*

13 Spring tableau setting, *The Sleeping Beauty and the Beast*, Drury Lane, 1900

14 Transformation scene, Beauty's Wedding Gifts, *The Sleeping Beauty and the Beast*

15 The Lorenz Platz: Faust greeting Margaret, *Faust*, Lyceum, 1885. From the *Illustrated Sporting and Dramatic News*

16 Martha's Garden, *Faust*. From the *Illustrated Sporting and Dramatic News*

18 Ellen Terry in the Dungeon scene, *Faust*. From *Pen and Pencil*

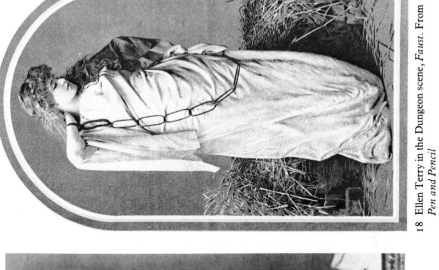

17 Ellen Terry in the Casket scene, *Faust*

20 The Brocken scene. From the *Illustrated Sporting and Dramatic News*

19 The Brocken scene, *Faust*, on a music cover

21 Archaeology in costume, *Antony and Cleopatra*, His Majesty's, 1906. From *Play Pictorial*

22 Archaeology in setting, *Antony and Cleopatra*. From *Play Pictorial*

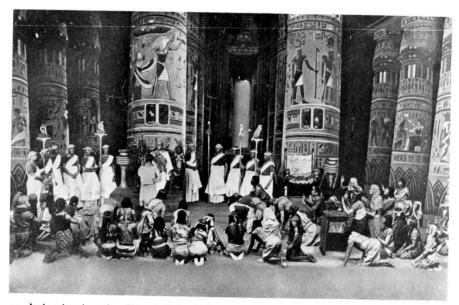

23 Archaeology in setting. Brieux's *False Gods*, His Majesty's, 1909. From *Play Pictorial*

24 Buckingham's final exit, *Henry VIII*, His Majesty's, 1910

25 Beerbohm Tree as Wolsey, *Henry VIII*

26 The Banquet scene, Hampton Court, *Henry VIII*

27 The Coronation scene, *Henry VIII*, with dummies in the back rows of the choir. From *Playgoer and Society Illustrated*

whose illustrations of Pandemonium – with Satan standing on a high flat rock on the right of the picture and flames licking the valley below – had been popular earlier in the century and were still widely known in the 1880s.

Crowds of hooded witches and their familiars arrived upon the rock and in the valley, moaning, shrieking, and howling. Mephistopheles fondled imps that crawled over his knees, and was caressed by a pair of monkeys who drew sparks from his body; gleams of red light emanated from the device in his cap. Faust was temporarily carried off by two or three beautiful young witches, but soon returned, he and Mephistopheles standing upon the topmost rock with their shadows looming spectrally upon the mist and cloud behind them. Nothing said was distinctly audible, and the mood of supernatural revelry was intensified by weird discords from the orchestra. A wild dance began in which Mephistopheles joined, the mass of revellers, in filmy grey-green garments, gyrating and tossing their arms in the air, now lit by the moon and now by the increasing redness of the rocks and the fires that glimmered among them. Most reviewers found this scene sublime – it gathered more power toward the end – but some remarked that it was only a short step from the sublime to the ridiculous, and comparisons to pantomime were again made. Indeed, the *Sporting Chronicle* (22 September 1887) amused itself by pretending that *Faust* was a pantomime, with Irving as Demon King, and reviewed it appropriately.[56] A small minority found the whole spectacle merely silly and an interruption of dramatic narrative. Henry James, who found nothing to praise in *Faust*, was horrified, and expressed his revulsion strongly:[57]

> We attach also but the slenderest importance to the scene of the Witches'
> Sabbath, which has been reduced to a mere bald hubbub of capering,
> screeching, and banging, irradiated by the irrepressible blue fire, and with-
> out the smallest articulation of Goethe's text. The scenic effect is the
> ugliest we have ever contemplated, and its ugliness is not paid for by its
> having a meaning for our ears. It is a horror cheaply conceived, and ex-
> ecuted with more zeal than discretion.

Fortunately for Irving, James was not the average Lyceum spectator, and there is no doubt that the Brocken scene set audiences absolutely agog. If possible, its spectacle content increased as the scene drew to a close, and its nightmare quality intensified. The dance ceased and the appalled Faust saw in the background, seemingly on the edge of a precipice, a vision of Margaret, dressed in white, with a red mark on her throat. At a command from Mephistopheles the whole scene suddenly vanished, and the devil was left alone in a desolate void. The Pennells found the extreme contrast between this moment of darkness, solitariness, and empty space and the ensuing renewal of the revelry compelling:[58]

> There is nothing more powerful than this single scene, – one minute a wild
> shrieking, singing crowd of misty shapes, moving hither and thither, clam-

bering over the rocks and up the trees, dancing and turning; the next, after one last shriek, wilder, shriller than the rest, a silent, storm-beaten mountain top deserted but for one flaming form. Then, summoning them once more, he himself plunges into the midst of the reveling. Now the dreary light, that has been strangely glimmering, here glows through film and haze, there sweeps in a rolling vapour; now creeps like a thread, now leaps and plays, lighting up the great mountain and all the rugged shapes, and finally gushes forth, a shower of fiery rain, over the wild and howling crowd of witches, while the rocky ramparts on all their heights are set ablaze.

Mephistopheles summoned his spirits once more, and the mad dancing briefly resumed. Thunder rolled again; the red glasses of twenty-five limelights shining through the background and upon openings in the rocks from which steam rose conveyed the impression that earth and sky were aflame. The rocks became molten and a rain of fire fell from the sky, scattered from bridges high over the stage by men with baskets of gold tinsel. At this sign of the supreme power of hell the weird host of revellers fell to their knees and raised their arms to their great leader, who stood alone on the summit in Miltonic majesty, his right hand flung aloft, outlined in relief against the background of fire. Thus ended a scene which, in its combination of spectacle, mass force and power, grandeur, and nightmare, many reviewers said had never been equalled on the stage. The Brocken scene was one of the great spectacles of nineteenth-century theatre, and probably the most extraordinary scene of its kind ever performed on the English stage.

One of the most remarkable things about it was the way in which Irving brilliantly solved, at least for this scene in particular and the production as a whole, the problem of the relationship between actor and spectacle, a problem that had been exercising critics and actors for a long time. How was an actor to control and rise above a spectacle so that he could be seen, heard, maintain his individual style, and not sacrifice himself entirely to lighting, mass effects, costume design, and stage carpentry? It is true that several critics believed that in *Faust* acting had indeed been subordinated to show, but no other spectacle production I have read about attracted so much critical attention to its acting; Irving's Mephistopheles, for instance, got far more space in the reviews than Tree's Wolsey. From a careful examination of the evidence it appears that Scott was quite correct in saying in the *Daily Telegraph* (26 December 1885) that Irving 'overmastered' the picture with a commanding presence. In fact Irving had obeyed the popular maxim, 'If you can't fight them, join them.' He overmastered not only by his acting, which will be spoken of below, but by making a spectacle of himself, by his superb sense of colour, design, composition, space, and light – the skills, it is worth repeating, of a painter as well as those of an actor and manager. This visual sense, together with a heightened use of mime and an enlarged pictorial acting method in such an extreme example of spectacle as the Brocken scene, was in perfect harmony with the spectacle style, and did not leave the actor uncomfortably isolated or, alternatively, engulfed by it. Yet Irving's identity and power were retained and even nourished by the effects of mass, colour, light, and sound all about him, of which he was always the visual centre. All this was thought out most carefully in advance. A fine instance of Irving's planning is given by Bram Stoker, the business manager of the Lyceum and Irving's constant associate at lighting rehearsals. At a very late stage of preparation for *Faust* Stoker expressed doubts about the possibility of success to his manager, advising him to have something else ready in case *Faust* should fail. In particular, he thought the Brocken scene, which had just been rehearsed in dress with Mephistopheles watching from the stalls, 'cold and unreal'. Irving's reply is instructive:[59]

I *know* the play will do. ... As far as tonight goes you are quite right; but you have not seen my dress. I do not want to wear it till I get all the rest correct. Then you will see. I have studiously kept as yet all the colour scheme to that grey-green. When my dress of flaming scarlet appears among it – and remember that the colour will be intensified by that very light – it will bring the whole picture together in a way you cannot dream of. Indeed, I can hardly realise it myself yet, though I know it will be right. You shall see too how Ellen Terry's white dress, and even that red scar across her throat, will stand out in the midst of that turmoil of lighting.

Tree, as will be seen in the next chapter, tried to use some of Irving's solutions, but because he did not have as much visual imagination or planning capability was not as successful.

The Brocken scene, massive though it was, took less than ten minutes to clear, and the fourth interval before the final act ('Nuremberg – Dungeon') was listed in programmes toward the end of January 1886, as twelve minutes. The dramatic and scenic contrast between this scene and the last was profound. The curtain went up on a prison cell illuminated by moonbeams. Margaret, condemned to die on the morrow, lay chained in straw in the foreground, wearing a long robe of coarse white cloth, on stage left a rude stone cross. The scene opened with her singing in a harsh voice a verse about her family; Faust, entering with a lamp, has difficulty in getting her to recognise him, and it is clear that she is mad. In the margin of Ellen Terry's first rehearsal copy, by Faust's remark, 'Alas! her mind is shaken', is the blunt inscription, 'Rather!' Several commentators noticed the resemblance in this scene between her Margaret and her earlier Ophelia, in both madness and pathos. Although her chains fall magically from her, she will not flee with Faust, despite his frantic urging as dawn grows near, and begins to tell him of the death of her family and how he should arrange the graves. This moment was, to many spectators, intensely moving. The speech is simple, and effective for being so:

To-morrow, I must die.
And I must tell thee how to range the graves,
And thou must see to it by break of day.
My mother, the best place – next her my brother:
Me well apart, but, dearest, not too far,
And by my side my little one shall lie.

Here Ellen Terry, two of whose main strengths, apart from looks and a beautiful voice, were pathos and romantic tenderness, rose to heights of simple sincerity and exquisite piteousness, climaxing, with the deepest feeling, in the phrase 'but, dearest, not too far.' Recovering her sanity somewhat, she refuses once more to escape with Faust and rejects him, preferring to seek God's mercy and meet her death.

The spectacle theatre was of course not content to leave it at that; a visual image of Margaret's essential purity and salvation would have to be found to complement the text, and the iconography of Margaret's apotheosis was by now, despite Goethe, well established in the theatre and opera house. Almost all critical attention was thus directed toward the end of the scene. A conventional ladder of angels appearing to take the soul of Margaret to heaven, set against a suitably rich allegorical background of heavenly beauty and promise, seemed the obvious solution, and Telbin set to work to produce just such a scene. He designed a huge and realistic rainbow of fine stuffs, linen, scrim, and tissue, painted and stained the colours of the prism. The result was splendid and elaborate, but did not satisfy Irving, who saw it for the first time the night before *Faust* opened. Bram Stoker tells the story of what happened next, which is not only remarkable and interesting in itself, but also provides an excellent example of Irving's visual and design talents – in this case exercised perforce on the spur of the moment. He ordered the whole scene struck except for the wings and ladder of angels, left starkly on the empty stage. Then he asked for a dark blue sky border as a backcloth, two if more height were needed. Sapphire mediums were put on the side limelights to make the backing a dark night blue, and all the white limes were turned full on the angels. The effect was simple but grand and beautiful: pure white angels floating radiantly in the empty heavens. The stage staff impulsively applauded; Irving asked Telbin to put stars in a new backcloth, and the scene was ready by morning.[60] Stoker also describes a 'ladder' of angels:[61]

For such a vision a capable piece of machinery has to be provided, for it has to bear the full weight of at least a dozen women or girls. The backbone of it is a section of steel rail which is hung from the flies with a steel rope, to this are attached the iron arms made safe and comfortable for the angels to be strapped each in her own 'iron'. The lower end of the ladder rests on the stage and is fastened there securely with stage screws. The angels are all fixed in their places before the scene begins, and when the lights are turned on they seem to float ethereally.

The ladder was revealed only at the end of the play. Mephistopheles entered the cell in pursuit of Margaret's soul. She clung to the cross as he attempted to seize her; lightning flashed and thunder rolled. Seeing the cross, he shrank back. Voices of demons cried offstage, 'She is lost!' and voices of angels replied, 'She is saved!' With a great cry ('shriek like a *Child*!'), Margaret fell at the foot of the cross. Lightning flashed in the dungeon itself, Mephistopheles seized Faust with a terrible command of 'Hither to me!', enveloped him in his cloak, and swept him into the wings. As he did so, the back wall of the dungeon opened (no doubt a backcloth was raised), rapturous music swelled in the orchestra, the voices of angels rose in the chorus, and the stage was 'gradually illumined by rays which seem to descend from a cloudless sun, and which grow in intensity and brilliance until they reveal the forms of beautiful angels, arms outstretched, and downy wings, descending with open arms to take her to a happier home'.[62] The silver-winged angels ranged diagonally from high above stage right nearly to the floor, reaching out their arms to Margaret, who was lying with her head at the foot of the cross. With this tableau the play ended, a beautiful morality painting of the frustration of evil and the salvation of good; the destruction of Wills's poor, weak, and helpless Faust was almost an irrelevance.

Faust was a great commercial success, and Irving's greatest hit. It was given 187 performances in its first season, 1885–6, and 209 in its second, 1886–7, which it opened. It went on a provincial tour to Edinburgh, Glasgow, Manchester, and Liverpool in the late summer and autumn of 1887, and then to America. It was revived at the Lyceum for thirty-five performances in 1888, with a major revival of seventy-six performances in 1894. The next year it was played three times, and the final Lyceum revival was sixty-seven performances in 1902. A provincial tour followed, and *Faust* was acted for the last time in Bristol on 10 December 1902. Altogether, there were 87 performances in the provinces, 128 in North America, and 577 at the Lyceum, for a total of 792,[63] the largest number of performances for an Irving production except *The Bells*, which achieved its early success under the Bateman management.

Naturally, such a popular production was a money-spinner. In its first season *Faust* did not drop below £300 at the box office until 5 July 1886, except for the first night, when half the house was occupied by invited guests. Ellen Terry's benefit on 31 July, the last night of the season, brought in an extraordinary £471, but several regular performances took over £400. Total box-office receipts for *Faust* in that first season were £69,447, an average of £346 a night, or a box-office average of 82.4 per cent, assuming an ordinary capacity of £420. Irving himself said that 350,000 people had seen *Faust* in its first season,[64] although judging by box-office and house capacity this figure seems high. With running costs at £41,723, including advertising, rent, taxes, insurance, wages, lighting,[65] orchestra, supers, ballet, printing, and a few minor extras; and a total Production and Preliminary account (the amount spent on the production itself, separate from daily running costs and including expenditure on costumes, materials, scenery, properties, rehearsals, and music) to July 1886, of £12,226, the net profit on *Faust* at the end of the first season was £15,948. In its second season, with much less spent on Production and Preliminary (£2,253) *Faust* took £57,016 at an average of £273 a performance, 65 per cent of capacity. It was no wonder that Irving toured *Faust* and revived it at the Lyceum. The 1894 revival was also successful; by the end of it *Faust* had been played 510 times at the Lyceum to total receipts of £157,547. The scenery of *Faust* was destroyed in the Lyceum warehouse fire of 1898, and production expenses for new scenery for the 1902 revival must have been heavy, but they are not recorded in the surviving Lyceum accounts. Before this revival the Production and Preliminary account for *Faust* totalled £16,878 over the years. With provincial and North American receipts added, *Faust*'s total box-office income until the end of its career was over £250,000.[66] The production was incidentally also responsible for a tremendous increase in the sales of Goethe's poem, a Victorian equivalent of 'the book of the film'.

Reasons for the great popularity of *Faust* are not hard to find. The spectacle effects were of course one reason, but the closely related and artistic pictorialism was certainly another. *Faust* probably came nearer to art – more specifically, to painting – than any other nineteenth-century production. Heightening the pictorialism, indeed an essential part of it, was the lighting. The Lyceum under Irving was well known for high lighting standards and the aesthetic quality of lighting effects, but again it is doubtful if the relationship between plot, characterisation, mood, and lighting had been so well thought out and so finely executed anywhere else on the nineteenth-century stage. The lighting of *Faust* was highly symbolic, a rare thing in the theatre of the period, and the prevailing pattern of overall gloom with fitful gleams of light corresponded closely to the moral pattern of the text. The *New York Times* (8 November 1887) said the play was really a series of dissolving views; 'the whole drama moved panoramically. The lights shift, the stage grows dark, the organ blares, stealthy and devilish figures flit in the shadows, angelic faces burn out on the canvas. ... While we gaze the stage grows black and the sun vanishes. So is the story told in pictures.' The fact that so many scenes were set at sunset, night or in the early dawn struck reviewers because it was so unusual. The last rays of the setting sun, cold moonbeams, the fire of a stove or a boiling cauldron, the gleam of a lamp, the light of a flickering torch, the flames of hell itself – these seemed the principal sources of light. The result was mysterious, magical, confusing, and frightening. *Faust* was, after all, a supernatural play, and the character of much of the lighting as well as the special lighting effects served to emphasise that; it could have been lit by the devil himself.

Not only the spectacle, pictorialism and lighting of *Faust* appealed to audiences, but the production also possessed two notable acting performances. Ellen Terry was of course overshadowed by Irving and her part was much smaller. Of the twelve scenes (including the Witch's Kitchen), she appeared in seven, in one of which she had two lines; Irving appeared in all. She was, however, a perfect foil for him, not only in character and moral position but also in appearance and acting quality. She too made room for herself on stage by the colours she wore, yellow in one scene or white in another when no one else on stage was wearing the same colour, or when her own colour stood out from the set. She too acted pictorially and struck attitudes. Sweetness, trust, tenderness, innocence, sincerity – in all these Ellen Terry excelled on stage; they were all needed in Margaret and were the opposite in every respect of Mephistopheles's characteristics. She was also very good at being in love and expressing warmth and genuine affection. The movement in *Faust* from the joy and happiness of reciprocated love to grief, remorse, despair, and madness particularly impressed critics.

If Wills's Margaret was a conventional romantic heroine invested with delicacy of manner and beauty of soul as well as body by Ellen Terry, Mephistopheles was played not as a heavy villain, but with a well-calculated mixture of the debonair man-about-town and the fiend, of a quite natural but unpleasant jocularity and a truly dreadful malignity. His mirth was as satanic as his rage; the difference was in degree, not kind. The mocking cynic, the kindly hypocrite, the sardonic tormentor, the practical joker, the reveller, and the destroyer were all the same person. After seeing his own play right through for the first time, Wills wrote to Irving (in an undated letter) that 'the suppressed gibber of hellish fun – the shambling limp of a wicked old magpie all over the stage – the sinister chaff and the concentrated malevolence of the demon which takes a terrible dignity and the weirdness which lifts and colours all are the simple outcome of genius.' With some exceptions, Irving's greatest powers as an actor were apparent in parts with a haunted, tormented, and sometimes devilish character to them – Mathias, Iago, Louis XI, Shylock, Robert Macaire – and his success in Mephistopheles was not surprising. Only one or two reviewers thought of him as sufferer as well as an agent of evil, marking a loneliness and isolation, and infinite sadness in the face. Some found him too flippant, too mocking, too inclined to pantomimic gesture and grimacing, too restless, 'a kind of Satanic Paul Pry constantly bubbling and fidgeting about the stage'.[67] Others found too much emphasis on comedy, too much of the clown. These tended to judge Irving's Mephistopheles by Goethe's creation rather than Wills's. Henry James was most disdainful. Irving, he said, had conceived and executed his part 'in the spirit of somewhat refined extravaganza; a manner which should differ only in degree from that of the star of a Christmas burlesque – without breadth, without depth, with little tittering effects of low comedy.'[68] The general verdict on Irving's performance was nevertheless highly favourable, and James was isolated from critical opinion as a whole.

The pictorial and picturesque character of Ellen Terry's acting was even more marked in Irving, since as we have seen the canvases of many scenes were not complete until Mephistopheles stepped into the frame. The *New York World* (8 November 1887) noted how Irving 'gets against those bits of background that will throw his pose into relief. ... Most of his endeavour was in the direction of posture and picture.' Mephistopheles did not give Irving the psychological opportunities of a part like Mathias in *The Bells* – such opportunities would have been wasted in a spectacle play in any case – so his emphasis had to be external and pictorial, stressing facial expression as well as bodily attitude. In a pictorial theatre the face was of course extremely important, and to use it expressively was another way in which the leading actor could identify himself distinctly on the canvas. Writing generally of Irving's powers of facial expression, William Archer commented, 'Hatred, malignity, and cunning dwell familiarly in his eye, his jaw can express at will indomitable resolve or grotesque and abject terror. Grim humour lurks in his eyebrows, and cruel contempt in the corners of his mouth. No actor had ever fuller command of the expression which has been happily called "a lurid glance".'[69] For Mephistopheles, Irving's pale face could be mask-like, with 'the thin mocking lips, and the fixed, impenetrable, lidless eyes',[70] or very mobile: a curl of the lip, a ghastly smile, a flicker of the eyes, an upward jerk of the eyebrows – all these worked out in exact relationship to posture and gesture, the hands as claws, the half-limp. Irving's gait bothered several reviewers; the hop-skip-jump progress across the stage was believed to detract from the majesty of the devil. But except at rare moments Irving never intended his devil to be majestic, and the peculiar walk was also a comic device. Similarly, 'his characteristic mannerisms of utterance – that jerky dislocation of syllables and catapult-like shooting up of words from the throat'[71] seemed to suit the part well. Irving was a notoriously mannered actor, and there was general agreement that his idiosyncracies were appropriate to Mephistopheles. They also served to give him even greater individual distinctiveness on the spectacle stage. Another way of achieving this distinctiveness – a method used by Tree in *Henry VIII* – was slowness of speech and gesture, a deliberate identifying mark in a production with a great deal of hurly-burly in it. Irving had the general reputation of a 'slow' actor, but this slowness, as we shall see with Tree, was a necessity in a pictorial theatre. Following in Irving's footsteps, Tree also did a highly pictorial and spectacular *Faust*, at His Majesty's in 1908, but it is his Shakespearean production methods that will next concern us.

5 · Beerbohm Tree's *King Henry VIII*, His Majesty's Theatre, 1910

Herbert Beerbohm Tree was generally regarded as Irving's heir and natural successor, and despite the difference between them and their methods a theatrical continuity and line of descent are easily recognisable. Tree further developed and extended Irving's techniques of pictorial romanticism, mass effects, adherence to archaeological and historical precepts, and their execution in design, scene-painting, costumes, and properties. In his maturity he dominated his profession as Irving did, and His Majesty's Theatre attained the pre-eminence of the Lyceum in the 1880s and 1890s. Tree was not so fine an actor as Irving, and did not on the whole enjoy so good a press. He was frequently accused of excessive scenic elaboration as a producer and of burying Shakespeare and other dramatists beneath a mountain of carefully conceived but essentially irrelevant effects – to us a by now familiar and historically consistent charge. As an actor and manager, he was supposed to perpetuate the worst sins of the actor-manager system, although in fact he chose good performers to act with him who later went on to star in their own right. He ran his theatre as extravagantly as Irving ran his, but usually at a profit, sometimes a very large one. His range of productions was wider than Irving's, his interest in experiment and the new drama infinitely greater – he produced, among others, Maeterlinck, Ibsen, Tolstoy, Brieux, and Shaw – and his commitment to Shakespeare even more substantial.

Twelve plays of Shakespeare were performed at the Lyceum under Irving's management; Tree did sixteen at the Haymarket and Her (later His) Majesty's. Furthermore, from 1905 to 1913 the annual Shakespeare Festivals at Tree's own theatre were major events: sixty productions of twenty-three Shakespeare plays were given over nine years, including ten by visiting companies, and a non-scenic *Hamlet* of his own.[1] Tree's major aim, and it was no unworthy one in spite of objections to his methods, was to make Shakespeare popular and accessible. In this he succeeded admirably. After he left the Haymarket his Shakespeares each ran for many months to large audiences, and he quoted early attendance figures with pride: 242,000 for *Julius Caesar* in 1898, over 170,000 for *King John* (a dark horse in any theatre) in 1899, and 220,000 for *A Midsummer Night's Dream* in 1900 – 632,000 for only three productions.[2] *King Henry VIII* broke all Shakespeare box-office records for Tree. Commenting on the record-breaking 168th performance, *Sporting Life* (26 January 1911) declared that 'a state subsidised theatre could have done nothing more worthy for the Shakespearean drama than has been done by Sir Herbert Tree. Bringing to his aid all the arts of the theatre, making his revivals spectacularly beautiful, he has carried Shakespeare to the people. He has achieved that which a few years ago was considered impossible – he has made Shakespeare popular.' Several years earlier, in defending his *Tempest* against *Blackwood's Magazine*, Tree stated:[3]

> I am at least entitled to maintain that I have done my best to present the works of Shakespeare in the manner which I considered most worthy, and I feel a certain pride in remembering that, be our method right or wrong, we have brought the poet's creation before hundreds of thousands. This version of 'The Tempest' has already been witnessed by vast multitudes, and if only a portion of these have been given a deeper insight into, and a wider appreciation of, this high fantasy, our labours to 'give delight and hurt not' will not have been in vain.

Those 'vast multitudes' kept the unsubsidised Tree in business and enabled him to do so much Shakespeare. To meet what he considered to be their taste and to ensure their continued and profitable attendance at his theatre he bent his efforts to establishing a performance pattern for Shakespeare that is now barely a distant memory on the English stage but in its time represented the theatrical establishment in its security and splendour.

That pattern was typified by *Henry VIII*, the culminating glory of twenty years of Tree's work with Shakespeare. Afterwards he revived earlier Shakespearean productions, but *Macbeth* in 1911 and *Othello* in 1912 were the only new ones to follow. The *Merry Wives of Windsor* (1889), *Hamlet* (1892), and *I Henry IV* (1896) at the Haymarket were unremarkable, and it was with *Julius Caesar* at Her Majesty's in 1898 that Tree first impressed the theatrical world with his abilities as a Shakespearean producer: the massive stage architecture; the Alma-Tadema designs, properties, and costumes; the well-disciplined and sizeable Roman mob; the acting of a superior company with considerable strengths apart from those of its star (in contrast to Irving's company) – all this really initiated Shakespeare according to the gospel of Tree. Later productions further developed and elaborated key elements of this one. *A Midsummer Night's Dream* was just as opulent, but the opulence was poetic and romantic rather than classical. The full Mendelssohn score was used, and the lighting attracted much more contemporary comment than the introduction of rabbits into the woodland scene, a vestigial memory of the modern Shakespeare devotee. The 'Wood near Athens' scene, according to the *Daily Chronicle* (11 January 1900) opened in darkness, 'but soon electric

lights on the heads and wings of the fairies – aerial and on foot – glint through
the trees. When illumination is increased tiny elves descend wooded shapes in
the rear, whilst from a pool in the centre overhung with trees rises Puck.' The
emphasis on the fairy aspects of the play was strengthened by an elaborate
finale. After the artisans' play and the sumptuous wedding festival of the final
scene, Theseus, Hippolyta, and their guests depart; then

> Puck with his broom cautiously peeps in and signals to the fairies. During
> the elfin dances the columns of the hall, the steps, and the festoons become
> illuminated. There is an abundance of light, but no suspicion of garishness.
> Oberon and Titania give their direction to the fays, who gradually disap-
> pear, the electric lights being extinguished until the stage is left in dark-
> ness, amid which (Puck's epilogue being omitted) the curtain descends.

In between these two scenes the reviewer found much to admire, especially
'the troops of children whose gambols show none of the customary effects of
lengthy preparation' and 'the lovely pictures of secluded glen and mountain
ridge overlooking the moonlit sea, the iridescent dresses changing their tint
with the movement of the wearers'. A special correspondent in the same issue
devoted three columns to an account of the costumes, being particularly
struck by that of Oberon, played by Julia Neilson, who, 'gorgeous in gold,
represents the sun, and the effect of cloth and trappings of bullion, jewels on
the corsage, pale-green wings, and a sun-crown on her head, is accentuated
by electric light cunningly introduced into her costume.'

After a *Richard II* (1903) in which Tree introduced live horses into the
lists at Coventry (a spectacle scene) and imitated Charles Kean's practice in
interpolating an elaborate processional entry, complete with mob, into
London by Bolingbroke and the deposed Richard – as he had also
interpolated a signing of of the Magna Carta into *King John* – the poeticism
of *A Midsummer Night's Dream* was made more fantastic in the 1904
Tempest, a production in the fairy tradition even more dominated by the
subtle use of beautifully conceived and executed romantic lighting effects. An
intensely realistic Kean-like shipwreck and straightforward expository scene
between Prospero and Miranda was followed by a blackout; purple light then
came up on nymphs playing in the water and on the sand, this taking place
behind a gauze with an offstage chorus singing 'Come Unto These Yellow
Sands'. Gradually, the purple was replaced by amber and the sands turned
golden.[4] Tree's Caliban was a highly fantastical monster with a costume of
seaweed and fish. The masque took place before a background of '*a fairy
glen and a lake, in which the Naiads of the winding brooks are playing
among the water-lilies.*' A lengthy ballet ensued in which Cupid became
involved with the Nymphs and Reapers; finally, '*the Nymphs assume the
marriage veils which they gather from the mists of the lake*' and the dance
ended happily. Tree added confidently in his stage direction that '*no excuse is
necessary for this introduction, which is in obedience to the author's*

directions.' To conclude, Prospero broke his staff after the words, 'I'll drown my book', at which there was lightning, thunder, darkness, and another vision through a purple haze of the yellow sands, with the nymphs once more singing the theme song of the island. Their song was interrupted by the *'homing-song'* of the sailors, and the departing ship was seen, viewed by a saddened Caliban and a singing, ascending Ariel. The final tableau showed Caliban stretching out his arms in despair to a distant vessel as night falls. Thus the play ended with Caliban rather than the epilogue or Prospero, an emphasis repeated by at least one modern director.[5]

This is by no means an account of Tree's pre-*Henry VIII* work in Shakespeare, but we should at least note a gorgeous and richly Eastern *Antony and Cleopatra* in 1906, appropriately opening on 27 December, Christmas pantomime time. Here Tree engaged in his usual heavy cutting and rearrangement of the text, nevertheless finding room for an interpolated return of Antony to Alexandria with soldiers, priests, dancing-girls, and a huge excited throng. Constance Collier, who played Cleopatra, remembered her appearance in the form of Iris:[6]

> It was the most spectacular scene in the play, where Cleopatra, robed in
> silver, crowned in silver, carrying a golden sceptre and the symbol of the
> sacred golden calf in her hand, went in procession through the streets of
> Alexandria, the ragged, screaming populace acclaiming the Queen, half in
> hate, half in superstitious fear and joy, as she made her sacrilegious ascent
> to her throne in the market-place.

Apropos of this production, B. W. Findon dismissed criticism of Tree's approach to Shakespeare as the futile objections of the pedant, the crank, the caviller, and the faddist, declaring[7] that

> If there were no other reason for the playgoer to visit His Majesty's he
> would be justified in paying his money to witness a series of scenes which
> revive in such a brilliant manner the pageantry and military glory of a far
> distant age. .... It was as if one breathed the air of Egypt and heard the
> murmuring of the placid waters as the stately vessel brought the lovers to
> the landing stage of Cleopatra's Palace.

The terms of such praise are familiar to us, and the living recreation of a past age was also said to be one of the chief virtues of *Henry VIII*, as it had been of the *Henry VIII* of both Kean and Irving.

Like *Antony and Cleopatra*, *Henry VIII* had always offered opportunities for spectacle, and in the nineteenth century at least three productions stood out from this point of view: John Philip Kemble's at Covent Garden in 1811, Charles Kean's in 1855, and Irving's in 1892. The *Times* (21 October 1811) said that Kemble's 'was the most dazzling stage exhibition that we have ever seen', praising the banquet tables covered with gold, 'the pomp of princely feasting', the glittering livery of attendants and guards, 'the rich tracery of the architecture', and 'the various and shifting splendour that fell from the chandeliers'. Kean's production was of course archaeologically and historically accurate as far as his own antiquarian spirit and scholarly research could make it, 'a perfect realization of history', according to J. W. Cole. Expanding on this point, Cole gave reasons for the success of the play, 'the life-painting, the vivid resurrection of persons, places, and events – the severe undeviating accuracy of the historical research, rather than ... dumb pictorial accompaniments, however appropriate and imposing, or ... new mechanical applicances.' Former generations, he added,[8]

> never witnessed the whole play illustrated, as now, by a succession of
> historical pictures, in which every person, group, and movement, is
> modelled from life, not taken from imagination or poetical resemblance,
> but embodied from the minute descriptions of those who had seen, known,
> and lived with the characters introduced: with whom they were as
> familiarly acquainted as with the places they inhabited and the costumes
> they wore.

Clement Scott, reviewing Irving's production, made the usual comment that 'we live once more in the days of bluff King Hal', but explained further:[9] Irving intended,

> with the aid of modern effects, by a lavish expenditure of money, a careful
> study of every possible archaeological authority, with Mr. Seymour Lucas,
> A.R.A., at his right hand, to guarantee correctness of every ruff, head-
> dress, sword-belt, shoe, to make this the most perfect reproduction of
> Court life, in the days of Henry VIII, that this stage, or indeed the stage of
> any country, has ever seen.

Tree, then, was no innovator in producing *Henry VIII*. He was following a trend of production that had been established since the middle of the nineteenth century, and, with reference to *Henry VIII* in particular, for a hundred years. The interest of his production in 1910 is partly in the completeness of the information available from which a reconstruction can be made, partly in the way he overtopped the spectacle of his predecessors and pushed their methods to their logical and ultimate conclusion, and partly in the chance it gives us to examine in detail what an Edwardian producer at the top of his profession, with the full resources of a major theatre behind him, would do with Shakespeare and how he would recreate him to suit his own predilections and his own theatrical style. Lastly, it is an opportunity to arrive at a full appreciation of a way of doing Shakespeare so entirely different from our own that the knowledge is instructively comparative.

On the production of *Henry VIII* Tree, who compensated for his own vague and chaotic way of handling financial affairs and running his theatre by retaining for many years the devoted loyalty of an extremely capable business and stage staff, had the additional assistance of three other people: Louis Napoleon Parker, Percy Macquoid, and Margaret Morris. A fourth, Edward German, contributed the overture, entr'actes, and incidental music 'selected from the original Music' already used for Irving's production; he also composed new pieces of incidental music and the anthem for the Coronation scene. The rights to the original music were obtained from the Irving estate. Parker, previously a pianist, organist, singer, composer, and early Wagnerian, turned to the drama in the 1880s. He collaborated with Tree on *Once Upon a Time* at the Haymarket in 1894, and after that wrote several plays for Tree, notably the pageant play *Drake* (1912) and *Joseph and his Brethren* (1913). His work on local pageant plays on a large scale was especially appropriate to a production of *Henry VIII*; he invented the form and before 1910 had devised six of these: at Sherborne (the first, in 1905), Warwick, Bury St Edmunds, Dover, Colchester, and York. He was also responsible for improving the historical section of the Lord Mayor's Show in 1907 and 1908. On *Henry VIII* he served in the capacity of assistant producer (without being given the title) and, obviously, organiser of the pageantry; he also had charge of rehearsals while Tree was away. For his services he received a fee of £350. Macquoid, an R.I., was an authority on tapestry, plate, needlework, costume, and furniture; between 1904 and 1908 he published a four-volume *History of English Furniture*. He had worked with Tree on several productions, most recently and impressively on the recreation of eighteenth-century Bath in the 1909 *School for Scandal*. His contributions to *Henry VIII* included the design of furniture, costumes, and properties; and although Joseph Harker painted the scenery it is clear that Macquoid had at the very least a considerable influence on its design. He was at any rate entirely responsible for the design of the Banqueting Hall of Act I, scene iii. Tree thanked him on the programme 'for his inspiring archaeological advice' and paid him a well-earned £250. Margaret Morris was a young dancer and teacher who had danced in pantomime before joining the Benson Company and going on to compose and arrange the dances for the first British production of *Peer Gynt* in Edinburgh in 1908. What probably brought her to Tree's attention was her success with the ballets in Gluck's *Orfeo* at the Savoy in April, 1910. For *Henry VIII* she choreographed the court dances in the Banqueting Hall scene and received £26 5s for her work.

The production concept of *Henry VIII* would have been generally apparent from Tree's previous experience with Shakespeare, but it became specifically enunciated during the course of rehearsals. On 26 July 1910, five weeks after rehearsals began, Tree and Parker held what amounted to a press conference on their plans. Parker told the *Daily Express* (27 July), among others, that the aim was 'to give an absolute reproduction of the Renaissance', that every detail would be realistic, and that 'we have ransacked every authority and obtained the most astonishing exactitude'. Archaeological accuracy and the recreation of history were, not surprisingly, the two artistic principles with which Tree began, as well as the opportunity for the sort of spectacle and pageantry which would both attract audiences and

constitute the only suitable style, as Tree firmly believed, for the performance
of the play. Tree was compelled to express these beliefs in print at an early
stage because of a published attack by a fellow-manager, Herbert Trench of
the Haymarket, whose views on staging Shakespeare have been referred to
previously. Trench argued for symbolic scenery and a rejection of the
spectacular approach; the passage in his article most relevant to the
forthcoming *Henry VIII* is as follows:[10]

> Presently we shall have upon us an avalanche of Shakespearian upholstery.
> There will be the familiar glitter of stage-crowds, betinselled cavalcades,
> 'built-up' palaces and chapels, of coronations modelled upon fancy balls.
> The cloth of gold in these will cost fabulous sums, and the lace and velvet
> robes of the cardinals will later furnish forth valuable dining-room curtains
> for illustrious actor-managers. Pictures galore there will be, in blazes of
> electric light so fierce that facial play is extinguished and grease-paint un-
> mistakable.

Since excerpts from this article immediately appeared in the *Era* and the
Stage only two weeks before the first performance, Tree had little time to
reply. However, he managed to tack on a postscript to a pleasantly readable
historical essay, *Henry VIII and his Court*, which he had written while on
holiday in Marienbad and put on sale in the theatre during the run of the play.
Having shown in the major part of his study that the daily life of Henry's
court was full of display and splendour, Tree went on:[11]

> *Henry VIII* is largely a pageant play. As such it was conceived and written;
> as such did we endeavour to present it. Indeed, it is obvious that it would
> be far better not to produce the play at all than to do so without these
> adjuncts, by which alone the action of the play can be illustrated. Of course
> it is not possible to do more than indicate on the stage the sumptuousness
> of the period of history covered by the play; but it was hoped that an
> impression would be conveyed to our own time of Henry in his habit as he
> lived, of his people, of the architecture, and of the manners and customs of
> that great age.

In the postscript Tree rejected the argument for symbolism and advanced the
counter-claims of full illusion: 'To attempt to present *Henry VIII* in other
than a realistic manner would be to ensure absolute failure', since the stage
directions alone demand the kind of staging appropriate to 'the pageantry of
realism.'[12] Since this was Shakespeare's intention it was not simply a matter of
a modern manager's unsupported theories. The Bard and history had already
spoken in Tree's favour.

The surviving evidence for the production is much richer and more varied
than for *Faust* or any pantomime. There is a promptbook which unfortunately
omits almost all lighting cues as well as the last scene; three preparation books
illustrating various early stages of the production in the hands of Cecil King,
the stage manager, Stanley Bell, the associate stage manager, and Claude

Rains, the assistant stage manager; and a rehearsal copy, annotated by Tree and marked for the part of Wolsey, containing some moves and business for other characters. In addition there is a scene plot, a lighting plot with some cues, a property plot, an acting plot and a costume plot, these last two showing what performers and costumes were required in each scene, including subplots for extra gentlemen, extra ladies, and children. The visual material, apart from the scene plans mentioned, comprises a large portfolio of costume designs by Percy Macquoid, and photographs of both the 1910 production and the 1916 replication in the New Amsterdam Theatre, New York. There are also three volumes of press cuttings relating to the productions in England and America. Various financial records are contained in six ledgers kept by the general manager, Henry Dana, and a useful typed summary of the final accounts for *Henry VIII* is preserved in a separate folder.

The main source of information for plotting the course of the production is the promptbook, which aside from a few lines of Act IV, scene i spoken in the production contains the entirety of Tree's text. His intention was to do the play in as close to the 'two short hours' — a phrase he underlined — of the Prologue as he could get, noting in his rehearsal copy that 'the play must be played swiftly & the waits quite short.' To save time, to allow for historical pageantry, and to eliminate passages considered uninteresting to a modern audience, Tree wielded such a mighty axe on the text that of Shakespeare's 2,810 lines he cut 1,323, or 47 per cent, an unusually high percentage even for the Victorians and Edwardians. Acts I, II, and III lost about one-third of their lines altogether, about the going rate for contemporary commercial Shakespeare, but Act IV was reduced by more than half and Act V cut entirely. All these cuts meant the elimination of a great deal of political intrigue, Gardiner and Cranmer (the latter retained only as a non-speaking ceremonial functionary), several minor characters, the whole of the plot against Cranmer, and the christening of Princess Elizabeth — which last Tree meant to include and only jettisoned at the very end of rehearsals. He followed his by now well-established custom of arranging Shakespeare in three acts: the first interval coming after the banquet at Wolsey's palace, the second after the trial of Queen Katharine. No doubt for reasons of theatrical climax and a rising crescendo of pageantry he reversed the order of the coronation procession of Anne Bullen (the Folio's IV.i) and the Queen's final scene at Kimbolton (IV.ii). The procession became a coronation in Westminster Abbey. Tree made no comment on this transposition, but defended his cuts generally by his usual practice of appealing to Shakespeare. What Tree called 'those portions of the play which deal with the Reformation' were omitted, 'being as they are practically devoid of dramatic interest and calculated, as they are to weary an audience.' However, Tree continued, there was no doubt that these passages were also omitted in

Shakespeare's time, since 'a considerable portion of the play was considered by the author to be superfluous to the dramatic action.' Developing this inspired strain of logic, Tree concluded that because Shakespeare's own theatre had played *Henry VIII* in 'two short hours', more of it must have been omitted than in 1910, and therefore 'we showed a greater respect for the presentation of the text than Shakespeare himself.'[13]

The theatre in which *Henry VIII* was performed opened as Her Majesty's in 1897. The foyer was compared to the entry hall of an old club, with oak panelling, thick carpets, armchairs ranged along the walls, and potted plants. The decorative scheme of blue carpets, red chairs and red wall-hangings was matched by the livery of the theatre servants in royal blue, red velvet breeches, and white stockings. The dress circle vestibule was decorated in the same French Renaissance style as the auditorium, in prevailing tones of red and gold. The auditorium hangings were of embroidered silk cerise and the walls were papered in the same colour. The seats in the stalls, dress circle, and family circle were armchairs covered in red velvet of the same shade as the curtain. The proscenium, the columns, and the pilasters were of *brèche violette* marble with ormolu mountings; the stage curtain was red velvet with wide bands of heavy gold embroidery, and behind it a drop curtain that was a reproduction of a Gobelin tapestry representing Dido receiving Aeneas. A hydraulically operated safety curtain could be lowered in thirty seconds. In addition to the overhead cut-glass and brass electrolier in Louis XIV style, the house was illuminated by reproductions of candle brackets at Fontainebleau, with electric lights instead of candles. The sight-lines were generally excellent, and there were six boxes, three on each side of the proscenium. An elaborate and expensive ventilation and hot-water heating system had been installed. The audience inhabiting this elegant and luxurious theatre paid prices for *Henry VIII* of 10s 6d for the stalls, 7s 6d for the balcony stalls on dress circle, 5s for other seats in the balcony, 4s, 3s, and 2s for the upper circle, 2s 6d for the pit, and 1s for the gallery; boxes were 31s 6d to 4 guineas.

The stage was the traditional kind of wood stage in use in nineteenth-century English theatres,[14] but a novelty in that Her Majesty's was the first English theatre since the Restoration to be built with a flat instead of a raked stage. This stage measured 50 × 70 feet, the 50 feet being from the curtain to the back wall; the proscenium opening was 29 feet 6 inches × 35 feet; from the stage floor to the gridiron was 60 feet, and from the floor to the cellar 23 feet. Like other stages, the stage floor at Her Majesty's was sectioned into movable platforms capable of bringing up scenic pieces, operated by lifts manually raised and lowered by a system of counterweights. In this case there were four such sections, each divisible into smaller sections.[15] The chief glory of the theatre was not its flat stage, however, but its electric stage lighting system, in 1897 one of the most advanced in Europe. The footlights, the six overhead stage battens, the two vertical rows behind and on each side of the proscenium, the wing lights, and a system of portable lengths were all controlled from a single and then highly sophisticated lighting board equipped with dimmers able to register light intensities from 0 to 10. The footlights, only two or three inches above the stage floor as compared to the greater and vision-obstructing height of the old style of reflector, were broken into three separate and independently controlled colour circuits, as was, indeed, each of the four other elements of the system listed above. All this electric lighting was supplemented by at least twenty-eight limelights operated behind the proscenium, from the fly-galleries, the perches, and occasionally on the stage floor itself. As will be seen, the lighting for *Henry VIII* was further reinforced by two limes located in the dome of the auditorium.[16]

Rehearsals for *Henry VIII* started at Her Majesty's on 21 June; Tree usually took about two months to rehearse a new production. Parker may well have taken some of the earlier rehearsals, and he certainly did when Tree was away for a week on his annual holiday in Marienbad at the end of July. On 4 August Tree assumed personal direction of rehearsals.[17] The course of Tree rehearsals ran far less smoothly than those in better ordered theatres like the Lyceum or George Alexander's St James's. They were, in fact, a byword in the profession for disorder and even anarchy, from which — somehow and miraculously — competent, attractive, and even splendid productions emerged at the very last minute. Several actors and dramatists who worked with Tree have left rather bewildered descriptions of the rehearsal process at his theatres. They all agreed that Tree was ruthless towards his actors and staff, never rested until he got the results he wanted, in spite of the chaos around him, and would often disappear for long periods, leaving the conduct of the rehearsal to God and his harried stage management. Yet undoubtedly there was purpose behind all this — Julia Neilson noted that 'it almost seemed as though the effects he achieved were accidental, but this was certainly not the case'.[18] Neilson had spent five years with Tree, but a newcomer could be overwhelmed. W. Graham Robertson, whose comedy *Pinkie and the Fairies* appeared at His Majesty's in 1908, was stunned by the early rehearsals:[19]

> All seemed confusion, everything drifted haphazard and apparently with-
> out a guiding spirit. Tree was, I suppose, producer; then there was an Act-
> ing Manager who had much authority, another Manager (what he managed
> I never found out), two very efficient Stage Managers, without whom
> nothing could have gone forward, the Composer, the Author, and, in addi-
> tion to these, any passing author, actor, newspaper man or critic, all of
> whom appeared at liberty to drop in and give advice. To me it seemed a
> return to back drawing-room theatricals or the charade parties of my
> youth.

Dress rehearsals were a terrible experience for all the acting, technical, and stage management personnel except for Tree himself. They would start in the morning and go on till two or three o'clock the next morning if things went well; if not, until five, six, or seven, with virtually no breaks. The cast of *Antony and Cleopatra* spent a week doing this and would sleep in boxes or in the wings to be woken for their cues. Constance Collier described what usually happened:[20]

> The men at their posts on the limelights would drop off to sleep, and the actors would lie about in the circle or in the boxes. Tree would disappear for hours to have supper or talk over some problem of the play, and return at three or four in the morning. The limelight men would spring to attention, the actors rush down on the stage, full of apologies for daring even to feel sleepy in his presence. And he would be as bright and energetic as ever.

Tree himself was inexhaustible and inextinguishable. Oscar Asche, who first joined him for Stephen Phillips's *Ulysses* in 1902, had an experience similar to Collier's, and recalled Tree's participation in rehearsals with amazement:[21]

> Tree never seemed inclined to work till after midnight. I know that the few days preceding production I was on His Majesty's stage from 12 noon till 6.30 the following morning. Tree would look in just before lunch for about ten minutes. His next appearance would be about nine, after dinner. He would then rehearse for two hours, and then to supper. About 1 a.m. he would turn up again, fresh and cheery, and say: 'Come, let's do some *work*!'

The rehearsals for *Henry VIII* were no different. When the play neared opening night, it became apparent that Tree had been wildly optimistic about running times. Tree's Act III originally concluded with two scenes: a brief one where Henry receives the news of Elizabeth's birth from the Old Lady, and a spectacle scene of the Princess's christening. In Claude Rains's preparation book the running time for the whole production, including these scenes, was estimated at 183 minutes. Cecil King estimated twenty-four minutes of waits and two eight-minute intervals; Tree's rehearsal copy put the waits at twenty-eight minutes. In the event, as Tree saw the total running time grow longer and longer, despite these calculations, he decided at the final rehearsal to cut the last two scenes. Perhaps he also thought that the audience would have had enough of pageantry by the end of the Coronation scene. *Henry VIII* opened on 1 September 1910. Quite 'done for', Parker had been carried out of the theatre after the last dress rehearsal and put to bed.[22] For the benefit of the critics, Tree advanced his starting-time on the first night by an hour, to 7.00. In spite of the last-minute cuts, of which he informed the audience in a curtain speech, the play lasted three and a half hours, for which Tree apologised − the very length of time that he accused Shakespeare of needing to perform the entire text.

Months before the first word of the Prologue was spoken to the fashionable first-night audience in His Majesty's, Percy Macquoid had been at work on costumes and properties; Maud Tree, in fact, called him rather than Parker 'Herbert's right hand in this production'.[23] Contemporary theatrical standards of historical and archaeological accuracy required a great deal of scholarship for a major production of this kind, and like Seymour Lucas before him for Irving's *Henry VIII* Macquoid had been carrying on extensive research in museums, art galleries, and Tudor buildings a long time before the first rehearsal. He had an immense number of properties to design: when the same production of *Henry VIII* went to America in 1916, 135 pieces of furniture, aside from the smaller properties, were carried with it, all especially designed for the play and none taken from stock. Many properties, like the embroidered chairs and tablecloths, required careful and patient work. A Chicago reporter noted that 'the cloth which covers the table is marked with the cardinal's hat and the letters "T.W." intertwined, a design which appears upon the backs of chairs and wherever the monogram is needed. From across the footlights it is unlikely that this can be distinguished, but it is an example of Sir Herbert's minute attention to detail.' (Or, at least, of Percy Macquoid's attention to detail.) The same reporter also observed that the gilded papier-mâché goblets and fruit dishes were 'ornamented with carving accurate even to the smallest detail'.[24]

The costumes were just as big a job as the properties. All the watercolour drawings do not survive, but the seventy-five sketches for men's costumes that do give an excellent idea of the richness and variety of design. Altogether there were about 375 or 380 costumes for *Henry VIII*, executed by the firm of B. J. Simmons, Historical Costumiers of King Street, Covent Garden. Their splendour attracted much press comment, and following the practice of the day several papers sent special correspondents to describe the costumes of the leading characters to their readers. The readership of such reports can be deduced from the fact that much the greater part of these descriptions is taken up by an account of female costumes. The number of costumes was not surprising considering that the number of the cast was 172: 24 speaking parts (5 of them doubling), 20 Extra Ladies, 12 Extra Gentlemen, 4 Chorus Ladies, 8 Special Chorus Gentlemen, 19 Boys, 8 Girls, 2 Trumpeters, and 75 Supers. The final cost of the costumes was £2,756 compared to £545 for the properties.

The already large stage on which *Henry VIII* was performed was further enlarged by a semicircular apron stage extending over the orchestra pit. This was indeed a novelty on a picture-frame stage but it was not of Tree's invention; the extension had already been used in April for the Shakespeare Festival appearance of Poel's *Two Gentlemen of Verona*. Commenting on the apron four weeks before opening night, the *Daily Mail* (5 August 1910) said that it came about 9 feet in front of the original stage, and added, 'By this plan the players will be brought more closely in touch with the spectators, and much of the dialogue, soliloquies, and speeches, instead of being spoken at a considerable distance from the audience, will be given in the auditorium itself.' This seems very obvious, even platitudinous, to us, but it must have been a newsworthy novelty for West End theatregoers in 1910, and it was unlikely that the readership of the Daily Mail had attended the *Two Gentlemen of Verona en masse*; Poel's production is not mentioned in the news item. Because of the apron the orchestra could be heard but not seen. The lights in the dome were essential for the illumination of the apron, but they were also used to light areas and actors much further upstage. They must also have been in place for the *Two Gentlemen of Verona*, unless Poel used lighting from the boxes for his apron. In any case they are an early example of front lighting in the West End and new enough to the public to call for an explanation from Tree that they were 'a device for throwing the light upon the faces of those on the stage'.[25]

The dome lights were in immediate use for the Prologue. After an eight-minute overture, an entirely un-Shakespearean Jester stepped in front of the drop curtain carrying a bauble and blowing a toy trumpet. He was lit by amber lime spots from the dome – which remained on until the end of the scene – and white and amber footlights, while the front chandelier in the auditorium remained up. The Prologue, spoken in a melancholy way (the 'two short hours' had been changed to 'three'), concluded with the Jester signalling the curtain to rise and then taking up a listening position by the doors of the church as the front chandelier was extinguished and the lights behind the proscenium came up.

Act I, scene i was set in red-brick cloisters, with a backcloth of flowering white chestnuts peeping over the tops of a slanting double row of arches, with church doors stage right and a stone seat down left. Buckingham, wearing black with gold lace and a mulberry cloak, talked briefly with Norfolk and Abergavenny until the church doors opened, the organ and singing within swelled, and Wolsey made a grand ceremonial entrance with a train that consisted, in the following order, of four guards with spears, twelve choirboys, two priests carrying crosses, two silver pillar bearers, Cromwell, two servants, a bearer carrying Wolsey's long train (the number of yards of expensive silk in it was a matter of dispute in the press), and two more servants – a total of twenty-nine to mark the first display of pageantry in the performance. However, Tree was using spectacle to illustrate character as well as to provide a pleasing show. By his initial entry with such a magnificent and ostentatious retinue, Wolsey was shown at once to be a great prince of the church with a vain love of pomp and the trappings of power – aspects of character repeatedly stressed in the production. The exercise of that power and the haughtiness, arrogance, and contempt for lesser mortals that went along with it, traits which Tree also emphasised in his acting, were briefly introduced to the audience by Wolsey's conduct in the rest of the scene. The choirboys sang until Wolsey spoke, but before he spoke he left the procession and, with an amber lime on him, came down to glare defiantly at Buckingham. The *Nation* (23 March 1916) objected to this business as too emphatic, too much of a theatrical point. Wolsey then rejoined the procession, which left the stage. Buckingham's arrest followed, and the scene ended with Wolsey's reappearance smelling an orange,[26] coming down through the centre arch of the cloister and imperiously holding out his hand for Norfolk to kneel and kiss it. One reviewer found this scene visually beautiful, and his description is couched almost entirely in terms of colours and materials: 'Red-brown brick walls, the green and scarlet and gold and grey of the nobles' dress, the slow plain song chant, the white-robed choir, sable-clad monks, and the resplendent crimson-gowned Cardinal, all this merges and blends into a glorious harmony, which needs no words to make it intelligible.'[27] The implications of that last remark with regard to the production as a whole are significant. Tree had hardly begun.

The second scene of Act I took place in the Council Chamber, a panelled room hung with tapestries, with a dais upstage centre and two rows of roughly semicircular benches opposite each other downstage. The curtain rose as a clock struck eleven, the Lord Chamberlain entered to inspect the premises, and to the sound of a repeated trumpet four gentlemen-at-arms and five bishops preceded the King, who leant on Wolsey's shoulders, followed by Cromwell, two secretaries, two more gentlemen, and Sir Thomas Lovell; a moment later the Queen, escorted by Norfolk, Suffolk, and two ladies-in-waiting, trumpets sounding again to mark her entrance. Wolsey was accompanied by his amber lime spotlight on his entrance, illuminated by a flood while seated, and followed on his exit by the faithful spot. However, this was really the King's scene – another amber spot was assigned to his throne – and Arthur Bourchier made the most of his entrance, which created a great stir in the audience. Bourchier had grown a beard for his part rather than stick on a false one every night, and this act of selfless devotion to the theatre aroused much press comment well before the first night; the progress of the beard was reported from time to time. It had been dyed red, and in a red wig and in a costume duplicated from the copy of Holbein's famous portrait (except for the codpiece), Bourchier stepped on stage for the first time to a spontaneous and long sustained outburst of applause: 'It was not merely a welcome to the actor. A whisper went round the pit "The King!" and the applause grew as he assumed the familiar attitude of his best-known portrait.'[28] The picture was being applauded, not the actor – or rather, the *coup de théâtre* of 'realising' the picture. Many reviewers admired this recreation and the legerdemain of Bourchier 'stepping from the frame' of the picture to become a living and moving Henry VIII. William Terris had done exactly the same thing in Irving's production.

To counterpoint the hearing of the charges against Buckingham and the investigation of Wolsey's unjustly imposed taxation, Tree had arranged for a great deal of offstage noise to convey the impression of a large and hostile crowd waiting outside. Shouts and crowd murmurs were cued by lights underneath the stage, where the aggrieved commonalty were also positioned. A white light cued cries of 'Buckingham!' a blue one 'Room for the Queen!' and a frequently used red one 'Angry murmurs' such as 'Give us bread'. There were also onstage murmurs, and all this irritated Wolsey, who according to the *Nation* (23 March 1916) 'exhibited an agitation and excessive by-play – patently theatrical – wholly unworthy of an experienced statesman.' An uproar broke out at the climax of the scene when the Surveyor, prompted openly by Wolsey, claimed that Buckingham had threatened the life of the King. All those seated, except Wolsey, the King, and the Queen, rose 'with an exclamation'. Henry and Wolsey left the stage together, the latter looking over his shoulder in triumph at the Queen, who sank into a seat. A final offstage hubbub and the sound of trumpets brought the curtain down.

The next scene, 'The Banqueting Hall, Wolsey's Palace', was one of Tree's great spectacular set-pieces, and of all the scenes it received the most comment from reviewers and was the most admired. With regard to properties it was certainly the most elaborate. On the banquet tables were no less than 235 separate properties – cold dishes, fruit bowls, a boar's head, fish, profile sweets, a dish of oranges for Wolsey, goblets, knives, etc. – all exact copies taken either from originals in museums or from paintings in the National Gallery. The gold plate that gleamed from tables and dressers was particularly impressive, shining in the light of an amber lime spot assigned to the dressers throughout the scene. The set itself consisted of two backstage galleries with choir, the dressers with plate below the galleries, in front of these and in the centre a canopied seat and table for the Cardinal on a rostrum, steps down to the main body of the hall, a long central carpet reaching from the steps almost to the proscenium, and on stage left and right two long tables with benches on the sides that faced the carpet. It appears from the scene plot that everything upstage from the rostrum was set up behind the backing for scene ii. This would have been essential if a long wait were to be avoided; as it is the wait was probably long enough, since putting the banquet tables and properties in place must have taken at least a few minutes. The hall had a fan-vaulted ceiling and its stone walls were hung with tapestries of velvet and gold. Over the length of the carpet – which might have been taken up for the dancing – hung four chandeliers of electric lights imitating candles. Twenty-five limes behind the proscenium, the two limes in the dome, a full array of amber and white floats and blue and white battens must have bathed the scene in the intense light often complained of by those sensitive to excessive brightness and glare in the theatre. The front house chandelier remained three-quarters up for the whole scene.

The curtain rose to reveal the musicians and choir in the galleries, guests entering to take their places, servants bringing on food, another servant perfuming the air with a scent brush, and a general hustle and bustle and merry chatter. After a few lines, trumpets marked the arrival of further guests, including Anne Bullen, who was wearing a costume of old rose satin with the overdress opening over a rose petticoat brocaded in white motifs, both overdress and petticoat outlined with jewels, a jewelled girdle, and a rose and white headdress. Laughing and talking, the guests took their seats at the invitation of the Lord Chamberlain, fourteen at each table, Anne Bullen prominently in view at the downstage end of the right-hand table. Wolsey then entered after a trumpet fanfare to occupy his seat of honour, his train carried by two bearers, to the accompaniment of more light than before: the friendly amber lime of the two previous scenes, the white battens slowly up to three-quarters on his entrance, and an amber lantern from the dome as he seated himself. (It is interesting to examine details of the customary practice – certainly followed by Irving – of giving the star more light than anybody else on the stage; Tree adhered to it in most of his scenes in *Henry VIII*.) The splendour of his silk robe, specially woven in Lyons, of a hue of flamboyant red far brighter than Irving's more conservative and intellectual Wolsey wore, stood out as it was intended to from all the other costumes. The *Irish Times* (2 September 1910) noted of this scene that everything was 'dominated by the crimson robe of Cardinal Wolsey, and nothing is allowed to clash with it. Therefore, reds and greens have been employed with a plentiful use of black and white, with sparkling gold and silver.' Another critic commented on the colour harmony of this scene, despite the brilliance of Wolsey's attire and his appearance 'against a background of translucent green and gold'.[29]

The banquet began with the choir singing a grace, 'Non nobis', and Wolsey pledging the company with a goblet of wine. One writer, not at all happy with the vaunted historical authenticity of the production, objected to the fact that the Cardinal did not remove his biretta or bless the food and drink.[30] After the grace, trumpets sounded again: 'all drink eat and talk', and upon Wolsey's

> Ladies, you are not merry; gentlemen,
> Whose fault is this?

'everybody kisses and laughs'. All that the actors could actually eat were sponge cakes and apples, distributed here and there amid the mounds of property food. An interpolated morris dance occurred after a flirtatious exchange between Anne Bullen and Lord Sands; there were eight female dancers and eight male, the women in blue and white, the men in blue and orange. For the succeeding court dances in this scene, according to the *Morning Advertiser* (2 September), Margaret Morris had examined 'every available picture of the Tudor period in which the dances of the day are illustrated'. After the dance the masquers, habited as sheep rather than as Shakespeare's shepherds, were ushered in by the Lord Chamberlain. 'Kneel

& Baa' is the direction for them in the promptbook, and the 'Baa' was repeated, with the disguised King giving a solo 'Baa' in the middle of the Chamberlain's speech. When Henry took off his full ram's-head mask and then his woolly robe to reveal his true self as well as a splendid green costume, the eight masquers did likewise. The critic from the *Daily Telegraph* (2 September) was quite overwhelmed by the cumulative effect of the scene to this point, describing the hall, the tapestries,

> the black velvet chairs trimmed with green fringe and embroidered with the Cardinal's hat – all these set off by the flashing radiance of colour introduced by the revellers, who came in to grace the banquet, from a colour-scheme of rose, red, and green, with the Cardinal himself, representing the apex as it were, or centre, as a point of vivid scarlet. This is assuredly one of the most brilliant stage pictures ever presented to a modern audience.

Immediately he had unmasked and been greeted by Wolsey, the King sat in the Cardinal's chair and listened to a part-song composed by his historical self, 'Pastime with good company'. This was sung to him by an onstage octet of four men and four women; Henry rose at the end of the first verse and conducted the singers in the second. When the song ended the company joined in two dances. The King, smitten with the sight of Anne Bullen, chased her through the crowd and led her out in the volta, an authentic period dance in which, as the press were assured, the real Henry and Anne were proficient, and which involved the dancers leaping into the air. Margaret Morris had to modify the more vigorous aspects of the volta because of the clouds of dust that rose from a stage heavily trampled by the historically accurate steps of the dance. However, it remained energetic enough. No doubt ignorant of the aerial requirements of the volta, the *Observer* thought that Laura Cowie as Anne was too riotous in her dancing,[31] and *Lloyd's Weekly* (4 September) was struck by the 'leaps and athletic gambols' of the dance. During the King's amorous pursuit of his lady, Wolsey occupied a chair down right and glared indignantly at the happy couple. In 1916 an American reviewer complained about the business involved: 'Ann [sic] kicks her foot at the cardinal and does a lot of "flirtation" business in the "ingenue" style that brought the whole thing down to farce comedy. Wolsey looks disgusted at Ann's behaviour and Henry does the infatuated in the most realistic manner.'[32] Another critic thought that Wolsey had come down stage for the sole purpose of being mocked by Anne and 'registering his own indignation and wrath in interpolated pantomime'.[33] In New York both Anne and Henry were played by different actors, and the business may have developed since 1910, but Tree was fond of underlining theatrical points, and the same thing probably happened at His Majesty's. At the end of this dance the King threw himself into a chair, proposed a health, gulped some wine ('everybody cheers'), and pulled a willing Anne onto his knee, 'like any scullion in his kitchen', as *Lloyd's Weekly* commented. Doubtless adding Henry's behaviour at this juncture to his conduct in the dance and his vocal performance as a ram, one or two critics thought that Bourchier's boisterous acting in this scene had a touch too much of the low comedian, but others approved the bursting energy and high spirits of the dances and the accompanying byplay. The scene ended with another general dance — the three last dances comprising German's still well-known dances for Irving's production — and the company exited singing and dancing ahead of Anne and Henry, who caught Wolsey's reproving eye as he resumed the chase. The curtain came down on the entrance of the Jester, pointing mockingly from the door at a vexed Wolsey standing stage centre. At this point the first calls of the play were taken in the customary form of tableaux, the first of a seated Wolsey smelling his orange, the second of Wolsey, Henry, and Anne.

The mood of Act II, scene i, 'The River Gate', was entirely different. After the first interval, the curtain rose to reveal the watergate at which Buckingham was to embark for his journey to execution at the Tower. A painted backcloth of the other side of the river hung behind a water cut and an arch cut in a painted cloth of the gate itself. House pieces flanked both sides of the gate, and when the scene opened a bell was sounding regularly and a crowd of over thirty citizens and boys was scrambling for places to see Buckingham pass; offstage murmurs growing louder are specified in the promptbook. It was a foreboding night scene, and the lighting was generally cold and blue.

In a moment Buckingham, holding a silver crucifix and wearing a black cloak, entered with a large escort of eight men carrying flickering torches, eight guards with spears, four miscellaneous lords, the headsman, a monk, Vaux, and Lovell. The headsman, in red, stood silently upstage, the blade of his axe turned toward Buckingham. The tolling of the bell, groans, sobs, and sympathetic murmurs from the crowd punctuated Buckingham's address, which he delivered up centre. The *Pall Mall Gazette* (2 September) thought Henry Ainley as Buckingham restless in this scene compared to the calm of Forbes-Robertson for Irving, but suggested that 'perhaps the torches, the semi-darkness, and the agitation of the stage-crowd detracted from the effect'. The majority of reviewers, however, were much impressed by the visual effect of the scene and the elocution of Ainley, who was nevertheless not to be compared with Forbes-Robertson. At the end of his speech all except the guards knelt to Buckingham, and he moved in dead silence to the barge, now visible in the water cut, a lantern gleaming in its bow. A boy cried, a woman kissed the hem of Buckingham's cloak, a blue lime from the flies followed him onto the barge and stayed on him as the barge moved off left, and the curtain fell slowly.

Both the second and third scenes of Act II were short (II.ii had been heavily cut) and played as front scenes while the carpenters were setting up the complicated Trial scene which required the whole depth of the stage. However, even the front scenes of this production were considered relatively elaborate, and the same standard of visual correctness and pictorial beauty were applied to them as to other scenes. Act II, scene ii was 'The Gallery' in the royal palace, with a large central window recess containing three chairs and a table; portraits of the King and Queen hung on either side of this recess, on a wall that was a painted cloth. The scene began with pantomimic comic business: Henry knocking a letter from the Lord Chamberlain's hand, the Chamberlain then in a fit of temper knocking the letter from the hand of a servant ordered to pick it up,. Accompanied by Cardinal Campeius, Wolsey entered with his orange and the papal commission, casting a defiant look at Norfolk and Suffolk before blessing them. The brief business between the King and the cardinals completed, the former delivered the lines

> O, my lord,
> Would it not grieve an able man to leave
> So sweet a bedfellow?

looking sadly at Katharine's portrait. After 'I must leave her' all three sighed, and as the cardinals followed the King off they smiled at each other, Tree once again stressing a hypocritical deference to his monarch.

In the next scene, 'The Pleasaunce at Windsor', a stone seat was placed in the centre in front of grassy banks to the left and right, a hedgerow, and a backcloth with a view of the Round Tower, the surrounding countryside, and the Thames. Downstage left and right were two rows of lilies. For this scene 'lights in front' – the chandelier or the house lighting generally – remained three-quarters up, and it is obvious from this and other references in the lighting plot that Irving's practice of darkening the auditorium, which he probably began in the 1879–80 season, was by no means universal thirty years later. When Anne Bullen had heard the news of her elevation to Marchioness of Pembroke and endured the banter of the Old Lady (whose sexual references were excised, as were all references of this kind throughout the text), she exited bowing left and right to the lilies, having picked one for a sceptre, a visual metaphor for her ambition that Violet Vanbrugh thought 'one of the prettiest and cleverest little bits of business' that Tree ever invented.[34]

Act II, scene iv, 'A Hall in Blackfriars', was the second of Tree's great spectacle scenes. At the very back of the hall, below a large stained glass window, stood a crowd of citizens flanked by two guards in red. Beneath them again were three tiers of seats; the upmost tier filled by lords and ladies and four monks in black, the middle tier by four more monks, an abbot, a peer, and twelve judges in red, and below them the Archbishop of Canterbury and five bishops, with five peers on each side. On the stage floor directly in front of the bishops stood five chaplains. The rise of the curtain revealed this entire body in place, and if in the photographs they look rather too like a large school assembled for the official photographer on speech day, there is no denying the spectacular effect of mass and colour carried straight up to the stained glass transparency, gleaming dimly with the light from white lengths behind it. In front of these spectators stood on a dais to the right the King's throne, with an ermine cloak over it from Tree's Richard II costume. A dais on the left contained two seats for Wolsey and Campeius, and in the centre, a little upstage, a chair for the Queen. Both daises had satellite tables and benches attached to them for lords and servants; there was a right-hand table for a scribe and a crier, already in place, and a left-hand table for Cromwell. Once again the audience saw tapestries covering the lower halves of the walls, and a heavily beamed ceiling stretched back from the proscenium.

For a spectacle scene of this size with several focal points of interest distributed about the stage, the lighting was appropriately large scale. Twenty-one limes were called into action, all with dark amber gelatines. Two were kept on the King, one spot and one flood, and five (two spots and three floods) illuminated the Queen's chair, the central area in which she moved, and, presumably, her attendants. Another lime was saved for Wolsey (none for Campeius), 'faint' on the Cardinal's chair before he occupied it, stronger as he took his place, The bishops had to be content with a single flood between them, and the *Church Times* (4 September) doubted if 'quite sufficient is made of the Bishops. Sir Herbert Tree puts the Bishops into a dim sort of background the while that the two Cardinals sport at the footlights.' Eight limes from the flies shone through the stained-glass windows on each side of the hall, and two amber lamps from the dome flooded the downstage area throughout the scene, in addition to blue light from the battens and blue and white light from the floats.

The action of the Trial scene began with no fewer than three separate processional entries. The leisured development of processions was characteristic of the unhurried rhythms of spectacle theatre, and Tree was as devoted to processions as was Augustus Harris in Drury Lane pantomimes. All three entered from the door half-way up on stage left between two guards in red. The largest number were, fittingly, in the first procession, Wolsey's: four halberdiers, two tipstaves, two silver-pillar bearers, a servant carrying the purse of Wolsey's office, two monks with crosses, the two cardinals, two bearers carrying Wolsey's train, four boys holding a canopy over the cardinals, and Cromwell. Directly after it came the second procession: four gentlemen-at-arms, Norfolk, Suffolk, and Sands carrying the crown, orb, and sceptre respectively, the Lord Chamberlain, and the King. Then came the Queen's much smaller contingent: Katharine herself, Griffiths, and five ladies-in-waiting. Once the principals were on stage, the riches of their wardrobe were as much an object of comment as in the banquet scene. The *Daily Chronicle* (2 September) said of the King and Queen that they move through the play – and this scene in particular – 'well-nigh encrusted with jewels and broidered gold'. Katharine's costume, the centre of interest, was described in detail by more than one paper. Our Lady Correspondent in the *Glasgow Herald* (2 September) enlarged upon 'the dignified richness of her attire'; it was a 'carefully accurate period dress of dull purplish red brocaded velvet, shimmering with gold and silver embroideries', the sleeves edged with fur and lined with gold gauze. Over this she wore a large sweeping cape, and a headdress with white facings studded with jewels.

When all had taken their places, the attendants and minor figures behind and to the sides of the three protagonists, the spoken text began as in Shakespeare, with the King's refusal to hear the commission read. Tree made Wolsey visibly annoyed at this; indeed, according to the ever-critical *Nation* (23 March 1916) 'with Campeius he was engaged in constant gesticulation'. Two blasts of trumpets summoned the Queen into the Court; as she rose a general murmur was silenced by cries of 'Hush!'; others whispered. Her speech, from which Tree cut only five lines, was accompanied by a full orchestration of 'very slight murmurs', 'slight murmurs', 'mixed murmurs' (whatever these might be), and 'loud murmurs'. The sympathy of the auditors was entirely with Katharine, and it was most vocally expressed by the citizens at the back. Half-way through her speech she knelt in appeal to the King, and on 'Please you, sir' tried to take his hand, but Henry turned away and gestured to her chair. At this, 'the crowd cry out in anger. The court ladies come forward but are moved back. ... Some ladies cry.' Wolsey, who had already been subjected to murmurs and 'slight laugh' when Katharine pointed 'He were mine enemy' at him, rose to murmurs of disapproval and a general groan when he finished his speech and motioned Campeius to rise and speak in his turn. The unfortunate Cardinal, very much Wolsey's puppet whenever he appeared, aroused murmurs of hatred which had to be hushed by officials. The cues for murmuring multiplied when the Queen rose again, forcing Campeius to sit 'with big gesture'; they rose to a crescendo on 'sparks of fire', and then ceased entirely. 'Excitement in court' is the direction at her second naming of Wolsey as her enemy – despite protests from a bishop – and upon 'from my soul/Refuse you for my judge' there was a 'sensation' and cries of 'Bravo!' from the crowd, whose mounting hostility Wolsey had to contend with when he spoke again. Katharine's denunciation of him was greeted with shouts of 'Aye, aye!' and 'loud noise and confusion' marked the end of her speech. Some critics blamed Violet Vanbrugh for speaking too much to the audience rather than to the Court; others criticised her for being too loud and slow. But the delivery of a text in spectacle theatre remained an extremely difficult problem, and it is not surprising that in a scene of this scale the actress would have simultaneously slowed textual rhythm and increased volume in order in some way to identify herself clearly in the sizeable pictorial canvas from which she could not escape.

The Queen's departure from the Court, with Griffiths and her attendants, was accompanied by cries of 'Long live the Queen!' and a sudden rush of female citizens from the back row, presumably to give her further encouragement offstage. Wolsey angrily stamped his foot on 'Most gracious sir' in addressing the King, but this was nothing compared to the latter's fury at the end of the scene. Much of his long speech beginning 'My lord cardinal,/I do excuse you' was cut, as were the Bishop of Lincoln's replies and indeed the Bishop of Lincoln himself. To sustain the mounting climax initiated by the Queen's abrupt and contemptuous exit, the confusion in the Court, and the noisy departure of the citizenesses, Tree jumped straight from

> Respecting this our marriage with the dowager,
> Sometimes our brother's wife.

to 'Prove but our marriage lawful' a few lines from the end. On

> I abhor
> This dilatory sloth and tricks of Rome.
> Break up the court

the King jumped to his feet, snatched the sceptre from Sands, and, pointing it at the Cardinals, shouted his lines. The direction is 'Uproar. Everyone rises in horror.' To quell the noise Henry waved the sceptre over his head, cried 'I say set on', threw away his cap, took the crown from Norfolk, jammed it on his head, and rushed off. 'Confusion in Court' naturally ensued; shouts of 'Long live the King!' and 'Down with Wolsey!' mingled with 'general uproar outside and trumpets'. The curtain came down on the sight of Wolsey downstage, smelling his orange as final 'murmurs' ran around the hall.

It has been worth noting at some length how Tree, who loved movement and bustle in large crowd scenes, dealt with a fairly static stage spectacle for much of this scene. He avoided the danger of tedium by carefully punctuating the text and lightening the immobility with a wide variety of individual and group vocal responses, themselves rising to a point of climax at the moment visual action and rapid movement took over the rest of the scene and precipitated a powerful and even violent curtain.

After the second interval, the last act of *Henry VIII* opened with a repeat of 'The Pleasaunce at Windsor', the same setting as Act II, scene iii, the only changes being the addition of a stool and bench on either side of the central stage seat and the replacement of the lilies by red and white carnations. These carnations caused some controversy. *The Times* (2 September 1960) was concerned that they were anachronistic, not having been introduced into England until much later. The *Star* replied the same evening, declaring that they were indeed cultivated in England at the time the play was set and that a carnation in a glass can be seen in the painting of a London merchant by Holbein. Two days later the *Observer* was convinced of an anachronism, but the *Star*, having obviously done further research on Holbein, who died in 1543, replied that this was not so since carnations could be seen in *two* of his paintings. There the matter rested, the anti-carnationists either routed or too uninterested to argue further. The dispute is an interesting example of public attachment to the principles of archaeological correctness in stage production.

The second Pleasaunce scene is of little concern to us except from a descriptive point of view. Commentators praised the scenic background, the 'old-fashioned garden in the shadow of a mighty cedar, the Round Tower rising majestically above, and the silver Thames winding through the meadow lands below.'[35] Perhaps they took more notice of the setting this time because of the more dramatic scene enacted in front of it: the unhappy Katharine striving to reject the insistent persuasion of Wolsey and Campeius. Tree conveyed the conflict in a strongly visual image which more than one reviewer admired: the Queen in black, on the stone seat, pressed closely on both sides by two blood-red cardinals, 'behind them the sombre wall of the castle and the sun gleaming on the distant river'. The scene ended on the same sombre note, the faltering Queen helped off the stage by Wolsey, and a 'very slow curtain'.

The second scene of Act III, which marked Wolsey's downfall, was listed on the programme as an 'Ante-Chamber with adjoining Chapel'. Tree had been puzzled how to locate and design a scene which seemed to him divided into two distinct halves, each related to the Cardinal's position: the arrogant Wolsey, still at the centre of authority and intrigue, dismissed by Henry and baited by the nobles, and the tragically self-aware Wolsey departing from the play and the world of power. The problem for Tree was to devise a stage environment suitable to express both these opposites in the same scene. 'Very difficult', he wrote in his rehearsal copy, and in spite of being the declared enemy of the symbolic treatment of Shakespeare decided to adopt an essentially symbolic solution. The stage was divided nearly into two: the ante-room on the right and a chapel on the left, the latter containing an altar with a cross and separated from the former by a grille running down at an angle towards the proscenium, continuing the angle of the wall that also marked off the division between the two areas. The ante-room was brightly lit, the chapel in semi-darkness. The lighting plot shows that except for two amber limes lighting the transparency windows on the chapel side and an amber spot for Wolsey wherever he went, the remaining eight limes illuminated the ante-room only. Except for the footlights, the only lighting indicated by the electric plot was white lengths full up in the stage right doorway of the ante-room, the entrance to the King's apartment, which blazed with a symbolic as well as a material light, including two floods from the flies as well as the lengths. The *People* (4 September) called this scene one of well-considered symbolism: 'King and servant stand in full light backed by the brilliant dresses of courtiers for this final meeting. ... As the sun of his power sets at the bidding of his master, the robbed and broken Wolsey staggers into the darkness of the sanctuary.'

To make it quite plain to the audience that it *was* a chapel they were looking at on stage left when the curtain went up, a monk came through a gate in the grille and crossed the stage to exit right, and 'Iste confessor' could be heard sung offstage. The nobles took shelter in the shadows of the chapel upon Wolsey's entrance, where they could observe him safely. During the exchange between Wolsey and the King they moved into the ante-room and stood up stage listening, laughing, and clearly treating the Cardinal with contempt. Henry remained in a jolly mood, 'lolling cheerily',[36] upon a settee at one point and putting his foot up to prevent Wolsey sitting next to him. He handed Wolsey the fatal letters almost as if the whole thing were a joke. The succeeding confrontation between the courtiers and the Cardinal was angry and bitter on both sides, with the latter at the height of his haughtiness and pride. His mood changed immediately they left, however, and he embarked upon 'A long farewell to all my greatness!' with leisurely deliberation. In fact many critics thought Tree too deliberate and too slow in this part of the scene. Visibly Wolsey 'tottered, in speech and bearing alike',[37] and after an emotional farewell to a stricken Cromwell passed from the radiance of the ante-room to the dark chapel, 'only a yard to walk into the darkness of despair, the calm of repentance'.[38] The scene concluded with a piece of interpolated pantomimic business characteristic of Tree. As the offstage music was heard again, Wolsey dropped his cardinal's robe to the floor and went slowly to the chapel door up left; the door was opened by a monk and the hymn 'Iste confessor' swelled in volume. Tree explained that 'I hope to have symbolised the tragic episode of his farewell to the world and his entry into the monastic life by my treatment. You will see Wolsey quietly disappear from the world, knocking at the door of heaven, as it were.'[39] Critics thought this ending highly effective, and only one noticed the strange juxtaposition of a monastery with a royal palace.

The penultimate scene of Tree's production (Shakespeare's IV, ii) was another front scene and revealed a room in Katharine's retreat at Kimbolton. A table, chair, and footstool were all the furniture required in the wide but shallow panelled room, and behind the furniture the rest of the setting existed for the purpose of realising the Queen's Vision: a gauze cloth for a back wall, a black drop cloth immediately behind it, a rostrum running nearly the width of the stage behind the drop, with steps rising almost from its centre toward the flies on stage left, these covered with velvet to kill any light reflection and deaden any sound the fifteen angels might make. This was evidently a proper set of steps rather than a *Faust*-like 'ladder of angels', no doubt secured at the top and with safety harnesses for the angels. Behind the rostrum was a 'batten with spangles', a cloth of light-reflecting sequins sewn onto a dark material; this in turn was hung in front of a velvet cloth, which would have absorbed light and made the reflections from the spangles even sharper. The whole effect must have been of a shimmering, starry heaven when the light behind the gauze came up. The velvet cloth would also have deadened sound, for on its other side the stagehands were quickly setting up the big Coronation scene, and scores of actors were taking their allotted places.[40] On stage torches provided 'the weird, mysterious shadows in Katharine's death chamber',[41] and the lighting was very subdued. An amber spot from the dome stayed a quarter up on the Queen in conjunction with a pinhole focus lime spot on her face.

Katharine heard the news of Wolsey's death seated weakly in her chair a little right of centre, a silver crucifix and flowers on the table next to her. Her lines condemning Wolsey had all been cut, but Griffith's praise, except for the reference to Wolsey coming from low stock, retained. Perhaps Tree did not wish the audience to hear any further blame of the penitent who had humbly sought monastic shelter only a few minutes before in stage time. Many reviewers thought Violet Vanbrugh too slow in this scene, which accordingly dragged, and they were not particularly struck with the Vision. It was thought conventional, and one critic objected that the angels did not dance as specified in the text. However, it is worth mentioning what actually happened on stage, since a vision scene behind gauze had been a standard feature of nineteenth-century melodrama and eagerly appropriated for drama with more elevated pretensions. At Katharine's lines 'whilst I sit meditating/ On that celestial harmony I go to' the sad and solemn music of the stage direction began at a cue from Griffiths to offstage musicians and all the lights in front of the gauze, including the footlights, began to check down slowly to out. The torches were taken off by Griffiths and Patience, to be restored when they returned. Almost simultaneously the black drop behind the gauze was taken up, the blue lights of no. 2 batten, which was directly over the rostrum and illuminated angels and spangled cloth alike, came slowly up together with two blue limes from the left- and right-hand flies, which shone only on the angels. The angels, themselves crowned with wreaths or garlands, passed down from hand to hand a crown of gold leaves with which to crown Katharine, the last angel doubtless holding it in the air in a tableau; from the audience it would have seemed as if she were holding it over the Queen's head. Then the lights behind the gauze went slowly out, the black cloth was dropped, and the stage lighting came up to its former level.[42] A dissatisfied American critic, who in any case thought the production scenically outdated, said that the Vision had 'a pronounced resemblance to an Easter card on sale at a drug store in Kansas City', especially when 'the white-robed angels began to wave their arms at the dying Queen'.[43] The scene ended, not with Katharine's exit as in Shakespeare, but with her onstage death in the flickering torchlight. 'Repeat heavenly music as scene darkens out' is the instruction in Tree's rehearsal copy, but there is no final music cue in the promptbook and no lighting cue there or in the lighting plot.

The dying fall of the two previous scenes, the atmosphere of loss and death, the dimness of the lighting that expressed these moods and provided a visual symbol of the decline of both Wolsey and Katharine, all this was sharply reversed by the apotheosis of Act III, scene iv, the exaltation of Anne Bullen, which took place in a veritable refulgence of glory. Tree had saved his greatest spectacle, his most lavish display of pageantry, for the last scene of all, although as we have seen it was not his original intention that it *should* be the last scene of all.

The promptbook ends with the death of the Queen, but it is possible to reconstruct the Coronation scene to some extent from other sources. Both the Tree rehearsal copy and the Cecil King preparation book preserve the same twenty-nine lines of dialogue between the First and Second Gentlemen of Shakespeare's IV, i. These were the last lines spoken in the production, and we know from reviews that this exchange took place, although it is not listed as a scene in the programme or anywhere else. It must have been played, as a brief prologue to what followed, on the apron in front of the curtain, illuminated by the lamps in the dome. When the curtain rose the audience saw an interior view of Westminster Abbey, with a decorated altar and steps up to it on stage right, a throne on a dais in the centre, and a raised box for the King on the left. Behind was a roughly triangular space for the large number of those attending, with a main entrance in the left wall of this triangle. At the back, to left and right, could be seen stained-glass windows, with smaller ones at the sides, and in the centre a tier of seats for the choir rising to a point below the great rose window in a backcloth. The sunlight streaming through this window created a splendid effect that was much admired. One reviewer was so impressed that he claimed the glass was real; it was actually painted parchment. Naturally, the lighting resources for this scene were at full stretch. To take only one example, the rose window required eight lengths of white light full up behind it, and nine of the thirty limes in use were directed at the windows. Another lime created a stained-glass effect at the base of a column; another was assigned to focus exclusively on the 'gold and green uniforms' clustered on stage right, and a third focused on the 'green uniforms' on the other side.

A large number of actors were already in place at the curtain, as in the Trial scene filling the back of the stage and leaving room for a processional entry at the front, a live backcloth to the main action. Not only did this device overcome the practical difficulty of opening a big spectacle scene with a bare stage and bringing everybody on at more or less the same time, but in a pictorial theatre it also provided the gilded frame − with the bottom section removed − of the stage painting, since Tree was careful, as we have seen in the Banqueting scene and the Trial scene, to fill in the sides of his human canvas as well. A sketch in Cecil King's preparation book shows that when the curtain rose two bishops were on stage right (one of these may have been the Archbishop of Canterbury), citizens up centre, monks, citizens, and two peers up left. Nine children played citizenesses and were placed on benches at the back in front of the choir, which must have already been in place in the lower tiers. The upper ones were filled with two-dimensional dummies, Tree continuing a practice that went back a long way of juxtaposing live actors with inanimate models and figures painted on scenery, and representing distant figures with small cut-outs. The Coronation procession itself then came through the entrance upstage left to the anthem newly composed by Edward German.

Tree had originally thought of putting the order of the procession on the curtain for the audience to examine before the scene started, but the idea seems to have gone no further than a jotting in his rehearsal copy. The full scope and detail of Tree's climactic pageantry can be seen by the order of the procession listed in Stanley Bell's preparation book:

4 Gents at Arms	Purse Bearer
2 Tipstaves	2 Canopy Bearers
4 Aldermen	Bishop–Anne–Bishop
2 Sheriffs	2 Canopy Bearers
1 Mayor	Duchess of N[orfolk]
2 Judges	Train boys white
1 Sergeant-at-Arms	Duchess of N[orfolk's] Page
Garter King at Arms	Dorset–Chancellor
Standard Bearer	3 Peeresses
6 Chaplines	3 Pages with Coronets
[10] Peers	3 Peeresses
Principal Gents	3 Boys and Coronets
Ring Bearer	4 Maids of Honour
Crown	3 Girl Pages
Lord Chamberlain	4 White Monks
Sceptre and Ivory Rod	

The property plot reveals that the ivory rod was carried by two supers, and an apparent omission in the order of the procession is the boy who carried a bottle of anointing oil on a cushion. A large number of gold and silver ceremonial properties were carried, and the property plot also lists ten cushions for the peers' coronets (perhaps carried by boys not listed by Stanley Bell), a standard, two flags, a cushion for Anne to kneel on, cushions for the crown and purse, a cloth of gold, eight crosses, a sceptre for the Garter King at Arms, two censers, and spears. There are about 88 in Stanley Bell's list, and the costume plot for the scene requires 119 costumes. As far as one can count from a photograph, approximately 122 are onstage in the New York Coronation scene, but it is hard to estimate the number in the choir, and given the total strength of the company as 172 and possible omissions in the preparation book it may well be that there were more than 119 on stage. The general critical praise bestowed upon the procession was not unanimous – one critic thought he had seen better processions in musical comedy[44] – and not to be found in a letter written by a correspondent in the Catholic newspaper, the *Tablet* (1 April 1911):

> Here they all come, in no apparent order, just higgledy-piggledy, rollick-ing along, all or most of the men with covered heads ... a sort of march past at a fancy dress ball or at the end of a popular 'pageant', some, as they pass right in front of and close to the high altar, bobbing to the archbishop, who returns their bob – like a celebrity at a big garden party.

As Anne Bullen was crowned and the peers and peeresses in crimson and ermine raised their coronets (historically inauthentic, according to the *Tablet*) and placed them on their heads, it was an opportunity for reviewers to remark the proud but menacing Henry watching from his royal box and a dainty, bewildered, and fearful Anne on the throne holding the ivory rod and dove of peace sceptre. She was wearing yet another gorgeous costume, a bodice enriched with jewels and 'a wonderful robe of rich white brocaded silk, with a very long train of cloth of silver, lined with crimson, and edged with ermine. Her huge drooping sleeves are turned back to show the deep ermine lining.'[45]

And so, near midnight every night except for the first night, the great red velvet curtains of His Majesty's closed on *Henry VIII*, probably not before time for a somewhat dazed and wearied audience, who perhaps left the theatre with the same impression as the reviewer for the *Manchester Courier* (2 September 1910), who concluded his praise of the 'kaleidoscopic tableaux such as have rarely been seen on any stage' on a note of visual satiation: 'Crowds brilliant with sheen of silk, lustre of velvet, and gleam of gems, pass and repass in bewildering succession, till the fall of the curtain comes as a positive relief.'[46] The feeling that the eye had been glutted with spectacle, rather as if one had eaten too many chocolates in the stalls, was reflected in several reviews. The *Daily Mail* (2 September), loud in praise, nevertheless said that 'for nearly three hours and a half our eyes were dazzled and overwhelmed'.

The phrase 'kaleidoscopic tableaux' was typical of several comments on Tree's production, which given its nature unsurprisingly evoked comparisons with optical shows and the still relatively new art of the cinema. In the initial press conference on *Henry VIII*, Parker told reporters that 'in this ceremony of the Coronation we will show you exactly what happened with the completeness of coloured cinematography.'[47] The fact that true colour film did not exist was one up for Tree. *The Times* (2 September) thought the production 'merely kinematographic', a 'polychromatic show'; the wise playgoer should 'let his mind drift along at the will of the showman'. The *Era* (3 September) concluded that 'it was not so much a drama as a moving panorama of the period', and the term 'moving-picture panorama' was used by *Vogue* (May 1916) in New York. The image of a historical peepshow was employed by the *People* (4 September 1910). Quite appropriately, then, Tree took his cast down to a studio in Ealing early in 1911 during the run of *Henry VIII* to make a five-scene film of his production for the Barker Motion Photography Company, with the scenes played exactly as they were on stage and the characters speaking their parts. The scenes were heavily cut, and the finished film, now lost, ran between twenty and twenty-five minutes. Tree himself was a strong supporter of cinema and especially keen to put Shakespeare on film; in 1917 he went to California to make a film of *Macbeth*, which was not a version of the 1911 production at His Majesty's.

Before the *Macbeth* film was made, *Henry VIII* had completed a highly successful American visit, opening at the New Amsterdam Theatre in New York on 14 March 1916, and running for eight weeks to crowded houses and a good profit. It then toured fifteen other eastern and mid-western cities, including Montreal and Toronto. It was a popular hit, but the American press was distinctly more critical than the English reviewers, and six years after the London production found Tree's scenic methods old-fashioned; unflattering comparisons with the new stagecraft were frequently made. By this time too the scenery was showing signs of wear, which did not escape the eyes of the sharper critics. One, indeed, condemned the production as 'the frumperies of a puppet stage', hitting Tree just where English critics thought him strongest with the sub-heading 'Pictorially His Production of "Henry VIII" Is a Worn Echo of Another Day.'[48]

General critical opinion of Tree's *Henry VIII* was favourable, both in England and America, and of particular interest is the way in which reviewers dealt with those questions of pageantry, pictorialism, historicity, and the relation of the text and the actor to spectacle that have been discussed elsewhere in this book, but here, even more than in the case of *Faust*, come to a valuable focus on a single production. The clamorous assault of those who usually condemned Tree for overwhelming Shakespeare with spectacle and rejected the spectacular method of production was not as loud this time, because there was broad agreement with Tree that *Henry VIII* had been written for pageantry, and that its very nature justified the taking of every opportunity for spectacular display. In this instance Shakespeare could not be subordinated to scenery and spectacle since there was nothing much of value in the play antagonistic to this treatment. As it was a poor play anyway – only Arthur Herbert in the *Dublin Daily Express* (20 February 1911) defended it – Tree's heavy cutting was not only excusable but laudable. Nobody was upset by the demolition of Acts IV and V. The overall view was that Tree had made a magnificent spectacle out of indifferent materials – 'this play of patches', as the *Daily Sketch* (2 September 1910) put it – and his arrangement of the text was held superior to Shakespeare's original.

The historical and educational value of the spectacle was stressed by many critics. *The Times* (2 September), which on the whole disliked the production for being too much 'a feast for the eye', grudgingly admitted that 'you have the historical *outside* of things quite faithfully presented.' Other reviewers praised the combination of history and visual splendour, and emphasised the merit of an instructive visualisation of an age. Such phrases as 'a succession of pictures from English history', 'a realization ... of the manners of an epoch', 'a splendid reincarnation ... of one of the most sumptuous ages of history', and 'a portfolio of Tudor views' can be culled at random from the reviews. The *Globe* (26 January 1911) summed up: 'We are shown Henry as one is certain he lived and loved, we are presented with pictures of his time that visualise for us the pages of history, and mark the production at His Majesty's as informative as it is entertaining.' Developing once again the still widely held principle of the illustrative ethic, the *Daily Mail* (2 September 1910) said, 'Never has any play of Shakespeare's been so sumptuously illustrated. The whole production is an edition de luxe of illustrated Shakespeare.' The *Standard* (2 September) noted that 'archaeology is correct as study and cultured imagination can make it, beauty of colour and movement, historical picturesqueness – all these appeal no less than the opulent spectacle.' *Outlook* (10 October) declared that 'each picture contains a wealth of minute detail that is in itself a liberal education in the customs and habits of the time.' The *Field* (10 September) elaborated the same idea:

> Such pictures are to be commended, not merely for their decorative and spectacular properties. They possess, also, a distinctly educational value, because of their historical accuracy, and because they are calculated to awaken the curiosity and the interest of the most superficial observer, whose knowledge of history is little more than surface deep.

An expert rather less than satisfied with Tree's production as a teaching device was G. Ambrose Lee, who wrote the aforementioned criticism in the *Tablet* of the very feature of the production upon which Macquoid, Parker, and Tree most prided themselves, archaeological accuracy. After detailed criticism of the ecclesiastical costumes and the Coronation scene, he concluded:[49]

> Those who look for some adequate measure of understanding and verisimilitude in representations of Catholic rites and ceremonies, put forward with most confident assurances of care and accuracy, will certainly find their just expectations unrealised ... while the close attention so successfully given to all the merely secular details disastrously emphasises the lack of similar care and knowledge as applied to the equally important ecclesiology.

The pictorial imagery of many of these critics is strikingly evident; the words 'picture' and 'pictures' frequently recur in descriptions of the production. They were, indeed, key elements of a theatre critic's vocabulary throughout our period. They were also extended to descriptions of the actor, and it was of course one of the aims of the serious nineteenth-century actor to compose his body in a continuous series of beautiful pictures. The creation of beauty was a vital principle in nineteenth-century theatre, and its visual realisation important for the actor as well as the scene painter. As we have seen with *Faust*, a pictorial acting style perfectly suited a pictorial production style, and it is hard to see what other method the actor could have adopted, given the fact that he was only one element in an elaborate and kinetic stage canvas.

It is not surprising, then, that Tree's performance as Wolsey was in part considered as picture-making, even though, as the *Star* (2 September) claimed in a comment that could serve as a critique upon the whole problem of acting in spectacle, 'there is no remarkable acting in this production. If there were the pageant would suffer.' Bourchier was considered from the pictorial point of view as well, with his realisation of Holbein's portrait, but the main focus of interest in this respect was Tree. The New York critics in particular were quick to comment on the virtues and defects of Tree's style, probably because they questioned the pictorial motivation of the production far more than did their English counterparts. The *Sun* (15 March 1916) noted that Tree played Wolsey 'with unfailing pictorial effect', marking the pictorial use of his cardinal's robe and 'the gestures with the flowing draperies of scarlet'. (It was not for nothing that there were so many yards of material in the robe.) With the *Nation* (23 March), Tree found favour only for his external and pictorial qualities: 'Pictorially, his embodiment was not unsuccessful – he is a clever actor, skilled in pose and gesture.' The *Nation*, however, objected to the performance as too restless, melodramatic, and pantomimic; in effect too emphatically theatrical. The *Evening Post* (15 March) came to similar conclusions. Tree's only fine moments were 'from the picturesque point of view'; otherwise he was too obviously a grimacing villain, too restlessly in motion, 'overdrawn, labored, self-conscious, and utterly theatrical and uninspired'. The *Toledo Blade* (20 March) commented significantly that 'whenever Shakespeare was silent, Tree got in his fine work'. A perceptive comment, because this was exactly Tree's style in Shakespeare, as Svengali in *Trilby*, and in other roles.

As can be seen from the promptbook of *Henry VIII* and the acting edition of *The Tempest*, to name only two sources, Tree was constantly inventing pantomimic business in order to illustrate Shakespeare; this was the actor's job as well as the scenery's, as he saw it. In order to play in spectacle at all and distinguish an individual part from the mass, the actor had to adopt a large, imposing, 'theatrical', and pictorial method. The deliberation and slowness of which critics accused Tree served several purposes. One was obviously to mark himself off in style, as star, from the rest of the company, and thus focus audience attention upon him as a very consequence of this difference. It is interesting that his leading actress, Violet Vanbrugh,

apparently did the same thing in the Trial scene and her death scene. It was
an old tradition, and something of a theatrical joke, that the nineteenth-
century star spoke more slowly than any other actor on stage, but it had its
basis in fact. Second, spectacle production was by nature unhurried and
leisurely in the unfolding: the rhythms of the leading actor must be in
harmony with the huge and deliberate rhythms of his own production. Tree
knew exactly what he was doing. If New York critics found him 'stagy' – a
word they used – they were quite right; he had to be. Some of his
interpolations and points of business were questionable at best, wrong-headed
and tasteless at worst – Tree never got very far from being an inventive and
sometimes lazy character actor – but his style had evolved in order to suit
performance conditions at his own theatre, and that was primarily a theatre of
pictorial pageantry and large-scale spectacle posing peculiar and difficult
problems for the actor. It would be unwise to reject Tree's solutions to these
problems.

    Henry VIII was given for the last time on 9 April 1911. It had been played
over eight months for 254 performances, and although still running to
excellent houses was taken off for a revival of *A Midsummer Night's Dream*
and the annual Shakespeare Festival.[50] Tree quickly tired of successes that
looked like settling in for long runs, and was always wanting to do something
new and different. However, he could hardly have afforded to take off *Henry
VIII* much earlier. We do not know the total number of spectators attending
the whole run, but 250,000 had seen it by the 168th performance, which
broke the record for a Shakespeare run at His Majesty's. Assuming little
diminution of business – and later in the run newspapers commented on how
good it was – this would mean a final total of about 375,000, far and away the
largest number ever to see a Tree Shakespeare, and probably the largest to see
the single run of any Shakespeare play. As far as can be ascertained, no other
production of Shakespeare had an uninterrupted run of 254 performances or
more in England. The nearest to *Henry VIII* was Irving's *Merchant of
Venice* in 1879–80 at 250.

    A run of 254 performances to near-capacity houses in a large theatre early
in this century meant a substantial profit, even for a production with such high
running and production costs as *Henry VIII*. Total box-office receipts were
£77,475, an average of about £306 a performance (one late matinée was
a free performance for children). The seating capacity of His Majesty's was
then 1,720, and because box-office seating capacity was £406,[51] this
represents an average box office of 75.4 per cent throughout the run. Bars
and programmes brought in an extra £2,222, souvenir books (*Henry VIII
and his Court*) £124, and opera glasses £119 – a total of £3,565. Both
audience and box-office percentages are extraordinary for eight months of an
allegedly mediocre Shakespeare play. The profit on *Henry VIII* was a tidy
£19,282, plus £793 for 'cinematographic rights' from the Barker Company.

Production and Preliminary, an account separate from that itemising the running costs of a production once it had opened, came to £7,204, far less than the £16,544 for Irving's *Henry VIII* eighteen years before.[52] The biggest single item, apart from Electricians' Wages and Materials, was Costumes (£2,756), not surprisingly, given the huge number used, the services of B. J. Simmons, and the price paid for fabric. (If the *Daily Mirror* (2 September 1910) is to be believed, Wolsey's robe of 'double-width specially woven silk' cost £1 a yard, with sixteen yards in the train alone. The King's shot-silk dress was £2 a yard, the Queen's specially woven silk underdress also £2 a yard.) Running costs amounted to £41,097. The size of the cast meant a high weekly wage bill after the first night. Tree said that 'there will be more people employed on stage in Henry VIII ... than in anything I have yet done',[53] and for three weeks in September 1910, the average weekly expenditure on wages was £1,110; for the 'artistes' – the category of performer above supers – it was £685. The seventy-five supers had a weekly wage bill of £59.

The three or four years before the outbreak of the Great War witnessed the final sybaritic glories of the spectacle stage. The apogee was reached, not in a production like Tree's *Henry VIII*, lavish though that was, but in the immense recreation of a Gothic cathedral in the vastness of Olympia offered by Max Reinhardt with the mime-play *The Miracle* in 1911. *The Miracle* was to *Henry VIII* as Belshazzar's feast to an Edwardian tea-party: production and running costs for eight weeks of £70,000, with £12,500 spent on costumes alone, a cast of 2,000, a choir of 500 voices, an orchestra of 200, 175 in the ballet, and enormously elaborate lighting installations.[54] To pursue the biblical analogy further, the writing was also on the wall. New concepts of theatre meant a sharp reaction against the spectacle style, and increasingly imperative economic considerations eventually made it prohibitively expensive.

As the Victorians and Edwardians knew it, the pictorial-spectacle style has disappeared from the dramatic stage. Superficially, there are signs of revival, as in the supremacy of the designer at the Glasgow Citizens' Theatre, the lavishness of recent productions by Planchon in Paris of *Pericles* and *Antony and Cleopatra* (traditional spectacle plays), and the richness of costume in such a production as the National Theatre *As You Like It* in 1979. However, there is every difference between the powerful but brief images of the modern stage, existing as they do in the context of a non-representational or selectively representational world, and the leisurely visual effects of a realistic scenic environment as complete and often as historically correct as its creators could make it. Victorian audiences were in no hurry, and quite content to sit with patience, interest, and enthusiasm through a procession requiring fifteen minutes of playing time or a pantomime transformation that took twenty minutes to unfold. They also accepted, as a necessary part of spectacular entertainment, the slow and massive rhythms of production, the long waits to allow for scenic display, the deliberate and expansive acting style of the major figures on the pictorial stage, itself perforce a highly pictorialised and leisurely style. The pace of production, the particular uses of mass, colour, light, and costume, the technique of the actor − all these elements of spectacle really have no parallel on the Western dramatic stage of today. The world of spectacle has gone, but in its time provided a rich visual feast the like of which the English stage had never known before and has never equalled since.

APPENDIX The costumes in *The Forty Thieves*, **Drury Lane, 1886**

The amount of precise information about costume that can be found in late nineteenth- and early twentieth-century theatre reviews is extraordinary, and contrasts sharply with the paucity of information of this kind available in the admittedly shorter reviews of today. The theatre historian of the next century will be hard put to reconstruct the costumes of any modern production by reading the press. He may have access to photographs and designs, but the former will tell him nothing about colour and the latter may not be helpful about fabric and texture. The modern reviewer is not very interested in what actors wear, or if he is does not think it worth space in his review. He also has little chance to see spectacle drama in which costumes are of crucial significance. His late Victorian or Edwardian counterpart was different, and his interest was not merely an aspect of the more generous review space generally available. Nor were costumes noticed only by lady journalists writing for a special section of the theatre public, although they were. Costumes were important to reviewers because they were an essential part of spectacle and archaeological recreation; they were important also because the theatre of this period coincided with a lavish, beautiful, and ostentatious mode of female dress, and like the theatre, critics were extremely fashion conscious. The detail of costumes was noticed in the same way other production details were noticed; reviews of this time are soaked in detail in a way they are not today, and again that is not just a matter of greater length. It was an age of great decorative and artistic detail, and this sense of detail is evident in theatre production as well as being reflected and faithfully reported in reviews.

Because all this is so we fortunately know a great deal about what costume looked like on the spectacle stage. The costumes of *The Forty Thieves* attracted so much attention that the *Era* published two special articles – it had already reviewed the play – on the subject under the heading 'The Dresses at Drury-Lane'. The first discusses the costumes of several scenes, especially the Cave scene. The second concentrates entirely on the costumes for the final pageant of the Jubilee; the pantomime was still running when it was printed.

For the light they cast on the richness and visual splendour of spectacle pantomime, they are reprinted here in full.

Era (8 January 1887):

As stated in our notice last week enormous expense has been incurred by Mr. Augustus Harris in the dressing of his pantomime *The Forty Thieves* at Drury-lane. The following particulars respecting some of the costumes will doubtless prove of interest to our readers :— Opening scene, Ballet of Almées and Houris, in four sets. Each costume consists of small Indian or Persian bodice, and trousers to correspond in satin, sleeves, loose bodice, and closely pleated skirts to the feet in gold-striped gauze, confined at the waist by silken sashes of a contrasting colour which tint is repeated in the head-dress accessories, jewelled crescents and gold coins. Colourings as follows: Bronze green costumes with pale aquamarine sashes. White dresses with gold sashes, deep cardinal, with delicate apricot and black, with an Algerian scarf of divers tints in stripes. Another set of dancers appears entirely in white silk gossamer draperies, with diamond tiaras and ornaments, and fringes of prismatic beads. The Forty Thieves in the Cave scene are clad in various Oriental styles of semi-military, semi-barbaric picturesqueness. They are armed with long Afghan guns, lances, scimitars, daggers, knives, &c. Their Captain Abdallah (Miss Blande) is clad entirely in heliotrope silk, embroidered in gold and gemmed with rubies; a drapery of heliotrope plush, lined with apricot colour and ornamented with a revers, richly embroidered in gold and rubies in a series of graduated crescents and stars. The Lieutenants are clad alike, but with a difference. Each costume is identical with its fellows in outward form, and also in that all alike wear white silk inner vests, embroidered in gold and silver, with boots, gloves, &c., to correspond. The colour of the headgear (adorned with two long bullion tassels in gold and silver), the jacket with pendant sleeves, and the sash and hose differ in each. Miss Dot Mario wears old gold; Miss Minnie Mario, deep peacock blue; Miss Marie Williams, delicate apple green; Mrs D'Auban, chestnut; and Mrs Inch, claret colour. As Ganem Miss Bruce appears in picturesque rags, blending many shades of deep and pale brown, Venetian red, and tawny orange. Later on a costume of pale electric grey throughout is donned, relieved with deep electric blue and rich ivory colour. Ganem's last dress is entirely in pale coral colour — tunic of plush, trimmed with silk pompons, sash and turban in broche Liberty silk, tights and aigrette to match; this costume is clasped here and there with clusters of brilliants. Miss Gilchrist's Morgiana makes her first entry in a costume which is a harmony in yellows. Vest and trousers in pale primrose silk, Zouave jacket and sash in sulphur, sash and turban in white and deep gold colour stripes, the jacket confined by a knot of pomegranate blossoms. Her second dress is very similar in form in white and salmon colour, the latter being exactly the shade of a species of flame-coloured

Azalea. The bodice is somewhat originally contrived to appear like a handkerchief knotted together at the bosom, in which a gardenia is worn, whilst another rests in the coils of her brown hair. Morgiana's fête dress consists of a bodice and peculiarly draped long full skirts of a sort of brocaded silk gauze in white, the latter weighted with small gold coins, which also reappear in the trimming of the small Zouave jacket of ruby velvet. The hips are encircled with a rich Algerian sash in white ruby and gold stripes, confined by a chased gold belt. The Persian trousers, which are scarcely revealed, are in red and gold shot silk. The Club Dress of the Forty Thieves is a species of modern 'masher' in Orientalised nineteenth century evening garb. The coats and tights are white; the inner garment, a 'combination' bodice in black velvet; centre stud, a large diamond crescent and star. Similar ornaments, but on a smaller scale, reappear on the black velvet cuffs. Abdallah and his lieutenants in this scene are similarly costumed, but entirely in black silk, with white striped satin vests. The coats have black velvet revers, adorned with graduated crescents and stars, the captains in brilliants, the lieutenants in gold. The waiters in this scene are attired in deep brown and gold, the vests striped; the pages very dark bottle-green and gold. The former have small belts on their shoulders. Waitresses, dispensing cigarettes, buttonholes, and perfumes, are daintily dressed in harmonies of réséda and turquoise, fawn and pale pink, and silver-grey and primrose. The cooks are entirely in white. The Bayadère ballet, which is supposed to be maintained by the 'New' Club, presents a mother-o'-pearl effect, with bodice and fringes entirely in iridescent beads of gold, silver, eau-de-nil, and pale rose, with gossamer sashes and draperies to match. It is very difficult to give a detailed description of the costumes in the great scene of the Cave, with its marching and countermarching and kaleidoscopic evolutions of hundreds of, doubtless, the most costly costumes ever seen on any stage. The most striking can alone be singled out for description. Each member of the Forty Thieves is followed by a retinue of twelve or upwards, whose dresses serve to repeat or intensify, either by harmony or contrast, those worn by their respective leaders. One set of costumes is entirely in white and gold, the draperies being in coral satin, showered with Persian devices in gold and pearls, and lined throughout with heliotrope plush. It should be said that the dresses of all the personages in this superb procession are supplemented by handsome draperies of the richest brocades furnished by the loom. Silk, satin, velvet, gold, and silver tissues are in turn employed separately and in combination, and all the emporiums of these rich stuffs have in turn been ransacked and exhausted for the selection of the most striking and characteristic patterns and materials. Mr. Harris, both in this scene and in that of the Jubilee, gave the designs *carte blanche*, and as the various designs (no inconsiderable number) have been handed in so they in turn have been as closely as possible reproduced in fabrics, armour, jewellery, and embroidery. A phalanx of dresses, which is always greatly admired, consists of silver grey silk costumes, richly embroidered with pearls. The ample cloak is in silvery grey plush, lined with rich primrose satin and bordered with swansdown pompons. The head-dresses consist of caps of pearls and satin, surmounted by a cockatoo-like crest of primrose-shaded white plumes. The captain of this little robber band is apparelled from head to foot in primrose colour, embroidered and fringed in pearls, the mantle being of the richest brocade in many shades of gold colour, primrose, and white, lined throughout with silver grey plush. A complete contrast to these may be found in a set of long sapphire velvet gowns, very deep in colour, richly embroidered in groups of quaint devices, such as in colour and form appear to so much advantage in Persian carpetings. A gold helmet, with aigrette of sapphire beads, and a mantle of gold brocade lined with sapphire satin further enriches these dresses. The draperies of another set of costumes are particularly *recherché* – in delicate sea-green plush, with a silvery sheen on it. On one side an exquisitely embroidered panel of lotus lilies in pale pink and white and bronze and gold-beaded leaves; these draperies are lined with the palest pink satin. A set of dresses in which terracotta and citron green velvet seem to struggle for prominence, subdued by silver bead embroidery, is striking; as is also a group in dull, pale lilac, showered with steel and gold, and draped with very pale turquoise, lined with deep violet velvet. Another fine effect is to be seen in a set of costumes in rich, soft brown, enriched with moonlight sequin pendants and bead trimmings, the draperies in a superb brocade, seal brown velvet on a pale electric blue ground, lined with shot blue and brown silk. There are three squadrons of armour dresses of a very fantastic and novel form, with bodices, sleeves, and long skirts in mail, and helmets, cuirasses, and other appointments in metal; one set, entirely in gold, wear crests of flamingo feathers and draperies of flamingo pink and gold brocade, lined with deep ruby plush, bordered with ruby silk and gold pompons. The second set, entirely in silver, wear draperies of brocade, the ground of which is deep ivory with scroll work in copper and olive; in the latter coloured plush lines these mantles. The third set appear in mail of alternate gold and silver linked pieces, and draperies of brocade (in which gold and silver almost efface a ground work of steel blue, lined with pale sky-blue plush). In this great procession Mrs D'Auban is superbly clad in white and gold throughout, cloak to correspond, lined with amethyst plush; Miss Dot Mario, in palest maize colour, with rich jewellery of topazes set in gold, small Persian helmet, with magnificent bird of Paradise plumes and splendid leopard-skin drapery, lined with fawn coloured plush; the very rich drapery is in pale apple green brocade strewn with cactus blossoms, appliqued in satin and gold beads; another in deep maize plush, with ornaments

in gold, bronze, and copper beads. In this big procession Miss Edith
Blande as Abdallah, Captain of the Thieves, is dressed entirely in black,
relieved with diamonds, diamond helmet, with rich aigrette of white osprey
feathers and ample mantle of gorgeous black and silver brocade, carried
train-wise by pages similarly apparelled. Her retinue consists of a regiment
of oriental military pages in gold and silver costumes, the close-fitting
bodice braided and beaded to correspond; gold and silver fringes also en-
circle this dress as well as the helmet, the former fringe terminating in
scarlet silk pompons, the silver in turquoise. A drapery of magnificent
arabesque brocade which more closely resembles the mural decorations of
the Moorish Alhambra than anything else completes this costume, and
each member of the group carries a damascened battleaxe. Another set of
dresses is entirely in silver chain mail, with diamond studded cuirasses and
helmets, draperies of silver brocade lined with deep sapphire plush.
Another set is in straw colour and golden brown with draperies of the
richest cream and gold brocade; contrasting with these are others in soft
pearl grey, sky blue and silver. A very handsome dress is worn by one of
the leaders, who is costumed entirely in réséda of a pale olive tone,
embroidered with gold and garnets – with this dress a drapery of rich brocade, in réséda and claret on a gold ground, lined with deep garnet plush.
In other groups may be noted effects of aquamarine beads on dull indigo
and gold brocade, outlining the pattern, the sparkle of gold and silver
spangled dresses, tight fitting, seen through the shimmer of bead net work
draperies of crimson and emerald respectively. A cameo-like effect is suggested in another group by pearl embroidery on deep fawn satin, contrasted with draperies of soft apricot brocade.

Era (26 March 1887):
Our readers have already been furnished with a detailed account of the
wondrously beautiful costumes introduced in the earlier scenes of the
Drury-lane pantomime *The Forty Thieves* and designed by the tasteful
and ingenious M. Wilhelm, who devoted to them many months of very
hard work. By the kindness of this gentleman, we are now able to satisfy
the curious with respect to the details of the extraordinary 'Jubilee scene',
the crowning glory of Mr. Augustus Harris's brilliant production as it was
presented on Boxing Night.

In the opening tableau of a ruined Indian temple, where the suttee is
prevented by civilisation, there is nothing remarkably noteworthy in the
costumes, save in the case of Mdlle. Aenea, the graceful flying dancer, who
impersonates the genius of civilisation. Her attire consists of flowing draperies of gold gauze, confined by bands of ivory satin, embroidered with a
pattern of olive and gold laurel leaves. A wreath of the same description
encircles her head, and soft white wings add to the illusion of her aerial

flights. The British rule having been inaugurated in India by a group of
Elizabethan merchant seamen planting the Cross of St. George, the scene
changes to the deck of a man-o'-war. Here Madame Lanner's clever little
pupils go through characteristic national dances. The English Jack tars appear entirely in white silk, with deep navy blue sailor collar and cuffs, and
large straw hat. The Scotch Highlanders in dark plaid (in which red pre-
dominates), Tam-o'-Shanters with eagle plumes, and carrying their circular metal-studded targes of leather and their quaintly hilted claymores,
escort Scotch fisher maidens of the 'caller herrin' ' type, carrying creels,
and wearing shepherds' plaid petticoats and three-cornered handkerchiefs
tied under the chin; tunics of red and black plaid turned up 'fish-wife'
fashion with red, short black velvet stay bodices, laced with red over a
white chemisette, and loose dull blue jackets. The Irish lads and lasses are
the next to put in an appearance, the former in stone grey corduroy coats
and breeches, with ribbed worsted stockings to match, dark green velvet
double-breasted waistcoats, orange silk neckties, grey felt hats, and the
latter in deep blue poplin petticoats, buff figured bodices, and scarlet silk
hooded cloaks. The Welsh girls are daintily apparelled in chestnut plush
bodices, brown and fawn striped velvet petticoats, flowered maize-colour
silk crossover kerchiefs, striped cream silk aprons, mittens to correspond,
market-baskets in their arms, and the national high hats. A change of
scene to the Temple of Fame reveals groups of vestals, in soft classical
dead-white draperies, whose choral apostrophe of England's fame melts
into the strains of the imposing march that ushers in the grand processional
entry of Great Britain and her Colonies. England leads the way. 'Jubilee'
heralds in white and gold and Royal purple precede trumpeters in black
velvet suits, with tabards emblazoned with the Royal arms, their trumpets
adorned with bannerets embroidered with the Royal crown and monogram
'V.R.' in scarlet, purple, and gold. Their hats are black velvet with flowing
white plumes. These trumpeters are followed by standard bearers, the
banners displaying the cross of St. George and the three Royal lions of
England. This latter device is repeated in gold on the cardinal satin tabards
of the standard bearers. Their epaulets are similar in colour, and are
decorated with the Tudor rose. Their hats are in Royal purple silk (to
match their court suits), surmounted by the English lion and crown in
gold. Then follows a regiment of yeomen of the guard, in costumes of the
familiar 'Beefeater' type adapted to the exigencies of the female figure, and
made entirely in the richest crimson satin, embroidered in gold and trimmed with black velvet. Tricolour ribbons adorn the black velvet hat and
form rosettes at the knees and on the shoes. A closely goffered white ruff
completes the dress. The yeomen carry picturesque steel halberds
damascened with gold, the poles being in gold-studded crimson velvet.
Four of their number carry canopy-wise an immense Royal Standard,

magnificently wrought in satin and gold, with most effectively appliqued devices, under which proudly walks Britannia, clad in rich white satin, the hem of the dress embroidered with gold anchors and palm branches alternately as a deep border. The skirt is drawn through a jewelled belt of sapphires and rubies. The bodice is confined by a cuirass of gold scales, and lions' head bosses secure on each shoulder a superb drapery of royal purple plush, showered with gold lions, bordered with a Greek key pattern, and lined with deep cardinal. The helmet is steel and gold, with cardinal plumes. The trident and Union Jack shield are of the conventional character. It should be added that the train of Britannia is carried by two little pages in white and gold, their tabards bearing the arms of the city of London. Britannia's attendants symbolise the rose, and are clad in soft white silk, embroidered across the corsage and around the border with detached conventional sprays of the Tudor rose and foliage in natural colours, accentuated with gold. A belt in deep crimson velvet and gold, sustaining a sword of justice similarly sheathed, and a rich drapery of soft rose-coloured silk, complete the dress. The classic sleeves are gemmed with rubies. The tiaras of gold and rubies consist of alternate crosses and fleur-de-lys, and their wands are gold surmounted by gold Tudor roses. Caledonia, preceded by Scotch pages in crimson court suits, and gold tabards with the red lion rampant thereon, and carrying banners (one with a similar device, the other the cross of St. Andrew) appear in classic robes of gold-coloured silk, the skirt bordered with silver thistles and crimson rampant lions alternately; a rich fringed drapery of silken plaid, white predominating, confined by a silver baldric set with cairngorms, and a silver morion on the head, with a tuft of heather on it; the auburn hair worn long and flowing. Her attendants, symbolising the thistle, wear amber silken robes embroidered with thistle sprays in glistening beads, and wear dark plaid draperies of rich dull purple and green, clasped with silver belt and ornaments studded with cairngorm stones. Hibernia's standard-bearers are clad in delicate apple green, with deep Irish blue tabards, one banner being the gold Irish harp, the other the cross of St. Patrick. Hibernia herself is robed in white silk embroidered with sprays of shamrocks in natural colouring. Her mantle is in delicate green satin showered with gold shamrocks and bordered by a quaint old Celtic pattern of interwoven devices in dull and bright gold. This is clasped by the Tara brooch. A diadem of emerald shamrocks set in gold, an emerald belt, and a wand surmounted by a Celtic cross, complete the equipment of Ireland's representative. Her attendants wear clinging robes of pale green, embroidered with gold shamrocks, and slightly opening at each side over an under skirt of deep blue. A baldric of gold and sapphires confines a flowing drapery of white silken gauze. Cambria follows next in pale sky blue, the skirt embroidered at the hem with alternate gold acorns and leaves and silver

Prince of Wales's plumes. A chased gold and silver belt clasps a rich drapery of white and gold brocade. Her wand is surmounted by a silver leek. The Welsh standard bearers wear white satin court suits and pale blue and silver tabards, with the triple white plumes and jewelled coronet. The banners repeat the latter device and the heraldic rouge dragon. Cambria's attendants wear classic robes of white, embroidered with sprays of acorn and leaves in bronze and gold, with fringe to correspond, draperies of pale sky blue and silver, wreaths of oak-leaves and acorns. These Welsh Druidesses carry silver harps surmounted by goats' heads. Malta, bearing aloft a gold key of office, is the next figure in the procession, represented in the black velvet robes of the Grand Master and a Portia-like cap to correspond. The attendant knights of Malta are in silver mail, with deep cardinal silk tunics reaching to the ankle, bearing the white Maltese cross on the breast. Hong Kong and the Straits Settlements are represented by single figures bearing their respective banners, the former in a richly embroidered silk Chinese robe, the latter in white jacket, figured silk turban and sash, brocaded skirt of red and gold, richly jewelled, pearl and gold necklets. The West Indies is portrayed by a female representative in a sort of Creole costume, skirt of striped turquoise silk and olive velvet, loose chemisette of white embroidered muslin and lace, a neckerchief of fringed apricot silk, embroidered with sprays of passion flowers. Gold and coral beads are twisted in the hair, and she carries a wand surmounted by a golden pine-apple. Her attendant banner-bearers are clad in an adaptation of the uniform of the band of the West Indian Regiment. Our important possessions in Africa are next represented by a group depicting Cape Colony, the leading figure clad in white draperies, with rich and massive Cape diamond ornaments, a tiara of diamonds with white ostrich plumes, a mantle of deep claret velvet, embroidered with gold antelopes, and carrying an arum lily wand. Her attendants are draped entirely in shot silk of pale coppery pink and steel colour, wearing baldrics of deep claret velvet, bearing the classic version of Good Hope, 'Spes Bona', in Cape diamond letters, supporting the Cape emblem, an anchor, in diamonds mounted in velvet. Each wears the hair coiled around a diamond arrow, and carries an antelope-headed wand. A troop of Zulus in picturesque native garb follow in the train of Cape Colony, brandishing their assegais and characteristic cowhide shields, their dusky skins showing off to great advantage their gaily beaded devices and fringes, their kilts of divers wild-beast tails, leopard-skin cloaks, uncurled ostrich plumes in their hair, necklets of teeth. Canada next engages the attention, clad in a robe of pale sky-blue plush, embroidered with silver lions and fleur-de-lys, wearing a rich mantle of white and silver brocade, deeply bordered with snow-white fur, and clasped with frosted-silver ornaments; a white fur cap in which a blue-plumaged bird is worn, and a silver harpoon is carried as a sceptre.

Canada's attendants are equipped in warm robes of plush to match their
leader, trimmed with white fur, and embroidered in chestnut and silver;
these dresses are draped over under-skirts of rich chestnut colour. The
Standard bearers carry beautifully embroidered banners of the various
states in the Dominion – the silver cod fish and thistles of Nova Scotia, the
bison of Manitoba, the golden maple leaves of Ontario, and the laurel
wreath of British Columbia amongst others. They are apparelled almost
entirely in white plush tunics, jelly-bag caps and hoods, bordered with
swansdown and trimmed with pale blue graduated stripes. These are
followed by a group representing the agricultural importance of Canada, a
trophy of wheat, maize, and apples being carried by bearers clad in tunics
and knee-breeches of réséda velvet, embroidered in North American
Indian devices in black, white, and flame colour. They also wear black fur
caps and leather belts, pouches, and high boots. Australia, preceded by a
detachment of the troops, whose juvenile representatives at Drury-lane
receive a cheer akin in heartiness to that which greeted the famous contingent in the Soudan, is followed by attendants who, in their deep violet
robes, embroidered in golden wheat ears and gold draperies, bordered with
vine leaves and purple grapes, typify the Australian vintage and harvest.
Australia herself is clad in classic garb of pale green, embroidered with
golden fern leaves and bordered with stars. A richly wrought belt of gold
emblazoned with the motto 'Advance Australia', and supporting a pendant
'Golden Fleece', maintains a superb mantle of rich gold brocade, lined
with deep golden brown plush. Australia's head-dress is the lyre bird, and
she carries as sceptre the caduceus of commerce, surmounted by the con-
stellation of the Southern Cross in diamonds. The resources of Australia
are further exemplified by a quartette of little miners in red shirts, buff
breeches, black felt hats, and high boots, bearing aloft a golden nugget,
and also by a party of pioneers in brown and grey, with sheep-skins slung
on their backs, and carrying picks, spades, and axes. The various banners
of the Australian colonies, Victoria, Queensland, New South Wales, &c.,
are massed picturesquely, their bearers being clad alike in fanciful costumes adapted from the beautiful emu egg ornaments. Their bodices, &c.
are in deep, dull bottle-green plush, richly trimmed with silver
embroidered fern-leaves, and their caps of plush are surmounted by silver
kangaroos. The group representing New Zealand is composed chiefly of
Maories, in white robes quaintly embroidered in scarlet and dull blue,
some wearing capes of straw, others mantles of fur. All wear the characteristic short plumes of black tipped with white in their luxuriant blue-
black tresses, they wear idol ornaments of greenstone suspended from
necklets, and carry curiously carved clubs decked with feathers. New Zealand herself is costumed entirely in pale pink, the mantle of plush
showered with silver stars. The most imposing phalanx of figures in the

Jubilee colonial procession represents the Indian Empire, headed by Burmah, who bears aloft the banner of pale crimson and gold, with the silvery white elephant depicted thereon. The Burmese are clad in national costumes, with the typical lofty pinnacle-shaped gilt metal head-dresses. The colours are pale rose pink showered with gold and silver — gemmed with rubies — contrasted with copper-brown. These Burmese dancers wear ruby girdles, and carry palm leaf-shaped fans in gilt metal. Burmah is followed by Ceylon, bearing aloft a huge ivory tusk. All the costumes in the group are clad in the sacred colour of Buddha — yellow, contrasted with ivory white — and with sapphire and pearl ornaments. The attendants wear the quaint headgear peculiar to the priests of Kandy. Next in the procession follow Hindoos in characteristic costumes — some part of their draperies being in crimson and black and orange figured stuffs, showered with morsels of looking-glass — carrying the banners of various native states, with their odd crests and devices. These are followed by a detachment of young Indian pages of rank, costumed in white brocade, turbans to correspond, richly jewelled belts and aigrettes; their sashes are in purple and pale green and scarlet brocade, and they carry fans and other insignia. India herself follows in a superb drapery of costly red and gold brocade, originally on exhibition in the Hyderabad court of the Colonial Exhibition. Her corsage and tiara are a blaze of jewels. From the latter a veil of white and gold gossamer falls around the figure, in one hand she carries a fan of Argus pheasant feathers, in the other an Indian battle-axe sceptre. Her attendants accentuate the colouring and effect of her dress in vermillion draperies embroidered with gold Indian pine patterns and 'saris' of indigo blue, partly veiling the face, which is framed in gold and pendant pearls. India is preceded by the banner of the 'star of India' in turquoise blue with device in gold and silver and the motto 'Heaven's light our Guide', carried by an attendant clad entirely in silver, with mantle of tiger skin. Following on India come an escort of native guards in steel armour — plate and chain — the former handsomely damascened in black and gold, carrying long lances and circular bossed shields. In attendance on India come the ballet, two groups of which represent the Punjab pottery and the Benares brass ware respectively. The former costumes are entirely in cerulean blue, relieved with emblematic devices in deep ultramarine and white. Each member of these groups carries a different jar or plaque, full of character in colour, form, and decoration. The porcelain vases are most skilful imitations of the original types, and the Benares brass ware reproductions are most costly. All these are on a very large and effective scale. The bearers of the latter are entirely in brass coloured satin, with appliqued and pendant ornaments in gold metal. The third group in the ballet harmonises the other two, and represents a party of nautch dancers, who, in their turn, typify the lotus lily, which, with its delicate coral flower and bronze foliage, each one carries, the water of the Ganges apparently dripping from its leaves and stems as if just plucked. The nautch dancers' costumes are white silk gauze draperies and long pleated skirts, showered with tiny gold coins, which ornaments, mingled with pearls, appear in their flowing hair and on their pale amber bodices and delicate turquoise sashes. Madame Zanfretta, the principal dancer in this group, wears a wonderful scarf of beetle wing and gold embroidery. The close of the scene brings a final effect of numerous coryphées attired in silver cuirasses and white classic draperies as the army of fame. Their heads are wreathed with gold laurel, they carry in one hand a palm branch of gold and in the other a magnificent banner of white satin, embroidered in gold with Royal monogram 'V.R.' encircled with laurel and surmounted by the Imperial Crown.

A note on bibliography

Nineteenth-century theatre production is an area that has attracted little scholarly attention; there are few recent works relating to it and no book on spectacle production. However, since it is necessary to know how the nineteenth-century stage worked in order to understand spectacle properly, several studies are important. Terence Rees, *Theatre Lighting in the Age of Gas* (Society for Theatre Research, 1978), provides a detailed examination of the development of gaslight, limelight, the carbon arc, and early electric stage and auditorium lighting, as well as discussing the various types of lighting instruments and the duties of the gasman. It is well illustrated, and easy for the layman to follow. *French Theatrical Production in the Nineteenth Century*, trans. Allan S. Jackson with M. Glen Wilson (New York, Max Reinhardt Foundation, 1976), is a translation of M. J. Moynet, *L'Envers du théatre* (Paris, Hachette, 1873), augmented by illustrations from other contemporary works. Moynet spends a great deal of time on the exact mechanics of spectacle production, and is particularly illuminating on stage machinery. Although Paris was not London, many French methods were in use on the English stage. English writers published almost nothing about such technical matters in book form, but there is valuable information in Percy Fitzgerald, *The World behind the Scenes* (Chatto & Windus, 1881), especially on traps, special effects, and the pantomime transformation scene. The most accessible account of how the theatre stage was constructed and functioned is 'The English wood stage', in Edwin O. Sachs and Ernest A. E. Woodward, *Modern Opera Houses and Theatres* (Batsford, 1896–8, repr. 1968, I, 9–14), a technical and highly informative summary. A simpler description of the same kind of stage aimed at the general reader can be found in an article, 'A new stage stride', in *All the Year Round* (31 October 1863, pp. 229–34), which concerns Charles Fechter's reconstruction of the Lyceum stage when he assumed the management. *All the Year Round* may not be very easy to locate; still in print is my own edition of the fifth volume (1976) of *English Plays of the Nineteenth Century* (Clarendon Press), which has an appendix, 'Pantomime Production, Rehearsal, and Performance', containing primary material that will amplify chapter 3. More contextual, but of the greatest relevance to chapter 1, is Richard Altick, *The Shows of London* (Harvard University Press, 1978), with much material on optical exhibitions, panoramas, and dioramas. Among the topics considered in John Stokes, *Resistible Theatres* (Elek, 1972), are the aesthetic and archaeological ideas of E. W. Godwin and the theatrical experiments of Hubert von Herkomer.

A fairly wide range of primary sources is indicated in the references for each chapter. Newspaper and periodical journals of course offer an immense amount of first-hand evidence of spectacle production; especially important in the periodical category are the *Era*, the *Stage*, the *Illustrated Sporting and Dramatic News*, the *Illustrated London News* and the *Theatre*. *Play Pictorial* and the *Playgoer and Society Illustrated* are largely picture magazines, but for that very reason valuable for visual evidence of Edwardian spectacles. Not as widely known, but often useful for descriptions of construction, alterations and redecoration in theatre buildings are the *Builder* and the *Building News*. There is real theatrical treasure trove in the *Scientific American* and the *Scientific American Supplement*, which frequently supply precise descriptions, sometimes with illustrations, of new lighting techniques, new stage machinery, and new special effects. Many reviews have been gathered in collections. The most helpful for the purposes of this book have been Henry Morley, *Journal of a London Playgoer* (Routledge, 1866, repr. 1974); Dutton Cook, *Nights at the Play* (Chatto & Windus, 1883, repr. 1971); and Joseph Knight, *Theatrical Notes* (Lawrence & Bullen, 1893, repr. 1971). Some reviews in *Victorian Dramatic Criticism*, ed. George Rowell (Methuen, 1971), are about production. Of the periodicals of the present day, *Theatre Notebook* and *Nineteenth Century Theatre Research* pay most attention to the nineteenth-century English stage.

Among other works cited, several are worth frequent consultation. J. W. Cole, *The Life and Theatrical Times of Charles Kean* (Bentley, 1859), although greatly prejudiced toward Kean, has still not been superseded as the principal record of his Shakespeare productions and views on theatre. Percy Fitzgerald, *Principles of Comedy and Dramatic Effect* (Tinsley, 1870), contains a thoughtful examination of the practice of realism in the theatre. Fitzgerald has the advantage over almost every nineteenth-century writer on theatre of being very specific when he is talking about production – a blessing for which modern scholars can only give thanks. Similarly specific when it gets round to production is Bram Stoker, *Personal Reminiscences of Henry Irving* (Heinemann, 1906 (2 vols), 1907 (revised, 1 vol.). Of the many books about Irving, this is perhaps the most informative on production methods at the Lyceum.

Notes

Chapter 1   The taste for spectacle

1 *Essays on the Drama* (Parker, 1858), p. 206.
2 J. W. Cole, *The Life and Theatrical Times of Charles Kean*, 2nd ed. (1859), II, p. 26.
3 *Report from the Select Committee on Theatrical Licences and Regulations* (1866), p. 136.
4 *Saturday Review*, 8 April 1899.
5 'London in January', *Blackwood's Edinburgh Magazine*, cxxxix (February 1886), p. 263.
6 *Principles of Comedy and Dramatic Effect* (Tinsley, 1870), p. 15.
7 For the uses of the magic lantern in the theatre, see Terence Rees, *Theatre Lighting in the Age of Gas* (1978), pp. 81–3.
8 Richard D. Altick, *The Shows of London* (1978), p. 176. My debt to this book in treating of the optical and pictorial nature of the new kinds of public entertainment in the early nineteenth century is considerable.
9 From his 1892 lecture, 'Scenic art', quoted in John Stokes, *Resistible Theatres* (1972), p. 90.
10 Ibid., p. 87.
11 Quoted in *The Golden Age of Melodrama*, ed. Michael Kilgarriff (Wolfe, 1974), pp. 87–8.
12 Louis N. Parker, *Several of My Lives* (Chapman & Hall, 1928), p. 245. For *Joseph and his Brethren* Parker had used as source material Tissot's illustrations to the Old Testament and models of furniture and accessories in the Metropolitan Museum.
13 'The drama', *Blackwood's Edinburgh Magazine*, lxxxix (January–June 1856), pp. 220, 226–7.
14 G. H. Martin and David Francis, 'The camera's eye', *The Victorian City*, ed. H. J. Dyos and Michael Wolff (Routledge & Kegan Paul, 1973), I, pp. 227–46.
15 *Treasure Trove*, 29 October 1900.
16 Fitzgerald, op. cit., p. 12.
17 Squire and Marie Bancroft, *Mr. and Mrs. Bancroft On and Off the Stage*, 4th ed. (Bentley, 1888), II, p. 308.
18 'Stage furnishing', *Stage* (25 January 1884). Even earlier, in 1876, the *Daily*

Telegraph (13 March), in noting the complete realism of stage interiors in a revival of Palgrave Simpson's *A Scrap of Paper* at the Court, nevertheless thought that 'they are not pictures of houses in which we dwell, but tantalising representations of the rooms we should like to possess.' The element of wish fulfilment may have been a strong one in the more sumptuous kinds of domestic stage realism.

19 *Journal of the Society of Arts*, xxxv (March 1887), p. 465.
20 Fitzgerald, op. cit., pp. 28–38.
21 T. F. T. Dyer, 'Foresters at home', *Art Journal* (October 1885), p. 301.
22 'Stage science', *Saturday Review*, 8 October 1887.
23 *Dramatic Review*, 26 December 1885.
24 *Umpire*, 25 September 1887.
25 Roy Strong, *And When Did You Last See Your Father?* (Thames & Hudson, 1978), p. 160.
26 J. R. Planché, *Recollections and Reflections*, 2nd ed. (Low, 1901), p. 170. The ladies of the court of Charles II also formed the subject of two contemporary paintings, by John Joseph Barker (1835) and Thomas James Barker (1847).
27 See Altick, op. cit., pp. 342–9.
28 Cole, op. cit., II, pp. 57–9.
29 *Western Daily Press*, 11 October 1864, quoted in Stokes, op. cit., p. 37.
30 *Dramatic Review*, 8 February 1885.
31 *Gaiety Chronicles* (Constable, 1898), p. 110.
32 *Nights at the Play* (Chatto, 1883), pp. 251–3. Spectacle had actually invaded comedy rather earlier than this, in the finished and elegant productions of Madame Vestris at the Olympic in the 1830s.
33 Bancrofts, op. cit., I, p. 418.
34 Archibald Chasemore, 'About stage costume', *Theatre* (October 1896), p. 188.
35 See Rees, op. cit., pp. 150–5 and 209–10.
36 C. Wilhelm, 'Art in the ballet', *Magazine of Art* (1895), pp. 50–1.
37 Donne, op. cit., pp. 77–8.
38 'The limitations of scenery', *Magazine of Art* (1896), p. 432.
39 'After the Play', *New Review*, I (June 1889), pp. 34–5.
40 *Saturday Review*, 20 January 1900.
41 Lyman Weeks, 'Scenic art in Mr. Irving's "Faust"', *The Dramatic Year*, ed. Edward Fuller (Low, 1888), p. 43.

Chapter 2   Shakespeare

1 'Mr Pearson on the modern drama', *Nineteenth Century*, xxxiv (October 1893), p. 545.
2 'The living Shakespeare: a defence of modern taste', [1901], *Thoughts and After-Thoughts*, 3rd ed. (Cassell, 1915), pp. 60–1.
3 Lady Pollock, *Macready as I Knew Him*, 2nd ed. (Remington, 1885), pp. 83–4.
4 *Leader*, 14 February 1852.
5 Tree, op. cit., p. 56.

6 *About the Theatre* (Unwin, 1886), pp. 243–4.

7 See Jan McDonald, '*The Taming of the Shrew* at the Haymarket Theatre, 1844 and 1847', *Nineteenth Century British Theatre*, ed. Kenneth Richards and Peter Thomson (Methuen, 1971), pp. 157–70.

8 'Our omnibus-box', *Theatre* (December 1884), p. 310.

9 *Shakespeare and the Modern Stage* (Murray, 1906), p. 6. Lee believed, in fact, that the fewer the number of supers by whom the necessary illusion was produced, the greater the merit of the performance and the greater the skill of the stage manager.

10 'Shakespeare and modern staging', *Saturday Review*, 13 August 1910.

11 On the subject of fairy painting, see Jeremy Maas, *Victorian Painters* (Barrie & Jenkins, 1969, repr. 1974), pp. 147–62, and Beatrice Phillpots, *Fairy Paintings* (Ash & Grant, 1978). I am particularly indebted to the latter.

12 See also Richard Foulkes, 'Samuel Phelps's *A Midsummer Night's Dream*, Sadler's Wells – October 8th, 1853', *Theatre Notebook*, xxiii (Winter 1968–9), pp. 55–60.

13 J. W. Cole, *The Life and Theatrical Times of Charles Kean*, 2nd ed. (1859), II, pp. 196–7.

14 *The Diaries of William Charles Macready*, ed. William Toynbee (Chapman & Hall, 1912), II, p. 18.

15 Quoted in Frederic Daly, *Henry Irving in England and America: 1883–84* (Unwin, 1884), p. 192.

16 Squire and Marie Bancroft, *Mr. and Mrs. Bancroft On and Off the Stage*, 4th ed. (Bentley, 1888), II, pp. 16–17.

17 *The Story of My Life*, 2nd ed. (Hutchinson, 1908), p. 106.

18 Bancrofts, op. cit., II, p. 22.

19 *Daily Telegraph*, 19 April 1875.

20 *Henry Irving* (Chapman, 1893), p. 185. The 'feast in the Louvre' is 'The Marriage at Cana'.

21 'Archaeology in the theatre', *Macmillan's Magazine*, liv (June 1886), pp. 126–34.

22 Quoted in George C. D. Odell, *Shakespeare from Betterton to Irving* (1920, repr., Constable, 1963), II, p. 164.

23 *Recollections and Reflections*, 2nd ed. (Low, 1901), p. 38.

24 Alan S. Downer, *The Eminent Tragedian* (Oxford University Press, 1966), p. 235.

25 A. H. Saxon, *Enter Foot and Horse* (Yale University Press, 1968), p. 157.

26 Cole, op. cit., II, p. 104.

27 Lewis Wingfield, 'Costume-designing', *Magazine of Art* (1894), pp. 406–7.

28 Seymour Lucas, 'The art of dressing an historical play', ibid., pp. 278–9.

29 M. H. Spielman, 'A Shakespearean Revival: "Macbeth" ', *Magazine of Art* (1889), pp. 98–9; *Pall Mall Budget* (3 January 1889). In view of Irving's careful working out of the relationship between his own stage-dominating costume and the lighting of *Faust* three years earlier, it is interesting to know that in the last act of *Macbeth* 'the golden armour of the now desperate king is in strong relief against the sadder hues' (p. 99).

30 I am indebted for much of this information to Sybil Rosenfeld, 'Alma-Tadema's designs for Henry Irving's *Coriolanus*', *Shakespeare Jahrbuch* (Heidelberg, 1974), pp. 84–95; see also Bram Stoker, *Personal Reminiscences of Henry Irving*, 2nd ed. (1907), pp. 284–6.

31 *Shakespeare in the Theatre* (Sidgwick & Jackson, 1913), pp. 120–1.

32 Cole, op. cit., II, pp. 216–17.

33 Clement Scott, *The Drama of Yesterday and To-Day* (1899), I, pp. 289–90. Kean had the bells specially cast, perhaps the first made for an English theatre.

34 *Shakespeare's Play of The Merchant of Venice* (Chapman, 1858).

35 *Macready's Reminiscences*, ed. Sir Frederick Pollock (Macmillan, 1875), II, p. 446.

36 Cole, op. cit., II, p. 379.

37 *Henry VIII and his Court* (Cassell, 1910), p. 104.

38 See Richard Foulkes, 'Samuel Phelps's *Pericles* and Layard's discoveries at Nineveh', *Nineteenth Century Theatre Research*, 5 (autumn 1977), pp. 85–92.

39 *Examiner*, 21 October 1838.

40 'Our play-box', *Theatre* (April 1882), pp. 235–6.

41 *Dramatic Notes* (1883), p. 51.

42 'Our play-box', *Theatre* (February 1892), p. 105.

43 'Our omnibus-box', *Theatre* (December 1884), p. 310.

44 *An Actor's Life* (W. Scott, 1902), p. 317. In 1890 at the Princess's, Wingfield included Cleopatra's barge, an Alexandrian Festival with an 'Interlude representing the conflict between Day and Night', and a triumphal reception for Antony after his victory.

45 See Russell Jackson, 'Shakespeare in Liverpool: Edward Saker's revivals, 1876–81', *Theatre Notebook*, xxxii, no. 3 (1978), pp. 100–9.

46 'Our omnibus-box', *Theatre* (April 1887), pp. 230–1.

47 'Plays of the month', *Theatre* (March 1894), p. 152.

48 Russell Jackson, 'The Shakespeare productions of Lewis Wingfield', *Theatre Notebook*, xxxi, no. 1 (1977), p. 30.

Chapter 3   Melodrama and pantomime

1 'Remarks', *The Woodman's Hut* (1818).

2 *The World behind the Scenes* (Chatto, 1881), pp. 52–3. In the same section of this book Fitzgerald explains the workings of stage thunder, lightning, rain, wind, ice-floes, rivers, waves, and waterfalls.

3 See my 'Irish landscape in the Victorian theatre', *Place, Personality and the Irish Writer*, ed. Andrew Carpenter (Gerrards Cross, C. Smythe, 1977), pp. 159–72.

4 *Morning Advertiser*, 7 December 1883.

5 Ibid.

6 E. W. Godwin, *'Claudian': a Few Notes on the Architecture and Costume* (1883), p. 3.

7 'Theatrical trades: no. V – Boots and shoes', *Stage*, 16 November 1885.

8 For spectacle melodrama at the Standard, see the brief accounts in Albert Douglass, *Memories of Mummers and the Old Standard Theatre* (*Era*, n.d.), pp. 88–92, and A. E. Wilson, *East End Entertainment* (Barker, 1954), pp. 124 ff.

9 'The National Theatre', *Fortnightly Review*, xxxviii (November 1885), p. 635.

10 'Our omnibus-box', *Theatre* (May 1882), p. 314.

11 *Nights at the Play* (Chatto, 1883), p. 466.

12 *Illustrated Sporting and Dramatic News*, 8 August 1881.

13 Cook, op. cit., p. 466.

14 *Illustrated Sporting and Dramatic News*, 13 October 1888.

15 *Illustrated London News*, 19 September 1885.

16 *Dramatic Criticism* (Long, 1899), p. 105.

17 'Our play-box', *Theatre* (September 1882), p. 184.

18 *Recollections and Reflections*, 2nd ed. (Low, 1901), p. 196.

19 A. W. Bean, 'Artistic stage interiors', *Theatre* (July 1891), pp. 19–20.

20 *From Studio to Stage*, 2nd ed. (John Lane, the Bodley Head, 1913), pp. 286–8.

21 'My first Drury Lane pantomime', *Old Drury Lane Christmas Annual* (1882–3), p. 5.

22 Joseph Hatton, *Cigarette Papers* (Hutchinson, 1892), p. 61. To accommodate this procession an archway was made in the back wall of the theatre into the adjacent scenery store, and the depth of the stage thereby doubled.

23 *Illustrated Sporting and Dramatic News*, 2 January 1881. It is not surprising that Harris worked himself to death at the age of forty-four.

24 'The hive of pantomime', *Theatre* (January 1880), p. 15. For further material on Victorian pantomime generally, see the Introduction to vol. V of my *English Plays of the Nineteenth Century* (Oxford University Press, 1976), pp. 42–63, and the Appendix on 'Pantomime Production, Rehearsal, and Performance' in the same volume, pp. 485–518.

25 *Daily News*, 31 August 1872.

26 *Daily Telegraph*, 30 August 1872. This scene was directed by Alfred Thompson, the costume designer.

27 Fitzgerald, op. cit., p. 109.

28 I am indebted for most of this information to Professor Theodore Cloak, who has in his possession a copy of the unpublished journal of Charles Stevenson, Boucicault's secretary at the time of *Babil and Bijou*.

29 The workings of the *parallèle* are explained in M. J. Moynet, *L'Envers du théatre* (1873), pp. 100–2, a book translated, enlarged, and given extra illustrations by M. Glen Wilson and Allan S. Jackson as *French Theatrical Production in the Nineteenth Century* (1976).

30 Fitzgerald, op. cit., pp. 89–90.

31 *Illustrated London News*, 2 January 1886.

32 Douglass, op. cit., pp. 29–30.

33 'Theatrical trades: no. IX – Limelight', *Stage*, 21 December 1883.

34 C. Wilhelm, 'Art in the ballet II', *Magazine of Art* (1895), p. 53.

35 *Illustrated London News*, 2 January 1886.

36 *Saturday Review*, 1 January 1898.

37 See B. R. Mitchell, *Abstract of British Historical Statistics* (1962); A. J. Bowley, *Wages in the United Kingdom in the Nineteenth Century* (1900) and *Wages and Income Since 1860* (1937); Phyllis Deane and W. A. Cole, *British Economic Growth: 1688–1959* (Cambridge University Press, 1962); William Ashworth, *An Economic History of England: 1870–1939* (Methuen, 1960).

38 C. H. d'E. Leppington, 'The Gibeonites of the stage', *National Review*, xvii (April 1891), pp. 245–61, and Charles Booth, *Life and Labour of the People in London*, Second Series: Industry (1902–4), IV, pp. 123–37.

39 'Illustrated interviews: no. VI – Sir Augustus Harris', *Strand Magazine*, II (December 1891), p. 561.

40 John Doran, *In and About Drury Lane* (Bentley, 1881), I, p. 3.

41 Leopold Wagner, *The Pantomimes and All About Them* (Heywood, n.d.)[1881], p. 32.

42 A. G. Bowie, 'Some notes on pantomime', *Theatre* (January 1882), p. 27. The total production and running costs of Augustus Harris Senior's most lavish pantomime, a *Robinson Crusoe* at Covent Garden in 1868, were £16,000.

43 Ibid.

44 See the diary entries relating to several pantomimes of the eighties in *The Life and Reminiscences of E. L. Blanchard*, ed. Clement Scott and Cecil Howard (Hutchinson, 1891), 2 vols. Blanchard wrote the scripts for Harris's pantomimes until his death in 1889.

45 Hatton, op. cit., p. 60, and 'Illustrated interviews: no. VI', p. 561.

46 See the *Builder* (18 September 1897, 17 December 1898, 4 July 1908), and the *Building News* (30 September 1898). In the five years after Harris's death in 1896, Arthur Collins spent between £40,000 and £50,000 on improvements to Drury Lane.

47 The text of *The Sleeping Beauty and the Beast* is printed in vol. V of my *English Plays of the Nineteenth Century*.

48 The Drury Lane 'Beauty's Awakening' tableaux must have at least owed something to the *Beauty's Awakening* staged by the Art Workers' Guild at the Guildhall in June 1899. This was a masque of Winter and Spring, highly allegorical in nature, and was designed by several artists, including Walter Crane, who chaired the design committee. It contained dances by the Forest Leaves (in four different colours) and by the Four Winds. Its chief objective was to produce 'an allegory of the Beautiful', and it was not concerned with the fairytale story.

49 *Sunday Times*, 30 December 1900.

Chapter 4   Henry Irving's *Faust*

1 'The state of the London theatres', *Saturday Review*, 2 July 1887.

2 See the *Builder*, 14 January 1882, and *Building News*, 11 September 1885. The alterations and redecorations of 1885 cost £2,632.

3 'Irving as stage manager', *We Saw Him Act*, ed. H. A. Saintsbury and Cecil Palmer (Hurst & Blackett, 1939; repr. 1969), p. 3.

4 *The World behind the Scenes* (Chatto, 1881), p. 42.

5 *Personal Reminiscences of Henry Irving*, 2nd ed. (Heinemann, 1907), p. 423.

6 For definitions and a discussion of the construction and use of each of these lighting devices, see Bram Stoker, 'Irving and stage lighting', *Nineteenth Century*, lxix (May 1911), pp. 903–12, and Terence Rees, *Theatre Lighting in the Age of Gas* (1978), pp. 20–41. See also Alan Hughes, 'Henry Irving's artistic use of stage lighting', *Theatre Notebook*, xxxiii, no. 3 (1979), pp. 100–9.

7 *Pall Mall Gazette*, 13 September 1887. In an answer to an enquiry on this very point, dated 20 January 1887, Irving put this figure at 'more than 400'. For *The Corsican Brothers* and *Romeo and Juliet* 'there are more than 500' (Irving Papers, 1887 file).

8 Stephen Fiske, 'The Irving influence in America', *Theatre* (February 1896), p. 77.

9 Fitzgerald, op. cit., p. 49.

10 'The Lyceum staff: a Victorian theatrical organization', *Theatre Notebook*, xxviii, no. 1 (1974), pp. 15–16. Apart from the light it casts on Irving as manager, the article is a valuable account of the ways in which a large Victorian theatre was staffed and operated.

11 Fitzgerald, op. cit., pp. 50–1.

12 'Irving and stage lighting', p. 912.

13 *Pall Mall Gazette*, 13 September 1886. In the same interview Irving said that 'as far as possible I do everything myself', which included archaeological study.

14 Ibid.

15 *Henry Irving, Actor and Manager*, (Field & Tuer, n.d.) [1883], pp. 96–8.

16 Lyman H. Weeks, 'Scenic art in Mr. Irving's "Faust" ', *The Dramatic Year*, ed. Edward Fuller (Low, 1888), p. 45.

17 'Pictorial successes of Mr. Irving's "Faust" ', *Century Magazine*, xxxv (December 1887), p. 309.

18 *The Lyceum 'Faust'* (Virtue, 1886), p. 20. This souvenir-book was revised when the Witch's Kitchen scene was added to the production.

19 *The Times*, 30 December 1885.

20 *Pall Mall Gazette*, 13 September 1886.

21 *Catalogue of the Valuable Library of Sir Henry Irving, Deceased* (1905).

22 Hatton, op. cit., p. 10.

23 *The Days We Knew* (Laurie, 1943), p. 99.

24 'Our omnibus-box', *Theatre* (October 1883), p. 223.

25 *Dare to be Wise*, n.d. [Hodder & Stoughton, 1925], p. 64.

26 Edward Gordon Craig, *Index to the Story of my Days* (Hilton, 1957), p. 67.

27 Pennells, op. cit., p. 309.

28 'Theatrical mechanism at the Lyceum Theatre', *Engineer*, 2 April 1886.

29 Pennells, op. cit., p. 309.

30 Manchester *Courier*, 20 September 1887.

31 *The Times*, 30 December 1885.

32 Weeks, op. cit., p. 47.

33 A comic kitchen scene in which imps and demons prepared potables and edibles and in which a major culinary accident occurred was a common feature of Victorian pantomime.

34 *New York Tribune*, 19 November 1887.
35 *Engineer*, 2 April 1886. Loveday said that much of the Witch's Kitchen scenery was sunk.
36 Weeks, op. cit., p. 44.
37 'On scenic illusion and stage appliances', *Journal of the Society of Arts*, xxxv, 18 March 1887, p. 460.
38 Pennells, op. cit., pp. 309–10.
39 *Daily Telegraph*, 21 December 1885.
40 *Shakespearean Representation* (1908), p. 106.
41 *Liverpool Mercury*, 4 October 1887.
42 Liverpool *Daily Post*, 10 October 1887.
43 In both *Henry VIII* (1892) and *Dante* (1903), Irving also wore costumes of a dominating shade of red.
44 Weeks, op. cit., p. 51. Henry James, however, a fastidious critic and a dissenting voice on *Faust*, thought the scene with the jewels 'obstreperous, and not in the least poetic in tone'. He found Ellen Terry generally 'much too rough and ready' ('The acting in Mr. Irving's "Faust" ', *Century Magazine*, xxxv (December 1887), p. 312).
45 *The Story of My Life*, 2nd ed. (Hutchinson, 1908), p. 240.
46 Hatton, op. cit., p. 20.
47 Pennells, op. cit., p. 310.
48 *Scottish Leader*, 24 August 1887.
49 'London in January', *Blackwood's Edinburgh Magazine*, cxxxix (February 1886), p. 261.
50 Pennells, op. cit., p. 310.
51 *Illustrated Sporting and Dramatic News*, 9 January 1886.
52 See Rees, op. cit., pp. 181–3.
53 *Pall Mall Budget*, 24 December 1885.
54 Terry, op. cit., p. 356.
55 Hatton, op. cit., p. 23.
56 The Christmas pantomime for 1886 at the Queen's Theatre, Manchester, *The Babes in the Wood and the Bold Robin Hood*, contained a Brocken scene on a burning mountain, with a set in imitation of Telbin's at the Lyceum. According to the *Pictorial News* (29 January 1887) the Demon King 'is surrounded by his slaves in large numbers, and they sing and dance, screech and yell in true demoniacal style. Thunder rolls and lightning flashes; the Demon, conspicuous in his mephisthophelean garb, waves his arms continuously, and assumes most grotesque and striking attitudes, and Mendelssohn's "Walpurgis Night" music is rendered by full orchestra and chorus. The scene is weird and impressive in the extreme.'
57 James, op. cit., p. 313.
58 Pennells, op. cit., p. 311.
59 *Personal Reminiscences of Henry Irving*, pp. 94–5.
60 Ibid., pp. 116–17.
61 Ibid., p. 117. For further information on the stage mechanics of such a vision, see also the account of the angels in Tree's *Henry VIII*, in the next chapter.

62 Manchester *Courier*, 20 September 1887. William Archer did not approve of what he called the Euclidean design of the ladder of angels, and said that there was no reason why Margaret should go to heaven on an inclined plane, 'like the Righi railway' (*World*, 23 December 1885).

63 The provincial and American totals came from Stoker, *Personal Reminiscences of Henry Irving*, p. 113.

64 *Pall Mall Gazette*, 13 September 1886.

65 In the first season gas and limelight expenses (exclusive of wages) for *Faust* in an ordinary week averaged between £61 and £62.

66 *Personal Reminiscences of Henry Irving*, p. 113.

67 Edinburgh *Evening News*, 24 August 1887.

68 James, op. cit., p. 312.

69 Archer, op. cit., pp. 51–2.

70 *Manchester Guardian*, 20 September 1887.

71 Manchester *Sunday Chronicle*, 25 September 1887.

Chapter 5   Beerbohm Tree's *King Henry VIII*

1 See George Rowell, 'Tree's Shakespeare Festivals', *Theatre Notebook*, xxix, no. 2 (1975), pp. 74–81.

2 'The living Shakespeare', [1901], *Thoughts and After-Thoughts*, 3rd ed. (Cassell, 1915), p. 46.

3 *The Tempest: as Arranged for the Stage by Herbert Beerbohm Tree* (printed by J. Miles, 1904), p. xii.

4 See Mary M. Nilon '"The Tempest" at the turn of the century: cross-currents in production', *Shakespeare Survey*, 25 (1972), pp. 118–23.

5 Jonathan Miller in his 1970 production concluded with Caliban and Ariel disputing for possession of Prospero's abandoned staff, the symbol of imperial and colonial power.

6 *Harlequinade* (Lane, 1929), p. 186. Having discovered that the real Cleopatra had five children, Tree insisted to the actress's horror upon her being followed in the procession by all of them, the two smallest splendidly robed in silver, miniatures of their mother. It was a typical example of Tree's methods.

7 *Play Pictorial*, no. 54 (January 1907), p. 226.

8 *The Life and Theatrical Times of Charles Kean* (Bentley, 1859), II, pp. 141–6.

9 *Daily Telegraph*, 6 January 1892.

10 *Saturday Review*, 13 August 1910.

11 *Henry VIII and his Court* (Cassell, 1910), pp. 89–90.

12 Ibid., pp. 106, 108.

13 Ibid., pp. 90–1.

14 See 'The English wood stage', in Edwin O. Sachs and Ernest A. E. Woodrow, *Modern Opera Houses and Theatres*, I (Batsford, 1896), pp. 9–14.

15 See the helpful isometric drawing of Her Majesty's (Fig. 169) in Richard Leacroft, *The Development of the English Playhouse* (Eyre Methuen, 1973), p. 272.

16 Information on the stage and auditorium of Her Majesty's is contained in the *Builder* (13 March 1897), *Building News* (30 April and 14 May 1897), Sachs and Woodrow, op. cit., II (1897), p. 36, and Georges Bourdon, 'Les théâtres anglais: Her Majesty's Theatre', *Revue d'Art Dramatique*, ix (March 1900), pp. 199–218. Bourdon is especially informative on the electric stage lighting.

17 *Daily Sketch*, 5 August 1910.

18 *This for Remembrance* (Hurst & Blackett, 1940), p. 48.

19 *Time Was* (H. Hamilton, 1931), p. 317.

20 Collier, op. cit., pp. 95–6.

21 *Oscar Asche: His Life* (Hurst & Blackett, 1929), pp. 98–9.

22 Louis N. Parker, 'A Tribute', *Herbert Beerbohm Tree*, ed. Max. Beerbohm (n.d.), pp. 211–12.

23 'Herbert and I', ibid., p. 149.

24 *Chicago Daily Tribune*, 7 December 1916. Mrs Macquoid, according to Maud Tree, had herself embroidered the tablecloth for the banquet scene (*Herbert Beerbohm Tree*, p. 149).

25 *Pall Mall Gazette*, 20 August 1910.

26 Tree had discovered the orange in Cavendish's *Life of Wolsey*. The real Wolsey had it filled with spices and kept it to ward off sickness and mitigate the unpleasant odours of daily life. Tree used it to emphasise Wolsey's fastidious arrogance and remoteness from others. Charles Kean's Wolsey had also used the orange.

27 *East Anglian Daily Times*, 3 September 1910.

28 *Liverpool Daily Post*, 2 September 1910.

29 *Outlook*, 10 October 1910.

30 *Tablet*, 1 April 1911.

31 *Observer*, 4 September 1910.

32 *Toledo Blade*, 20 March 1916.

33 *Nation*, 23 March 1916.

34 *Dare to be Wise*, n.d. [Hodder & Stoughton, 1925], p. 93. She also pointed out how often Tree used flowers to add significance to a scene or mood.

35 *New York Evening Post*, 15 March 1916.

36 *Daily Chronicle*, 2 September 1910.

37 *Sunday Times*, 4 September 1910.

38 *Daily Chronicle*, 2 September 1910.

39 *Daily Express*, 27 July 1910.

40 His Majesty's carpenters must have been much quieter than those at the New Amsterdam Theatre for the New York production, where several critics complained about backstage noises.

41 *Art Chronicle*, 10 September 1910.

42 When the production was revived in 1915, the vision was transposed to the end of the scene, and this was the order followed in New York.

43 *New York Times*, 19 March 1916.

44 *Court Journal*, 7 September 1910.

45 *Daily Chronicle*, 2 September 1910.

46 After describing the final scene, Clement Scott ended his review of Irving's *Henry VIII* in exactly the same way: 'By this time the audience is pretty well tired of pic-

tures and pageantry, although they represent stage pictures unparalleled in the history of the stage' (*Daily Telegraph*, 6 January 1892).

47 *Daily Express*, 27 July 1910.

48 *New York Evening Mail*, 15 March 1916.

49 *Tablet*, 1 April 1911.

50 Tree's poster for the revival of the *Dream* was a reproduction of Landseer's painting, 'Titania and Bottom'.

51 Both figures are from *The Stage Year Book* (1911), p. 331.

52 Alan Hughes, 'Henry Irving's finances: the Lyceum accounts, 1878–1899', *Nineteenth Century Theatre Research*, I (autumn 1973), p. 82.

53 *Standard* (27 July 1910). For futher financial information, see Richard Foulkes, 'Herbert Beerbohm Tree's *King Henry VIII*: expenditure, spectacle, and experiment', *Theatre Research International*, iii, (October 1977), pp. 24–7.

54 See Huntley Carter, *The Theatre of Max Reinhardt* (Palmer, 1914), pp. 228–40, and the *Playgoer and Society Illustrated*, V, no. 28 (January 1912), p. 110. The production of *The Miracle* in London was widely documented.

Index